The Romans

The Romans: An Introduction, 3rd edition is a concise, readable and comprehensive survey of the civilization of ancient Rome. Covering more than 1,200 years of political, military and cultural history, it explores the religion, society and daily life of the Romans, through a study of their literature, art, architecture and technology.

This new edition contains extensive updated and revised material designed to evoke the themes and debates which resonate in both the ancient and modern worlds: class struggles, imperialism, constitutional power (checks and balances), the role of the family, slavery, urbanization and religious tolerance.

New features include:

- Expanded historical coverage of republican history and the legacy of Rome.
- An expanded introduction to the ancient source materials, as well as a more focused and analytical approach to the evidence, which are designed to engage the reader further in his/her interaction and interpretation of the material.
- New maps and a greater variety of illustrations have been added, as well as updated reading lists. A further appendix on Roman nomenclature has also been provided.
- The book's successful website, www.routledge.com/cw/kamm, has been updated with additional resources and images, including case studies which provide closer 'tutorial'-style treatment of specific topics and types of evidence.

Those with an interest in classical language, ancient history, Roman art, political and economic systems or the concept of civilization as a whole will gain a greater understanding of both the Romans and the model of a civilization that has shaped so many cultures.

Antony Kamm read Classics and English at Oxford University. He was Lecturer in Publishing Studies at the University of Stirling 1988–95. His publications include the *Collins Biographical Dictionary of English Literature* (1993), *The Israelites: An Introduction* (1999), *The Last Frontier: The Roman Invasions of Scotland* (2004) and *Julius Caesar: A Life* (2006).

Abigail Graham is Lecturer in Ancient History at the University of Warwick. She specializes in the epigraphy and monumentality of the ancient world and conducts a biennial postgraduate course in epigraphy for the British School at Rome. She has published *The Roman Empire: A Brief History* (2008).

THE ROMANS
An Introduction

Third Edition

Antony Kamm
and
Abigail Graham

Routledge
Taylor & Francis Group

LONDON AND NEW YORK

First published 1995
Second edition published 2008

This third edition published 2015
by Routledge
2 Park Square, Milton Park, Abingdon, Oxon OX14 4RN

Simultaneously published in the USA and Canada
by Routledge
711 Third Avenue, New York, NY 10017

Routledge is an imprint of the Taylor & Francis Group, an informa business

British Library Cataloguing in Publication Data
A catalogue record for this book is available from the British Library

Library of Congress Cataloging in Publication Data
A catalog record for this book has been requested

ISBN: 978-1-138-77667-8 (hbk)
ISBN: 978-1-138-77668-5 (pbk)
ISBN: 978-1-315-73992-2 (ebk)

Typeset in Avenir and Amasis
by Keystroke, Station Road, Codsall, Wolverhampton

To the memory of Antony Kamm: author, teacher and poet

Maioresque cadunt altis de montibus umbrae

Virgil, Eclogue 1.84

CONTENTS

LIST OF FIGURES

LIST OF MAPS

ACKNOWLEDGEMENTS

Antony Kamm, author of the first two editions of *The Romans* (1995 and 2008), left a wonderful legacy that I have tried to continue with the generous advice and support of his family, especially his wife, Eileen. Whilst expanding sections on history and architecture, greater focus has been placed on specific case studies and analysing different types of evidence, attributes that are often acclaimed as 'transferable skills'. I have augmented The Romans website, incorporating new didactic tools and weblinks, to connect the reader with a growing number of internet resources (though I feel I have only scraped the surface).

In undertaking this project, I am grateful to academics in the USA and the UK who responded to the publisher's request for suggestions – notably Jeffrey Brodd, Garrett Fagan, Amanda Krauss, Teresa Ramsby – and to colleagues at the University of Warwick: Alison Cooley, who provided helpful comments and expertise through-out the editorial process, Clare Rowan, who advised on all things numismatic, and Clive Letchford, who provided a number of literary translations and comments. For translations I owe a special thanks to Robert Garland and Bruce Cobbold, who not only provided translations and comments for this work but accomplished something far more difficult: teaching me how to create these when I was student.

For images, I have benefited from the generosity of a number of individuals and organizations: Barbara McManus (VRoma), Allan Kohl, the IMAGO database from the Society for the Promotion of Roman Studies, Gregor Kalas, Diane Favro and Christopher Johansen's 'Visualizing Statues' project for the Experimental Technologies Center at UCLA, the Ancient World Image Bank, the Classical Numismatics Group and the American Numismatic Society as well as Cristian Chirita and Eric Galba, who have generously shared their work. I am also indebted to my students (particularly those from the City of Rome trip, 2014), whose enthusiasm and curiosity (in addition to sharing their photos) reminded me why I became a teacher of the Classics.

My editor, Matthews Gibbons, has been a fount or wisdom and experience (and was also willing to overlook first impressions), guiding me through the process with helpful suggestions and seemingly endless patience. Amy Davis Poynter (assistant editor) has also been wonderful, kindly explaining a number of obvious things to me. I would also like to thank the thoughtful and diplomatic readers of the manuscript: Phillip Parr (copyeditor) and Graham Bradbury (proofreader).

Finally, I would like to thank my husband Martin and my children Lucy and Basil for putting up with late nights, burnt dinners and countless field trips to Roman sites, which they endured with remarkable enthusiasm.

Abigail Graham
July 2014

A NOTE ON ANCIENT SOURCES: *CAVEAT LECTOR* (READER BEWARE)!

Reconstructing a picture of the ancient Romans is a challenging process in which one must reconcile different sources and types of evidence, each of which has its own perspective and limitations. Imagine if all that survived of our world today were a single newspaper: whose image of the world would it represent? Where it was written, the opinions of its writers (men or women, old or young, wealthy or poor, liberal or conservative) would fundamentally alter the portrayal of information to the audience. This book and its accompanying website, which provide focused studies of different types of evidence (from passages of literature to 'on-site video' lectures on material evidence), aim both to provide the reader with a good sample of material and to demonstrate how this evidence is used to reconstruct the Roman world. The following discussion offers a brief introduction to the benefits and limitations of historical, literary, epigraphic and archaeological sources.

A fundamental factor in assessing both ancient and modern accounts is to understand the lens through which an author presents his view. Observing how a lens is shaped by an author's agenda and his audience, how it defines and distorts the information, allows the reader to understand better both the evidence and how we interpret it. One of the most dangerous things we can do as readers is to assume that, simply because something survived thousands of years or has been written in the medium of stone, it is more 'true' or less biased than a modern account. Livy (Chapter 1), like many ancient historians, wrote about events 500 years before his lifetime, making him one of the fathers of 'revisionist history'. What Livy chose to record or omit, and how he presents his history (often in a moralizing tone), may tell us as much about the values of his audience in imperial Rome as it does about the subjects of Rome's early history. Suetonius, the author of *The Twelve Caesars* (Chapter 3), had access to the imperial archives (unlike many other historians), yet his work reads more like a spicy imperial exposé than an 'official' historical narrative. From gossipy letters and heartfelt advice for his friends and family to lofty public speeches, Cicero's work provides a colourful and multifaceted illustration of both the man and the politician (Chapter 2).

Similarly, literary sources such as Juvenal and Martial (Chapter 8), who bemoan their status as impoverished writers, relied on the support of wealthy patrons – men who could dictate the subjects of their works. Their embittered lampooning of the rising middle classes and freedmen, often cited because they are among the only surviving literary sources we have on the subject, were designed for comic effect rather than to provide an accurate account. Similarly, Virgil's epic poem the *Aeneid*, set after the Trojan Wars (more than a millennium before the author's lifetime) was composed to honour the Emperor Augustus. Ancient authors, like modern ones, were also subject to censorship. The poet Ovid was exiled by Augustus for his racy love letters and 'Art of Loving', which offers advice about how to pick up girls at the theatre. The Stoic philosopher Seneca, once the tutor of the young Nero, and Petronius, an author of satire and *arbiter elegantiae* ('style guru') at Nero's court, were both ordered to commit suicide. While court satires, outrageous poetry and Ovid's pop fiction guides to what women want provide some delicious romps, we have to appreciate them for what they are: works of great men composed for the edification and delight of a small, elite audience. The literacy rate in the ancient world was much lower than it is today, with 15 per cent being an optimistic figure. Many Romans' lives and views are not represented by these sources.

Literary and historical evidence is also subject to the circumstances of its survival – through a series of copies made during the medieval period. The modern concept of the 'butterfly effect' certainly operated in the copying of manuscripts: a monk might sneeze, fall asleep, spill ink, misspell a word or omit a passage, resulting in two different versions of the same text. In turn, the second text might then be copied, perhaps with even more mistakes, again and again. The more versions of a text (often called a codex) we have, the more complicated the situation can become, and we seldom have an author's complete corpus. For example, the historian Cassius Dio wrote eighty books of history, of which only twenty-five survive, along with summaries (about forty books) of the extant works from the medieval period. Why weren't the rest of his books copied? Were they boring? Were they accidentally recycled in the monastery latrine? Roman historical literary accounts are the products of numerous revisions, which makes them fascinating but at times unreliable.

This leads to the final area of distortion: the translation. To some extent, difficulties in translation, an issue throughout history, have been exacerbated by the internet, which offers translations of works that are out of copyright (at least a hundred years old). For example, the most popular search result for Plutarch's *Lives of the Caesars* is Dryden's translation from 1683. Using a translation can be challenging enough without having to translate early modern English into more contemporary idiom. Some authors (not all of them linguists) will offer a translation of their own, which conveniently conforms to their argument. Penguin and Oxford World Classics translations are widely available, reasonably priced, and provide not only clear English translations by leading scholars but indexes, timelines and introductions to the authors (very useful in understanding their 'lenses'). Regard translations (especially those online) with care: if it is not good English, then it is not a good translation.

Epigraphic evidence, objects from the ancient world that were 'written on' (principally building or monumental inscriptions, but also graffiti, text on pots, coins, etc.), can seem more 'legitimate' as voices that have come to us directly from the ancient world. These sources, sometimes the sole voices of slaves, women and lower-class citizens, represent a broader spectrum of society. Monuments set up in a public venue, where they were meant to be seen (although not necessarily read), had a wider viewing audience and tended to be written in a simple and formulaic language, which could indicate a wider readership. This broader 'social network', while offering a more expansive view of Roman society, can also make epigraphic sources more prone to record aspiration than truth. Funerary monuments (Chapter 6), in particular, can bear an uncanny resemblance to a Facebook page in their efforts to showcase a person's literary, educational and social achievements. These invaluable sources illustrate not necessarily who a person was 'in reality' but who that person wanted (or claimed) to be. Epigraphy is also a foil for literary accounts, both when the two accounts agree and when they contradict each other. As it involves analysis of both text (the subject of linguistic and historical studies) and material objects (the subject of archaeological studies), epigraphy stands at the crossroads of numerous disciplines, where the arguments between scholars are often 'monumental' in scope.

The circumstances of survival shape these sources as well. Many inscribed texts survive only in fragments. These are 'restored' by scholars, who make assumptions about what any missing text might have said based on information from similar texts; these assumptions are then added in square brackets alongside the extant text. While such restorations can be quite accurate, that is seldom guaranteed. Classical scholars, for example, used to 'restore' names of famous Romans like 'Quintus Horatius Flaccus' (the poet Horace) whenever they came across the name Quintus. That was a bit like adding '[Washington]' to anything from eighteenth-century America that included the name 'George'. So be wary of drawing too much 'fact' from any text in square brackets. Despite the implied permanence of writing in stone, a number of statue bases, buildings and funerary monuments were reused and even recarved. Suetonius (*Domitian* 23) describes Romans gleefully hacking Domitian's name from his public monuments and toppling statues in an act of desecration called *damnatio memoriae* that still resonates in modern contexts – such as the iconic toppling of Saddam's statue after the second Iraq War.

Archaeological evidence represents all the material evidence that survives from the Roman world. It is the props and stage upon which Roman life was set. This type of tangible evidence allows us to reconstruct and experience Roman life in a different way: by sitting in at the back of a Roman theatre and hearing a pin drop on the stage. Artefacts are also a check for the literary record. Vitruvius' treatise on architecture gives the dimensions of the 'ideal' Roman theatre. Yet, of over one hundred surviving Roman theatres, not one matches the plan or dimensions he provides. It is also illuminating to compare the public portraits of the Roman emperors on statues and coins with the physical descriptions provided in Suetonius' account. Did Augustus really have a six-pack at forty? Coins depict many monuments that no longer survive and illustrate how an emperor or a politician could 'spin' a victory or foreign policy to a broader audience. This evidence can also corroborate the historical record. Metal slingshots (*glandes*) record the names of individuals (e.g. Octavian and Fulvia) as well as the parts of their anatomies that were the weapons' targets (see Chapter 3).

Archaeology is a guide to aspects of everyday life that can be neglected in literature. What was it like to live in an apartment block? Surviving blocks in Rome or Ostia provide only a shell, like a student dormitory on the first day of term. Without the beds, furniture and personal items, it can be very difficult to assess living conditions (e.g. how many people lived there and how was it ventilated?). Sites such as Pompeii and Herculaneum, preserved at a single moment in time, provide dozens of homes, decorations, even furniture through which we can contextualize Petronius' depiction of a middle-class dinner party in the *Satyricon*. Shops and taverns allow us to stand in the space, see the wall painting depicting a bar fight, a mosaic floor saying, 'Drink up!', amphora which contain wine resin and graffito that boasts about a good shag with a barmaid. Maritime archaeology (e.g. excavating a shipwreck) can help scholars understand trade routes and which luxury items or commodities were exported. Women and freedmen, whose voices are rare in literature, come to life as public benefactors, owners of property and religious leaders in the archaeological record.

Archaeological evidence is also subject to its survival and its conservation. Many early excavations were little more than glorified treasure hunts, with beautiful and/or valuable objects stripped from sites and few records kept as to where they were found. Moreover, many artefacts are not found in their original locations because they were discarded or reused, which limits our ability to associate any object with its original context, owner and function. Imagine finding a toilet seat a thousand years from now in a landfill: would its original function be clear? Faced with a marble throne, archaeologists might label it a ritual headdress or religious item (translation: we don't have a clue what it is!). The most well-preserved temples in Rome, such as the Pantheon, survive because they were converted into churches. The bronze statue of Marcus Aurelius outside the Capitoline Hill (now kept indoors) was spared in the

Middle Ages because it was mistaken for a statue of Constantine (a later, Christian, emperor). The haphazard survival of artefacts can result in a distorted image of what the ancient world actually looked like. Archaeology is a learning process, and the use of tools such as shovels and trowels means some destruction is inevitable. For this reason, many modern surveys involve excavating, documenting, then reburying materials, as this is the best way to save them for posterity.

Reconstructing the world of the ancient Romans is like trying to piece together a hopelessly incomplete puzzle from disparate and often conflicting sources. Each of these sources has a unique contribution to make and it is only by integrating all of them that we can generate a picture of Roman life. It is this rigorous and inter-disciplinary approach, involving the analysis of politics, literature, history, religion, economics, art and architecture, that has made the Romans a keystone in education for so many careers over the past millennium.

COMPANION WEBSITE

The Romans third edition is accompanied by a companion website (found at www.routledge.com/cw/kamm) that provides a wealth of extra information to support the text. The book's website also features a new didactic component: case studies. Portions of the text which have accompanying online case studies and additional resources are indicated by the companion website logo in the margin.

Following recent trends in evidence and research based learning, these case studies offer a detailed analysis of specific types of evidence, events and individuals in Roman history. Expanding upon materials from the book, the case studies illustrate how we use evidence to reconstruct the ancient world and encourage students to question the evidence; considering what 'proof' it provides. How do we reconstruct the image of Romulus' hut? How do we prove the Capitoline Bronze Wolf is a fake? Did Caesar want to be King? What is 'Roman' in Roman architecture? How did the Roman 'testudo' formation work in an ancient battle? How many people were literate in the Ancient Rome?

The website is organised by chapter and there you will find:

- Additional images and discussions on material from the book
- Didactic Case studies which feature
  - Research and evidence based learning through a thoughtful treatment of specific events, concepts, individuals and material evidence.
  - Word documents (*ca.* 2,000 words) which set out a question, a clear line of argument, as well as an illustration of how different types of evidence are used (and what each type contributes) to the discussion.
  - Accompanying PowerPoint presentations with additional images and labels to illustrate the evidence and the analytical process.
  - Additional reading, including online articles and publications, research projects, video lectures, as well as additional teaching materials.

This resource in an invaluable aid for students and also a repository for material that will be useful for instructors teaching a course on Roman civilization, developing knowledge as well transferable research and analytical skills.

GENERAL INTRODUCTIONS AND WEBSITES

Please note that websites are subject to change over time. Please see The Romans companion website for more weblinks (which will be edited regularly).

ARCHAEOLOGY OF THE CITIES OF ROME, OSTIA AND POMPEII

A number of online websites allow students to visit ancient sites virtually, combining building and urban plans with images of surviving remains, such as wall paintings, furnishing and inscriptions.

Rome

- Aicher, P.J., *Rome Alive*, Bolchazy-Carducci, 2004.
  This guide to Rome, organized spatially, provides descriptions and translations of ancient accounts for a number of areas and buildings in Rome. The translations are available online, along with building reconstructions of dubious quality: http://romereborn.frischerconsulting.com/ge/RomeAlive.html.
- Claridge, A., *Rome*, Oxford Archaeological Guides, Oxford University Press, 2010.
- Platner and Ashby's *Topographical Dictionary of Rome* (1929) is now available online: http://penelope.uchicago.edu/Thayer/E/Gazetteer/Places/Europe/Italy/Lazio/Roma/Rome/_Texts/PLATOP*/home.html. While information about (and identification of) a building can change, the primary sources that record it (e.g. passages in Cicero) remain constant.

Ostia

- www.ostia-antica.org/. This site is incredible and continues to develop: it now offers didactic videos about buildings such as bakeries. It boasts an interactive and colour-coded urban plan which allows you to view hundreds of different buildings as well as graffiti and structures that are closed to the public.

Pompeii

- www.pompeiiinpictures.com/. This offers a detailed treatment of individual houses and buildings as well as virtual three-dimensional tours of some of the rooms.

EPIGRAPHIC EVIDENCE

Often called 'inscriptions' (on account of being 'inscribed'), these objects are used in a number of ways to inform our knowledge of the ancient world. The reference numbers used in this work (e.g. *CIL* 6.344) refer to large volumes, 'the Corpus of Latin Inscriptions' (*Corpus Inscriptionum Latinarum*). While these are helpful for finding inscriptions, they do not provide translations and the commentary is in Latin. However, there are a number of good books and websites.

- Bodel, J.P., *Epigraphic Evidence: Ancient History from Inscriptions*, Routledge, 2001.
- Cooley, A.E., *The Cambridge Manual of Latin Epigraphy*, Cambridge University Press, 2012.
- Gordon, A.E., *An Illustrated Introduction to Latin Epigraphy*, University of California Press, 1983. Many of the inscriptions are accompanied by translations and commentaries.
- http://odur.let.rug.nl/~vannijf/epigraphy1.htm is an absolute beginner's guide to epigraphy.
- Oxford's Centre for the Study of Ancient Documents at www.csad.ox.ac.uk/ is useful for case studies of inscriptions from across the Roman empire (including some in this book, such as the Vindolanda tablets (Hadrian's Wall), British curse tablets and the Oxyrhynchus Papyri project).

COINS

Coins are also an invaluable source and are often cited in this work with specific catalogue references: RRC = Roman Republican Coinage; RIC = Roman Imperial Coinage. As with inscriptions, these refer to large corpus publications, which set out specific coin types, considering dates, styles and weights for Roman coins. A number of published works and websites that help to explain how to use coins are listed below.

- Burnett, A., *Coinage in the Roman World*, Spink and Son, 2004 (reprint).
- Howgego C., *History from Ancient Coins*, Routledge, 1995.
- www.humanities.mq.edu.au/acans/caesar/Home.htm and http://andrew mccabe.ancients.info/ are both good introductions to the coins of Caesar and the Roman republic.
- http://numismatics.org/ocre/ is useful for Roman imperial coins.

HISTORY (SOCIAL, POLITICAL, ECONOMIC, MILITARY)

- Alföldy, G., *A Social History of Rome*, Routledge, 1988.
- Beard, M. and Henderson, J., *Classics: A Very Short Introduction*, Oxford University Press, 2000.
- Boardman, J., Griffin, J. and Murray, O. (eds), *The Oxford History of the Roman World*, Oxford University Press, 2001 (new edition).
- Boatwright, M.T., Gargola, D.J. and Talbert, R.J.A., *A Brief History of the Romans*, Oxford University Press, 2006.
- Garnsey, P. and Saller, R., *The Roman Empire: Economy, Society and Culture*, University of California Press, 1987.
- Goodman, M., *The Roman World, 44 BC–AD 180*, Routledge, 1997.
- Huskinson, J. (ed.), *Experiencing Rome: Culture, Identity and Power in the Roman Empire*, Routledge, 2000.
- Jones, P. and Sidwell, K. (eds), *The World of Rome: An Introduction to Roman Culture*, Cambridge University Press, 1997.
- Kelly, C., *The Roman Empire: A Very Short Introduction*, Oxford University Press, 2006.
- Lane Fox, R., *The Classical World: An Epic History from Homer to Hadrian*, Penguin, 2005.
- Le Glay, M., *A History of Rome*, Blackwell, 2004 (third edition).
- Mackay, C.S., *Ancient Rome: A Military and Political History*, Cambridge University Press, 2005.
- Wacher, J. (ed.), *The Roman World*, Routledge, 2001 (reissue).
- Wells, C., *The Roman Empire*, Fontana, 1992 (second edition); Harvard University Press, 1995 (second edition).
- Woolf, G., *The Cambridge Illustrated History of the Roman World*, Cambridge University Press, 2003.
- Woolf, G., *Rome: An Empire's Story*, Oxford University Press, 2012.
- Perseus: a digital library of classical texts: www.perseus.tufts.edu/hopper/.

MAP 1 Italy: showing places and other geographical features mentioned in this book.

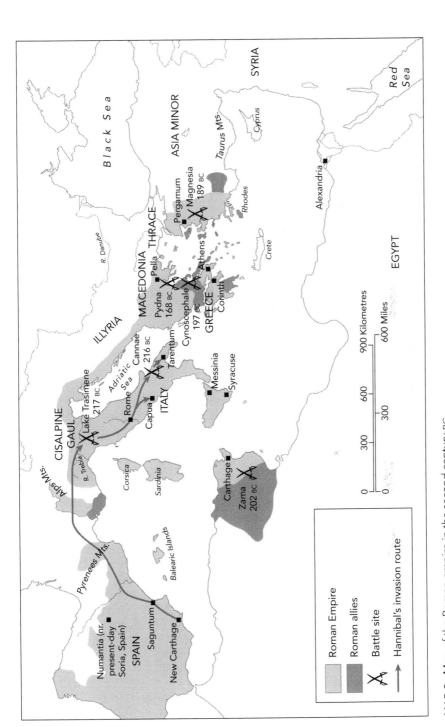

MAP 2   Map of the Roman empire in the second century BC.

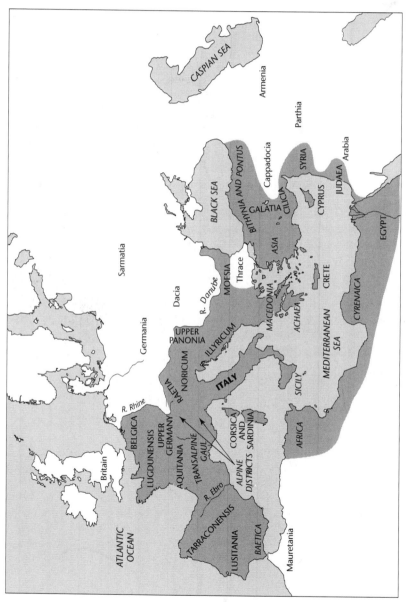

MAP 3 The Roman empire in AD 14 at the death of Augustus: imperial provinces are in Roman capital letters; senatorial provinces are in italic capital letters.

MAP 4   The extent of the Roman empire during the rule of Hadrian, including places and people outside Italy mentioned in this book.

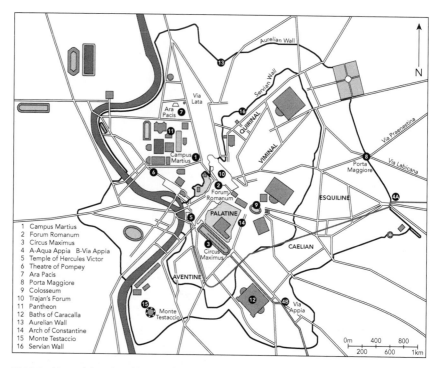

MAP 5 Map of the city of Rome, showing a selection of the buildings and geographical features discussed in this book

1 THE ORIGINS OF ROME

Rome, the city that would become the centre of a vast empire, was not built in a day. It took the better part of a millennium for it to reach its apex, then several more centuries to devolve and deteriorate into a series of smaller empires. The period of time between the foundation of the city in 753 BC to the ultimate destruction of her empire (for the purposes of this work, on the death of the last Western Emperor, Romulus Augustus) in AD 476 spans nearly 1250 years. To put this era in perspective, roughly the same amount of time elapsed between the actual fall of the Roman Empire and the publication of the modern era's first comprehensive history of Roman civilization, Edward Gibbon's *The Decline and Fall of the Roman Empire*, published the same year as the American Declaration of Independence was signed (1776). That the Romans continue to play a crucial role as a benchmark for the successes and failures of modern society, both in Gibbon's time and today, demonstrates the power and influence that the legacy of Rome continues to hold in Western society.

In the past, Romans have been viewed as merely imitators of the Greek culture, which reached its zenith between the start of the fifth century BC (the beginnings of 'democracy' and the Persian Wars) and the death of Alexander in 323 BC. However, this type of comparison often falls apart upon closer inspection. To examine how Rome adapted aspects of Greek culture, from its mythical foundation in the Trojan Wars to its laws, public buildings and foreign policy, is to see how Rome acted as an innovator. From the very beginning, Romans sought to define themselves as distinct from those who had come before. Many modern concepts of Roman culture or Latin language have been taken from the late republican/early imperial period (first century BC–second century AD), a time which falls more than 700 years after the founding of the city. Early Roman Italy was, like colonial America, defined primarily as a 'melting pot' of different cultures and languages that made up its people (such as Etruscan,

Oscan, Latin and Greek). It is doubtful than many, or indeed any, of these early settlers would have seen themselves as 'Roman'.

The Roman era is generally divided into three parts, based on the type of government. The regal period extends from the founding of the city in 753 to the expulsion of the last Etruscan king by Lucius Junius Brutus in 510 BC. The republic lasted from 509 until 27 BC, the date Octavian assumed his title Augustus as well as numerous constitutional powers, making him effectively the first emperor. Augustus did not formally spell the end of the republic; in fact, he claimed to have 'restored' it. However, when his extraordinary powers were passed on to his successor, Tiberius, in AD 14, imperial rule appears firmly established. This system of government lasted until 476, when Romulus Augustus, the last western emperor, was deposed by Odacer, a German mercenary who did not take the title of emperor but preferred to rule as a king. This decision is often seen by scholars as a testament to the impotence that the term 'emperor' had acquired. The eastern part of the Roman empire, based at Constantinople (Byzantium), carried on as an independent political entity into the Middle Ages, until the city fell to the Turks and the Ottoman empire in 1453.

FOUNDATION LEGENDS AND THEIR SOURCES

There are two key events in the mythological foundation of Rome: the arrival of the Trojan hero Aeneas in Italy (c. 1200 BC +/– fifty years, depending on which date one accepts for the Trojan Wars) and the founding of the city by Romulus (21 April 753 BC). The gap of 500 years between these two events is largely undocumented and although Virgil and others have sought evidence of a Greek foundation, the five 'wretched shards' of Mycenean pottery found in Latium do not make for a compelling argument. Archaeological studies have revealed hilltop settlements on the Capitoline, Palatine and Quirinal hills as well as burials in the Forum and the Esquiline hill from the tenth century BC. While the approximate date of the city's foundation is well documented as the starting point of Livy's history *Ab Urbe Condita* ('On the Founding of the City'), our evidence for this period is limited. A dirt wall, a monumental gate and a series of huts and pens for livestock on the Palatine support the concept of defined agrarian-based settlements, but not necessarily a thriving metropolis. Perhaps what is most informative about these mythological foundations is observing how Romans chose to represent their city and their culture. To understand the function and meaning of these mythological events, we must first consider the sources from which they came.

Accounts of these foundation myths, which represent some of the earliest works in Latin literature, date to the third century BC: 500 years after the founding of the city and nearly a millennium after the arrival of Aeneas. This was the time when Latin began to emerge as the 'linga franca' of Italy and Rome began its accumulation of a global empire, extending its reach into modern Sicily, Sardinia and Corsica. Early authors such as Fabius Pictor (mid–late third century BC), who began his history with Aeneas' arrival in Latium, wrote in Greek and relied upon earlier Greek sources, which survive either in fragmentary form or as references by later authors. So we must turn again to the foundation myth accounts written in the first century BC, between five and eleven centuries after the events in question. Similar difficulties pervade the studies of the Norse colonization in the Americas, where the events of the eleventh century were not recorded until the fifteenth century, and these accounts were not the subject to further scholarship until the nineteenth and twentieth centuries. In both cases, modern science and archaeology can corroborate *some* aspects of the settlements, but other elements have been disproven and numerous fakes and forgeries exposed in the process. Finding the truth is always more difficult when there is a particular version that people want to believe. Nevertheless, though facts and evidence may be scant, these tales make for a thrilling adventure; and this virtue was not lost upon Roman writers.

Although Titus Livius (Livy) (59 BC–AD 17) and Virgil (70–19 BC) are often classed as a historian and a poet, respectively, these distinctions, like those of church and state, are not always so clearly drawn in the ancient world (for further details on both authors, see Chapter 8). The Roman world was much more interdisciplinary in terms of politics and the arts: in addition to writing an epic poem (the *Aeneid*), Virgil wrote a treatise on farming; Livy, an Italian-trained scholar from Padua, devoted his life to research, which was more extensive than that of many of his predecessors (who tended to be retired politicians in Rome looking for a hobby). Both men sought to impress a powerful figure (Augustus) and rather than composing an accurate account of past for the present, they wrote with a sense of predestination, tracing Rome's recent triumphs to the past. Tying in with Augustus' new moral legislation on 'traditional' family values, these stories sought to illustrate quintessentially 'Roman' values in the city's prestigious ancestors. The resulting works are fantastic mythical tales that abound with moral messages and allusions to Rome's imminent glory.

AENEAS ARRIVES IN ITALY: VIRGIL AND THE TROJAN WARS (c. 1250 BC)

It is not surprising that Rome sought to trace her history through the same events that defined the Greek world: the Trojan Wars. The narrative and imagery of those wars were recognized throughout the Mediterranean and some of the finest surviving Greek vases depicting these events have been found in Etruria (Tuscany) in sixth-century BC Etruscan tombs. Integrating themselves within this epic tradition need not be taken as lack of originality on the part of the Romans, but should probably be viewed as a canny political move, which placed Rome within an internationally recognizable historical context and a pre-existing framework of epic tradition. In selecting the Trojan underdog Aeneas, however, Romans deliberately set themselves apart from Greek heroes such as Achilles and Odysseus, as well as the tendency of Greek literature to recall a lost 'Golden Age' of wealth, palaces and glory. The most iconic **image of Aeneas**, attested on Greek vases from as early as the sixth century BC, depict the hero in full battle regalia carrying his father on his back from the ruins of Troy (sometimes accompanied by his son Ascanius, and his divine mother Venus; Figure 1.1). This scene, the most common in Roman depictions of Aeneas, was also represented on the coins of Caesar and on popular commodity objects such as oil lamps, which, like the literature that describes them, date from the first century BC to the second century AD. In the quintessential role of *paterfamilias* ('head of the family'), Aeneas leaves Troy with nothing but his family (and his armour). He wanders through the Mediterranean, not coincidentally encountering the lands and foes that will eventually become part of Rome's vast empire. After a series of delays, adversities and divine interventions, he reaches Italy and meets King Latinus of Latium, who promises his daughter Lavinia in marriage. Sadly, our hero's hardships are not at an end, as a rival leader, Turnus of Rutuli, challenges Aeneas. Reluctant to go to war, Aeneas seeks help from King Evander (a Greek exile from Arcadia) on a mission that will lead him to the nascent city of Rome (*Aeneid* 7.29–36). A sense of destiny and divine approval is conveyed by the river god 'old Tiber', who addresses Aeneas in his sleep (*Aeneid* 8.35–49):

> Night: when the birds and animals were everywhere at rest, Aeneas lay on the riverbank under the cold stars, heartsick and restless with plans for the impending war. At last he fell asleep. In a dream he saw the god of the place [Old Tiber] rising from among the poplar trees . . . 'Son of Venus' he said in a soothing voice 'You have brought Troy here, safe from her enemies and here you will rebuild her to stand forever. On the soil of Italy, in the Land of Latium, we have been waiting for you. This is to be your home and here your household gods will find protection. Look at me: you must not be frightened by any threats of violence . . . To prove to you that this is no false dream, I promise that soon among the oak tress on the bank, you will find a great white sow; she will be lying on the ground suckling her piglets – 30 of them . . . This will be the site of Alba Longa, the famous city which Ascanius will found, 30 years from now.'
>
> **(*Aeneid* 8; trans. G.B. Cobbold (2005), p. 202)**

When he awakes, Aeneas ventures through the outskirts of Rome, discovering the prophetic white piglets and entering the city at the Forum Boarium (near the Temple

FIGURE 1.1 Black figure oinochoe (a type of wine jug popular in Greece) by the Louvre Painter, 520–510 BC, Musée du Louvre, Inventory Number: F118. This vase depicts a fully armoured Aeneas carrying his father on his back, with one arm, while in the other he holds his shield (futher identifying him as a 'protector'). Greek vases, popular objects in Etruscan tombs, illustrate the prominence of trade links between Etruscans and their Greek neighbours. Photo © RMN-Grand Palais (Musée du Louvre) / Hervé Lewandowski.

of Hercules Victor; see Map 5), where he dines on beef (a reference to the original function of this forum as a cattle market), noting various features such as a crevice in the Aventine, supposedly torn by an angry Hercules. The aim of this journey seems to be an exploration into the humble nature of Rome's origins: 'What Roman power has now raised to the heights of the sky, in those days was poor land ruled by Evander' (*Aeneid* 8.100). Aeneas' path through the landscape of the future city of Rome takes him on a journey through time and space: past the Porta Carmentalis, where a temple of Apollo will be built (and later restored by Augustus), past the sacred Asylum grove and the cave of Pan Lycaeus 'the wolf god' (both references to Romulus' foundation), past the Capitoline hill 'now all gold but in those days was bristling with rough scrub' (*Aeneid* 8.348–350). The tour proceeds through the Roman Forum (Map 5, no. 2), which is filled with grazing cattle, ending at Evander's humble hut on the Palatine hill: 'Talking this way they were coming up to Evander's humble home . . . "Come into my poor home and do not judge it too harshly"' (*Aeneid* 8.360–367). Virgil is laying it on a bit thick here, contrasting the humble agrarian setting of his story with the

Palatine hill that would have been familiar to his readers, home of Romulus and, later, Augustus (and root of the modern word 'palatial').

After recruiting King Evander, Aeneas is given a shield by the goddess Venus (his mother). This event clearly echoes the shield offered to Achilles in Homer's *Iliad*, with a few minor alterations. Instead of giving the earth and the cosmos a central position, surrounded by general scenes of daily life, Aeneas' shield places Augustus' achievements in the centre, with other key events in Roman history scattered around the edges (*Aeneid* 8.620–730). The episode represents a further way in which Roman authors could manipulate a Greek tradition to serve their own purposes and propagandist overtures. In the end, Aeneas gains support from the Etruscan king Tarchon (perhaps foreshadowing their prominent role in the regal period) and reluctantly goes to war against Turnus. After many casualities on both sides, Aeneas triumphs.

While it is difficult to accept many aspects of Virgil's *Aeneid* as truth, the story has a number of historical benefits. It correctly identifies the different cultures (Latins, Samnites, Etruscan and Greeks) living in Italy in the relevant period, and the inevitable conflicts that would arise between them. It illustrates the role of destiny and divine intervention that was used to legitimize Rome's place as a world power. One can also see how a Greek literary tradition is not simply mimicked but manipulated by Romans, to suit their own agenda. The reconstruction of Rome's natural features and her humble origins allows for a powerful juxtaposition between past and present that serves to connect and glorify both versions of the city. Readers in Virgil's day, like archaeologists today, could fancifully try to retrace Aeneas' steps through the city, identifying remaining features. It was this recognition of and pride in Rome's humble origins as an agrarian society that set the Romans apart from the Greek epic tradition of a 'Golden Age'. This humility is exemplified not only in the image of the early city but also in the world-weary character of 'Pious' Aeneas, who is not always heroic in the conventional sense. When in trouble he lifts his hands up in despair and wishes for death (*Aeneid* 1.91–104); he compromises an African queen and then jilts her because the gods command it (*Aeneid* 4: perhaps the origin of the dreaded cliché 'It's not you ... it's me'); his final defeat of Turnus represents a loss of self-control; and rather than showing mercy for his enemies (a trait exemplified in Greek literature when Achilles returns the body of Hector (his enemy) at the end of Homer's *Iliad*), a bloodthirsty Aeneas slaughters the wounded Turnus. Arguably, it is his despair, reluctance and begrudging acceptance of his burdens that make Aeneas a sympathetic character, especially for a ruling figure such as a Roman emperor, with whom Aeneas was a consistently popular figure. Although it was published posthumously, possibly against the wishes of the author (it was later claimed that he wanted to burn it), Virgil's *Aeneid* became the national epic of Rome, and to this day it remains the most famous poem of the Roman era.

Little is known of Aeneas' fate. The Greek historian Dionysius of Halicarnassus, who lived at Rome in the first century BC, records that a tumulus (a large earth mound) was dedicated to Aeneas in Lavinium (*Roman Antiquites* 1.64). This is likely the tumulus, excavated in 1968, that dates to the seventh century BC, with a later restoration in the fourth century BC. Yet again, there is a significant chronological chasm between the life of the Trojan hero and the surviving remains. It is generally believed that the Romans invented the string of monarchs between Ascanius (son of Aeneas) and Numitor, grandfather of Romulus, our next great founder and the namesake of the eternal city: Rome.

THE STORY OF ROMULUS: LIVY ON THE FOUNDING OF ROME (753 BC)

In the preface of *Ab Urbe Condita* (1.1) Livy recognizes that his early history is a story where human elements mingle with the divine, illustrating the lives and morals of a community, rather than a fact-based account:

> I neither affirm nor refute the events that took place either before the city was founded or was about to be founded – events that are adorned with poetic fables rather than handed down with incorruptible testimony. It is the right of antiquity to make the birth of cities more august by mixing divine occurrences with human occurrences. And if it ought to be permissible for any people to consecrate its beginnings and make the gods their originators [it is our own].
>
> **(Trans. R. Garland)**

Like the Greek historian Thucydides, Livy believed that human nature was constant; so recreating a past character or event based on a modern one was still an accurate portrayal. These characters (and their speeches) were so popular that even a century later Romans carried them around in little 'pocket books' (Martial, *Epigrams* 14.190). Like Virgil's, many of Livy's stories appear to have been rescripted from Greek history or mythology (for example, the famous '300' Fabii at Cremera (2.50) bear striking similarities to the Spartans at Thermopylae). However, the sentiments and the ideology at the heart of these stories and characters were distinctly Roman.

The myth of Romulus' birth and the foundation of Rome (Livy, 1.3–7), like the story of Aeneas, can be traced to the historians of the third century BC. Originally thought to be from the sixth century BC, the most iconic image of Rome's foundation (Figure 1.2) is the **Capitoline Wolf**, a bronze sculpture of a she-wolf suckling twin boys, which has been proven, by scholarship and modern science, to be medieval in date (eleventh–twelfth century AD). Even to the naked eye, the bronze wolf is quite

FIGURE 1.2 The bronze sculpture of Capitoline wolf and twins is one of the most famous symbols of Rome. The wolf (85 cm high) was believed to be a fifth–sixth-century BC Etruscan work (based on eighteenth-century scholarship) until 1996, when closer examination revealed it was cast as a single object (a process from the medieval period). Further scientific analysis in 2008 using radiocarbon dating and accelerator mass spectrometry confirmed a date between the eleventh and twelfth centuries AD. The figures of the boys were likely added in the fifteenth century, before Pope Sixtus IV paid a handsome price for this 'genuine' artefact. Photo © Deutsches Archaologisches Institut, Rome; Guidotti, Neg. D-DAI-Rom 1953.0434.

static in comparison with genuine Etruscan bronzes and when compared with Roman depictions of the suckling wolf, found on Rome's first coins in the early third century BC. Artistic depictions of this myth, like literary accounts, leave a substantial gap in chronology.

The setting, a world of farmers and huts, does not seem very different from the settlement Aeneas found. The world Livy describes is treacherous, superstitious and seemingly without much respect for family or human life. Numitor, descendant of Aeneas' son Ascanius (many times removed), is ejected by his younger brother Amulius, who kills his nephews and prevents further offspring by confining his niece Rhea Silvia as a Vestal Virgin (1.3). The penalty for violating the vestal vows was a gruesome death. However, the insouciant and randy god Mars came to Rhea Silvia as she slept (or so she says; Livy clearly had doubts about the twins' divine paternity) and the outcome of her unconscious celestial experience was twin boys: Romulus and Remus (1.4).

For her many sins, Rhea Silvia was duly tossed in the old Tiber, and the river god decided to marry her (that's one way to try to redeem this sordid tale). Meanwhile, her sons were placed in a reed basket. There are many interpretations of what happened next: first the basket was caught in a fig tree (the word for fig remains slang in Italian for the female genitalia); then the twins were suckled by a 'lupa', which refers to either an actual 'she-wolf' (sacred to Mars) or the Latin slang counterpart – a prostitute – until they were rescued by a shepherd. From these insalubrious beginnings, Romulus and Remus grew to manhood and, when Numitor regained his throne, they decided to found a new city (1.6). Romulus favoured the Palatine hill (Map 5), while Remus favoured the Aventine (1.7). This is clearly a reference to the division of the Roman social classes: the patricians (founding fathers) favoured the Palatine, while the plebs (working class) favoured the Aventine. To settle the dispute, the brothers sought an omen. Remus saw six vultures on the Aventine, then twelve appeared on the Palatine. An argument erupted between the rival supporters: the pro-Remus faction claimed, 'Our vultures came first!' while the pro-Romulus group shouted, 'We had twice as many!'. Two versions of Romulus' fratricide are provided, one involving this dispute and the other happening when Remus cheekily hopped across his brother's mud wall. In either event, Romulus murders Remus, patron of the Aventine, and makes the Palatine the home of Rome's glory.

Romulus' wall, perhaps larger than it needed to be, provoked him to recruit more settlers. Livy's account of this recruitment drive (1.8), which resulted in the original founding families of Rome (*patres*), provides an illuminating perspective on Rome's patrician class as well as the process of city founding:

> Next, so that his great city should not be devoid of inhabitants, Romulus, adopting a plan for increasing the size of the population that was well established by those who found cities, namely that of gathering together people of humble origin and pretending they have been born from the earth, opened up an asylum at a place that is enclosed between two groves as you ascend (i.e. the Capitoline hill). To this spot a rabble fled from neighbouring peoples, both freeborn and servile, eagerly seeking a new life. These people constituted the first expansion towards the greatness that was now under way.
>
> **(Trans. R. Garland)**

It is noteworthy that Romulus' reliance on exiles, 'a mob', is cited here as a step to Rome's greatness. The model for a new settlement is probably taken from the Greeks, who were colonizing southern Italy (and elsewhere) at this time. Greek colonies, which often maintained economic and religious ties with their mother cities, offered increased opportunities for social mobility and economic prosperity to dis-enfranchised Greek citizens. However, this came at a cost: colonizers lost citizenship rights in their mother city (unlike many modern colonizers). This was a risk, as many of the places they chose to settle were already inhabited and skirmishes with the 'locals' were common. As Romulus and his successors expanded, they offered something different to defeated populations (locals and Greek exiles alike). Perhaps more along the lines of the 'American dream', Romans offered acceptance as well as an opportunity to participate and prosper in the Roman community. Rome's policy of absorbing different cultures and forging alliances as she expanded would offer vital economic and military strengths, though this did not always include citizenship (a subject of many debates in the republic).

Having collected a dignified body of citizens, Romulus would need women to perpetuate his noble families (founding a city without females was, perhaps, a small oversight). He invited the neighbouring Sabines to a programme of games and then abducted 600 women, all but one of whom were allegedly 'virgins' (Livy, 1.12–13). The Sabines (quite understandably) sought vengeance, and in the ensuing battle it is not the Romans but the Sabine women who, with dishevelled hair and torn robes, run fearlessly into the fray of flying spears and try to broker peace. The women speak beautifully, reinforcing values of the family:

> We are mothers now . . . our children are your sons and grandsons: do not put on them the taint of patricide . . . We are the cause of discord; on our account our husbands and fathers lie wounded or dead, and we would rather die ourselves than live as widows or orphans.

Livy, who composed many compelling speeches, has created a touching scene that, true to his claims, is more of a fable about virtues and family values than a historical account. This episode, often referred to as the 'rape of the Sabine women', does not necessarily imply the same connotations which that term has today (regarding a violent sexual encounter), though clearly the Roman men had dubious intentions. The Latin verb *rapio* means to 'seize' or 'carry off in a hurry'. Depicted on coins during the civil wars in the early first century BC with two men, each casually carrying a woman, the rape of the Sabine women does not appear to be an episode associated with violence but with the fruits of alliance. From the murder of his brother to the epic rape of the Sabine women, Livy's racy and audacious tales create a memorable example of Romulus as a maniacal yet oddly charismatic urban leader, which Roman emperors would struggle to surpass.

It is difficult to substantiate specific aspects of these accounts with contemporary archaeological evidence from the eighth century BC. Excavations in and around the Palatine reveal huts and pig pens from that century, including the '**Hut of Romulus**', an oblong hut made of wooden poles interwoven with twigs and branches, then covered in clay. Since wood and other organic remains (leaves and skins) seldom survive, archaeologists must work with a network of holes (where the wood used to be). This hut, like the humble hut of Evander described by Virgil, was probably based on the hut of Romulus, noted by Dionysius of Halicarnassus (and many others) on the Palatine. Like a modern historic site, such as the Lincoln Log Cabin Site in Illinois, Romulus' humble hut (or a reconstruction) was maintained and restored by appointed guardians as a monument of Rome's humble past (*Roman Antiquities* 1.79). Models of these homes have also been found as burial urns on the Esquiline and Palatine hills, where two different cultures of burial practice emerge (perhaps evidence of the Latin and Sabine cultures). These remains allow archaeologists to connect a few dots but there are also contradictions. For example, burials and alluvial deposits (from flooding) suggest the Roman Forum was uninhabitable, probably until the early sixth century BC. Though settlement patterns and a dirt wall at the Palatine do not contradict the date of the city's mythological foundation, the supporting evidence for specific events is less conclusive.

Some consistencies arise between the two myths and the archaeological sources: the image of an archaic landscape with simple and scattered farming communities; a society based around small *gentes* (clans) or tribes (and the bitter struggles between them); and the significance of omens and divine intervention. These factors illustrate the similar agendas of Virgil and Livy as writers of salacious yet propitious accounts of Rome's history, both of which aim to reinforce Roman family values and the sense of predestination for the greatness of Rome and her leader Augustus. Each account is clearly an exercise in using history as a propagandist device, tracing the origins of the Roman culture with a view to reinforcing a cultural or political agenda salient at the time the history was written. Nevertheless, insofar as these sources reflect the fundamental values of a civilization, they are informative.

ROME: CENTRE OF THE UNIVERSE

Even before all roads led to Rome, the location of the city was ideal (Map 5). A cluster of hills, each between 60 and 100 metres high, stood on a plateau above a surrounding plain, enriched with fertile volcanic soil deposits from the Tiber. A series of hilltop settlements, separated by marshy ground at the foot of the hills, allowed trade and communication between early settlements. Access to the sea was only a few miles downstream and the hills overlooked some of the best natural shallows for crossing the Tiber, which also made it an important point for travellers along the western coast of Italy, including from Greek settlements in the south (e.g. Cumae in the Bay of Naples) and Etruscan settlements in the north (Etruria, modern-day Tuscany). Both these cultures and their languages would fundamentally shape the development of the Roman world. Perhaps, as Livy and Virgil suggest, Rome was from its beginning destined for greatness.

ETRUSCAN INFLUENCE

Who were **the Etruscans**? Our largest limitation in understanding the Etruscans is how little we know about their culture. As in so many disciplines, what we know shapes not only how we view things, but what we see. Few Etruscan sources survive and most accounts of the Etruscans, written by outside observers such as Greeks or later Romans, tend to be judgemental and moralizing, without attempting to explain or understand the culture. The Greek historian Herodotus (fifth century BC) claimed that the Etruscans, whom he called 'Tyrrheni', came as colonists from Lydia (modern Turkey), which is corroborated by other sources, while Dionysius of Halicarnassus (first century BC, who hailed from the same city as Herodotus) says they were the local Italian population (called Villanovans) (*Roman Antiquities* 1.26). Modern genetic studies support both theories of origin. These accounts may help to provide context for the early foundation myths of Rome. Troy (Aeneas' home), situated in an area called Troad, which shared a western border with Lydia, could provide a link between the Etruscans and the mythological Trojan foundation (though the arrival of Etruscan culture in Italy is generally dated to the eighth century BC). Colonies were often founded by men, so marriage with women from a local tribe was a necessity for survival, which places the rape of the Sabine women in a different context as an event that was neither isolated nor unprecedented in Roman history. There is often a grain of truth or plausibility in even the most seemingly fantastical myths.

The fact that classical scholars (and Rome's historians) tend to be more well versed in Greek culture can result in accounts that give more attention to the Greek origins of Roman culture while neglecting the role of the mysterious Etruscans. More commonly known in literature for their gory sacrificial cults and gloomy religious figures, surviving material evidence, such as cheerful wall paintings of dining and hunting scenes, often contradicts this macabre image. The Etruscan Sarcophagus of the Spouses at the Louvre (late sixth century BC) captures the skills, mysteries and unique cultural pastiche of the Etruscans (Figure 1.3). The sarcophagus, which may have contained urns (used for cremation) rather than bodies, depicts an intimate moment as a husband and wife embrace on a dining couch, perhaps sharing perfume (there is also a wineskin on the couch). This beautifully painted and sculpted clay portrays the man and the woman smiling, in what is often called 'the archaic smile', a characteristic of Ionian and Lydian art. While their image and hairstyles resonate

FIGURE 1.3 The Sarcophagus of the Spouses. This terracotta sarcophagus comes from the Etruscan city of Caere and is dated to the end of the sixth century BC. It features a husband and wife, tenderly entwined on a banqueting couch. The archaic style (evident throughout the Mediterranean at this time) can be seen in their smiling faces, almond-shaped eyes, and imperfect geometric-shaped bodies. Paint can still be seen on the blankets, the pillow, the wife's skin and their hair. Musée du Louvre, Inventory Number: CP5194. Photo © RMN-Grand Palais (Musée du Louvre) / Hervé Lewandowski.

with Greek archaic art, the subject of the event is distinct: the participation of women at Greek dinner parties was limited to courtesans and flute girls, while the Etruscans included spouses. Appreciation of a good dinner party became an integral part of Roman society, and it is a nice contrast to the stoic and austere male/female relationships we often encounter in literature.

Whatever their origins, Etruscans came to be regarded as a separate culture, whose practices were not definitively eastern, Greek or Italian. Despite the numerous controversies that surround the Etruscans, their contribution to Roman culture, especially the urbanization of the city of Rome in the seventh and sixth centuries BC, is undeniable. Etruscan culture had a fundamental economic, religious and cultural influence on Rome, including trade agreements with the Phoenicians, water management, the paving of roads, the plan of a Roman temple, the Roman arch, games and the triumph. These elements shaped Roman culture in many ways, from their government to their social organization and religious practice.

ROME UNDER THE KINGS: A CITY OF MUD

Unlike Augustus' Rome, which he claimed to have 'found a city of brick and left a city of marble', archaic Rome was a city of mud. The same flooding Tiber that prevented the development of the Roman Forum until the sixth century BC also brought a glorious bounty in the form of alluvial clay deposits. These would make mud walls, roof tiles, the clay pipes of the first drainage systems, as well as the beautiful coloured statues and decorations that adorned Rome's early temples, fashioned by imported Etruscan sculptors. Local building stone, such as tufa, was rough and unsightly (grey or yellow), but it was covered by brightly coloured terra cotta tiles that were light, durable and easily replaced. Much later, in the fifteenth century, Pope Sixtus IV, more widely known for his funding of the Sistine chapel, would claim that he had found Rome 'a city of mud and left it a city of brick'. While this is a pun on Augustus' accomplishment, it is also a reflection of the original urbanization of Rome, carried out by her early kings moving from waddle-and-daub habitations to buildings of clay and stone.

After Romulus founded Rome on 21 April 753 BC, a government of kings was established, and the names of Rome's first seven kings are recorded: Romulus, Numa Pompilius, Tullus Hostilius, Ancus Marcius, Tarquinius Priscus, Servius Tullius and Tarquinius Superbus in numerous historical sources. Descriptions of these kings, who appear to have ruled in convenient blocks of around thirty to thirty-five years each, are somewhat suspect. (For comparison, the average ruling period for an English monarch in the modern era is twenty-one years, and more contemporary lists of Spartan kings reflect even less longevity.) Many historians would like to consolidate this period of 240 years to 140 years to fit with the surviving archaeological remains, which attest to significant growth in the late seventh and sixth centuries BC.

Rome's early kings are generally associated with military conquest, and some time in the seventh century BC scattered Latin settlements in Rome were invaded and/or formed an alliance with the neighbouring Etruscans from the north. More attention is given to the last three kings, starting from the end of the seventh century BC. At this time it seems that Rome was not only extending her territorial boundaries south of the Tiber but developing into both a city and a cohesive urban community in the swamp land between her hillside towns.

According to the sources, Rome's original social organization under Romulus comprised three ethnic tribes: the Sabines (Tities), Latins (Ramnes) and Etruscans (Luceres). Each of these was divided into ten *curiae*, whose representatives were responsible for civil affairs and met, as and when the king required, to discuss (but not decide) matters of national importance. The tribes were also committed to provide military support in times of war (fairly often it seems) in the form of 1000 infantry and 100 cavalry. While Rome's kings were nominally elected and advised by an appointed council of advisers (selected from the 100 most important families in the city – the patricians), at best the system was an oligarchy (rule of a few: namely, aristocrats). In practice, Rome's government under the kings probably had closer parallels with basic economic or domestic class systems. The *paterfamilias* was the head of the household with absolute power, including the right to pronounce death upon members of his own family. In true *Godfather* style, wealthy Roman landowners supported hundreds of *clientes* (farmers, artisans and warriors), who needed patronage or had been made an offer they 'couldn't refuse'. In the first century BC, the politician Cicero (*De Republica* 2.16) argued that this system worked well in practice, as the people were 'kept in order':

> [Romulus] dictated that nobles should act as patrons and protectors to lesser citizens, their natural clients and dependants, in their respective districts; a measure whose advantage I will note later. Judicial punishments were largely fines of sheep and oxen, for the property of the people at that time consisted of fields and cattle, a situation that produced the terms which, even today, define real and personal wealth. And so the people were kept in order by fiduciary penalties rather than physical punishment.

Cicero's opinion is contested in other accounts.

The king's role was multifaceted, including military, political, social and religious authority. The king's political power was expressed in the state chair (the 'curule' chair), a purple-lined toga and the *fasces*, a bundle of rods with an axe in the middle, carried by his attendants (lictors) as a reminder of punishments: all of these are attributed by Livy to the Etruscans (1.8). The king's religious role is attested in one of the few surviving Latin inscriptions from the archaic period, found buried under later paving works at the heart of the Roman Forum (in front of the Senate house (*Curia*; Map 5; Figure 1.4). Called the **Lapis Niger** ('black stone'), this obeliskoid slab of grey tufa commemorates a sacred place for the king, though what it represents is debated (possibly the site of a king's assassination?). It is very difficult to read, not only because the language is so unusual (a mix of numerous tongues) but because it is carved left to right, then right to left (called 'boustrophedon': like the pattern made by a plough in ancient Greece or a lawnmower in the modern world). There are no spaces or stops between the words, either. Scholars can make out only a few key words, such as King (*Recei*), Sacred (*Sacros*) and Priest/Servant (*Kalator*). The presentation of writing on this oddly shaped monument, combined with its location in the pavement, makes the thought of someone trying to read it seem ridiculous. It is important to remember that writing, especially on public monuments, can serve a symbolic role, which supports but is by no means vital to understanding the message. The same is true of modern monuments, such as the Vietnam War memorial in Washington, DC: one need not read every name to understand the broader meaning of a commemorative act.

FIGURE 1.4 Lapis Niger. This photo depicts a cast of the Lapis Niger on display at the Il Museo Epigrafico (Museo Nazionale Romano). The actual monument, dated to the sixth century BC, is inscribed on unsightly 'grotto oscura' tufa from Veii and remains in situ beneath the paving in front of the Senate house in the Forum Romanum. The size (c. 60 cm in height), shape, and style (right to left; then left to right) of this monument make it nearly impossible to read (even if we knew what it said). It is the epitome of a monument that was meant to be seen, rather than read. Photo © Ministero dei Beni e delle Attività Culturali e del Turismo – Soprintendenza Speciale per i Beni Archeologici di Roma.

At least two of the last three kings of Rome were Etruscan (the Emperor Claudius and others would argue that Servius Tullius was also an Etruscan mercenary). The Etruscans, who built a series of hilltop fort settlements in Etruria (the word 'Etruscan' refers in Greek and Latin to these towers – *tursis*), had extensive experience mining tunnels for water and drainage, as well as building platforms and arches (some Etruscan arches still survive in Volterra and Perugia) and administering a large population. Tarquinius Priscus' initiatives, including the plunder of rebel Etruscan towns, would set an irrevocable precedent of using the fruits of victory to finance public and religious projects. He began work on the Temple of Jupiter Optimus Maximus ('Jupiter Best and Greatest') on the Capitoline hill, which was constructed on a platform 60 metres long and 55 metres wide, as well as the Cloaca Maxima (the Greatest Sewer), an open sewer that drained into a series of tunnels leading into the Tiber (the opening can still be seen today). Pliny the Elder would later describe these tunnels as 'large enough for a loaded hay wagon to pass through' (*Natural History* 36.24). The Circus Maximus, its chariot races and the procession of a triumphant victor in purple robes all claim origins in Etruscan traditions (Livy, 1.36) (Map 5, no. 3). The king's palace, known as 'the Regia', in the Roman Forum, was built in Etruscan style; and the Vicus Tuscus, which marked out Rome's Etruscan neighbour- hood, ran from the Regia to the Forum Boarium on the other side of the Palatine.

The most important political, social and military reforms are associated with Servius Tullius, who may or may not have been Etruscan and/or a king (some have argued that he was not an official king but an appointed 'dictator'). Tullius was unique in many ways: he was from a servile class and he was the only king elected by popular demand (without the approval of the Senate). His class reforms, which included a greater portion of the city's inhabitants in state participation and military service, his dedication of the Temple of Diana on the Aventine (associated with the plebs) and the myth of his divine birth by a giant phallus that rose out of the ground defined him as the patron of the plebs. Frankly, the legends fit a bit too neatly, and again we have the sense that Roman historians are using history to create a prophecy or to trace the origin of existing conflicts. Despite these problems, fundamental roots of the Roman constitution emerge at this time, and the tensions between a small privileged elite and the broader urban population were certainly real.

Servius Tullius' efforts to reorganize the population into five classes on the basis of wealth (a bit like modern tax brackets), rather than ethnic tribes, reflect the needs of a growing population in Rome and its hinterland. However, like Kleithenes' contemporary reforms in Athens, a more inclusive aristocracy still excluded many people (women, slaves and those who did not own land) and those within the five classes were not equal: greater wealth carried greater privilege and obligation. The definition of wealth is also revealing. While sources refer to asses (*Aes*, bronze, being the main material for coinage), we know that money, in conventional terms, did not exist. Common measures of wealth were tied to the land (*iugera*) and livestock (*pecus*, 'a head cattle', which is the origin of the Latin word *pecunia*, meaning 'funds'). Pliny the Elder credits Servius Tullius with the invention of Roman money in the form of metal bars (*Natural History* 33.13): 'King Servius put a stamp on copper . . . like that of an ox or sheep.' This passage, which describes the branding of money, is often misinterpreted. These chunks of bronze (called *Aes rude*; Figure 1.5), like the Spartan currency of iron bars, were hardly functional for everyday transactions and were often broken into smaller bits, like a *libra*, or 'pound' (327 grams – roughly three-quarters of a modern pound). In the past, decorated bars, called *Aes signatum*, with pictures of oxen, were associated with Servius Tullius, but none of these date before the mid-fifth century BC, and they were used through to the third century BC (see Figure 2.1). However, some *Aes rude* appear to have countermarks or stamps, which could have been the branding to which Pliny refers. Romans, unlike Greeks, did not mint coins until the late fourth century, and the first coins made in Rome would not follow until the start of the third century BC. In many respects, the Romans as we know them – an internationally respected, Latin-speaking economic superpower – did not yet exist. Divisions between the wealthy patricians and the common plebs, both economically and spatially (between the Palatine and Aventine hills), however, were real; and the issue that divided Rome's founding brothers would continue to tear her people asunder for centuries to come.

The last king, Tarquinius Superbus ('the proud'), earned his name by refusing to bury his predecessor (not the sign of a 'good' hero in epic terms). Despite many successful military campaigns and diverting the money generated by them to public works, including improvements to the Temple of Jupiter Optimus Maximus and benches for the Circus Maximus, his attitudes towards the people garnered contempt from both classes.

> Having selected the plebs who were loyal to him and fit for military service, he put the rest into forced labour on public works. For he believed that kings were most vulnerable when the poor and needy were idle . . . The poor were set to work for a miserable ration of grain: quarrying stone, cutting timber, leading wagons filled with these materials . . . Others were put to work digging underground conduits, constructing arches and supporting walls for them and assisting the various craftsmen, copper-smiths, carpenters and stonemasons, all forcibly removed from their private business to labour for the public good.
>
> **(Dionysius of Halicarnassus, *Roman Antiquities* 4.44)**

Moreover, Tarquinius Superbus did not treat members of the Roman or Latin aristocracy much better. He did not consult the Senate before declaring war or concluding treaties. Also, having made alliances with the Latin tribes, he called them

FIGURE 1.5a The *Aes rude* was generally an uncast slab of bronze of varying weight and size, sometimes decorated like a seashell (but often plain and unsightly). It appears to have been the most common medium for large-scale transactions (one would not carry a bag of these to the local market). That Latin term *rudera* may refer to the colour of the uncast bronze – 'red' – rather than the rough nature of the metal. This trade of raw materials, which was common between the eighth and the fourth centuries BC, represents not so much a lack of trade by the Romans but a rudimentary form of monetary exchange that is not, perhaps, so surprising in a primarily agrarian-based economy where silver was scarce and gold a rare commodity. Photo © CNG Coins.

FIGURE 1.5b This silver didrachm with the suckling she-wolf was one of the earliest coins minted in Rome in the mid 3rd century BC. Although this image of the wolf is often cited as an 'early Roman imagery', it dates to 500 years after Rome's foundation. Modeled on the Greek monetary system of drachma (a didrachm was worth two drachma) this coin illustrates the necessity of currency for trade with a Greek audience, indeed Rome's first coins in the late 4th century were minted in Naples. The small didrachm weighed less than 7 grams, compared with the Aes *rude* (ranging from 10–300 grams), and stamped bars (Aes Signatum, some weighing more than a kilo) used in central Italy and Etruria. Photo © CNG Coins.

to a meeting at dawn but did not turn up himself until the evening, prompting one Latin leader to observe: 'No wonder that Rome has called him Tarquin the proud!' (Livy, 1.50). He is an interesting foil for the republican dictator Sulla, who, after numerous military successes, marched on Rome, dug up and burned the bones of his predecessor, then promoted several of his cronies, killing off his enemies with public death lists.

Livy (1.58) has another yarn for the fall of the kings, involving (yet again) the rape, sacrifice and death of a virtuous Roman woman: Lucretia. The tale, probably much more interesting than the truth, describes how Superbus' unruly son Sextus falls for a virtuous wife, who dutifully accepts him into her home in her husband's absence. When she refuses his advances, he threatens not only to kill her but to kill a slave and place the body next to hers (worse, by far, than death was to be caught consorting with a slave). Bound to lose her honour either way, Lucretia submits to Sextus but afterwards calls for her husband and her father (who still has primary authority) and confesses. After demanding reparation and unable to live with the shame, Lucretia kills herself. On hearing of this, Lucius Junius Brutus, rather than Lucretia's immediate family, leads a group of noblemen to avenge her honour in a *coup d'état*, probably with an ulterior motive. In trying to understand the subtleties of this account, we are drawn back to Livy's preface (1.1) on Roman history:

> Let each of my readers attentively direct his thoughts to what sort of life and morals were in place, and to the types of men and by what policies, both domestic and military, our empire was acquired and extended.
>
> **(Trans. R. Garland)**

The rape of Lucretia, which does follow more conventional definitions of 'rape', is not a straightforward account of a historic event, but rather a moralizing fable about Rome's virtues and vices. One can see why facts and/or evidence are rather scarce, but at least Livy is up front about it.

Rome's last king, unlike his predecessors, was not assassinated: he was driven from the city to live in luxurious exile, first in Etruria, then, after a failed attempt to return, in the Greek colony of Cumae. Roman historians can proudly note that in 509 BC, a year after Athens removed its tyrants and a year before that city took her first steps towards 'democracy' with Kleithenes' reforms, Rome expelled her kings and gave birth to a republic. There is an important difference between setting oneself within the context of the Greek world and shamelessly mimickng its achievements. Rome's origins, while set within the historical and epic framework of the Greek world, are different in a number of respects. Regardless of the moralizing tendencies of Roman authors, Rome's heroes were not the victors of the 'Golden Age' and her city was not a palace capital with golden riches. Rome's legacy was a series of huts and scrubby hills, colonized by exiles and asylum-seekers from across the Mediterranean. Her defining features were not her commonalities with the Greek traditions but her differences, and the diverse cultures of Etruscans, Sabines, Latins and Greeks who came to live together. These men, who would become Romans, were united not by a culture or a language but by a prosperity that was a product of their own toil (and divine prophecy, of course). Emily Lazarus' poem, now on a bronze plaque at the base of the Statue of Liberty, would have fit equally well on the gateway of Rome at the twilight of the sixth century BC as the city began her next step towards becoming a nation with the founding of the republic:

> Not like brazen giant of Greek fame,
> With conquering limbs astride from land to land . . .
> 'Keep, ancient lands, your storied pomp!' cries she,
> With silent lips. 'Give me your tired, your poor,
> Your huddled masses yearning to breathe free,
> The wretched refuse of your teeming shore.
> Send these, the homeless, tempest-tost to me,
> I lift my lamp beside the golden door!'

FURTHER READING

Barker, G. and Rasmussen, T., *The Etruscans*, Blackwell, 2000.

Carandini, A. (trans. Sartarelli, S.), *Rome: Day One*, Princeton University Press, 2011.

Cobbold, G.B. (trans.), *Vergil's Aenied: Hero, War, Humanity*, Bolchazy-Carducci, 2005.

Cornell, T., *The Beginnings of Rome: Italy and Rome from the Bronze Age to the Punic Wars (ca. 1000–264 BCE)*, Routledge, 1995.

Forsythe, G., *A Critical History of Rome from Prehistory to Early Rome*, University of California Press, 2005.

Macmullen, R., *The Earliest Romans: A Character Sketch*, University of Michigan Press, 2011.

Smith, C.J., *Early Rome and Latium Economy & Society 1000–500 BC*, Oxford University Press, 1996.

Wiseman, T.P., *The Myths of Rome*, Exeter University Press, 2004.

2 THE REPUBLIC (510–60 BC)

The Latin term *respublica* is usually translated as 'state' or 'commonwealth'; it was not a 'democracy' in a modern sense. Rome's rigid social classifications, with people divided by wealth (usually landownership), status (freed or enslaved) and class (patrician or plebeian), was not necessarily less 'democratic' than contemporary Greek democracies, which had similar social divisions and excluded the poor, foreigners, women and slaves. At a time when Greece would move from democracy, to oligarchy, to a Macedonian hegemony under Philip and Alexander the Great (mid-fourth century BC), the Roman republic would develop in many ways, but would remain dominated by members of the upper classes, especially the patricians and the *equites* (the second class of citizen, who were provided with horses by the state). The republic began at the end of the sixth century BC as a fledgling collection of agrarian communities (509 BC) and ended as vast empire across Italy, Europe and the Mediterranean, including millions of people.

This chapter will consider how the republic, like its citizens, grew and evolved over the course of 450 years in three periods: the birth of the Roman constitution (509–281 BC); Roman warfare and imperialism (281–121 BC); and the twilight of the republic (121–49 BC). In the first period we see a culture that is struggling to survive; in the second we witness the rapid expansion of Rome's culture and her borders; and in the third we encounter new adversities, as Rome struggles to administrate her empire.

THE BIRTH OF THE ROMAN CONSTITUTION (509–281 BC)

Now I will retrace the political and military history of a free Rome.

(Livy, 2.1)

Contrary to what Livy's remark may suggest, neither the republic nor the city of Rome was born in a day. The transition from monarchy to republic was a slow and difficult one. The fifth century BC was a period of experimentation in Rome's offices and the idea of a fixed yearly consulship is not fully attested until the following century. The period from 500 to 300 BC is often referred to as the 'obscure centuries' in Roman history and most of our sources, with the exception of Polybius (*c.* 200–118 BC) and Cato the Censor (234–149 BC) come from the first century BC (e.g. Livy (see Chapters 1 and 8), Dionysius of Halicarnassus and Cicero (see Chapter 8)). At this time, the Romans engaged in a number of battles with neighbouring Sabines, Latins and Etruscans, and they suffered the Gauls' sack of Rome in 390 BC (followed by a second sack in 358), events which led to the destruction of many early records. Constant warfare continued to strain the relationship between the working-class plebs and their wealthy patrons (the patricians), resulting in a number of conflicts throughout the fifth century BC and on into the mid-fourth century, when a compromise was finally reached (367 BC). The most significant outcome of this early period (aside from military conquests) was a series of legal and social reforms which included the drafting of Rome's first law code (the Twelve Tables) and the **Roman constitution**. The legal structure and the system of checks and balances lay at the heart of Rome's success during the early to mid-republic period (500–200 BC) but proved fatal flaws as her empire expanded (200–59 BC).

OFFICES AND ASSEMBLIES IN THE ROMAN CONSTITUTION

Rome's mixed constitution, often compared to the Spartan government, created a series of checks and balances between executive (consuls), legislative (the assemblies) and judicial (praetors) powers (see Appendix 1). Polybius' account of the Roman constitution, written in Greek to explain Rome's government to the eastern world, remains a key source for scholars and was also consulted during the drafting of the United States' constitution. A key point in the transition from monarchy to republic was the transfer of power, including full military command, from a single king to two individuals whose role was based on consultation: 'the consul was so named because he consults the people and the Senate' (Varro, *On the Language* 5.14). Among the most important powers was *imperium*, often translated simply as 'power', which was a specific legal authority awarded by the state to an individual to run the state. Outside the *pomerium* (the sacred boundary of the city) this power included capital punishment. The politics of the republic were inextricably linked to power and prestige, and to be elected consul was often regarded as the pinnacle of the Roman career ladder (called the *cursus honorum*). Jealously guarded by Rome's leading families, the highest offices were not unattainable, but any outsider who did succeed (e.g. Gaius Duilius, Marius and Cicero) was sneeringly referred to by an elite majority as a **novus homo** 'new man', someone who was the first member of their family to be elected consul and/or to serve in the Senate.

Of fundamental importance in the republican system was a series of checks and balances that allowed magistrates to veto the actions of equal or lower magistrates. A further check, meant to give the plebs a voice, was added in the early fifth century: the tribune of the plebs.

Offices

Consul (two)
- Term of office: one year. Later restrictions would limit continued tenure.
- Powers and perks: each had twelve lictors who carried *fasces*. They presided over the assemblies, the Senate and judicial matters, and they could propose laws. They were also military commanders, leading troops into battle.
- Checks: each consul could veto the other, and they were accountable for their actions after their term of office. During office they were also subject to a *provocatio* (literally a 'calling out'), whereby the people could appeal against a decision.

Dictator (one), plus master of the horse (an assistant to carry out the dictator's commands)
- Term of office: six months (maximum).
- Powers and perks: twenty-four lictors (equivalent to two consuls). In times of crisis, particularly in war, a single dictator could be nominated by the two consuls. This individual had chief executive and military powers, including the power to kill a Roman citizen. Free of the tribunes' veto, a dictator could appoint an assistant – the master of the horse – who, though not elected, often exercised similar powers (as the executor of a dictator's command). (This 'grey area' in the Roman constitution will be examined later.) According to Livy, dictators were appointed throughout the fifth century, primarily to wage war, from which they returned in triumphal processions. The procession not only celebrated victory but was a symbolic return of the *fasces* (the symbol of *imperium*) at the city gates.
- Checks: a dictator was meant to return his powers as soon as the emergency for which he had been appointed was resolved. Perhaps surprisingly, Rome's dictators generally followed this principle and it was only in the first century BC, with the arrival of Sulla, who was granted the title for life, that the term acquired the negative connotation it has today.

Censor (two; instituted in 444 BC)

- Term of office: eighteen months, every five years.
- Powers and perks: chief registrar, financial and tax officer, who was responsible for supervising the Roman census as well as public morality. Though the term was only eighteen months, the acts remained in force until the next election. Censors had wide powers not only in classing individuals – 'They shall divide citizens into tribes and list them according to wealth, age and rank' (Cicero, *On the Laws* 3.2) – but in disciplining them: 'Anyone who let his land grow wild and was not giving it enough attention . . . became a matter for the censors who could reduce him to the lowest rank of citizen' (Aulus Gellius, *Attic Nights* 4.12). Censors were also in charge of public works, such as roads and aqueducts, which required time to complete and afforded great power through the awarding of building contracts to private individuals.

Praetor (six; after 197 BC)

- Term of office: one year.
- Powers and perks: six lictors. A chief law officer in the courts, judge and understudy of the consuls. Like consuls and dictators, he was given *imperium*. Power in the courts, even the ability to schedule the order of trials, was crucial (see discussion of Cicero's *In Verrem*, below).

Aedile (four)

- Term of office: one year.
- Powers and perks: supervisor of public works, temples, markets and games. Two of the four were usually plebeians.

Quaestor (four after 421 BC; eight after 267 BC; twenty after Sulla (80 BC))

- Term of office: one year.
- Powers and perks: Assistant to the consuls, particularly controller of the military or civic treasury, and keeper of records.

Tribune of the Plebs (two)

- Term of office: one year.
- Powers and perks: as direct representatives of the people (elected for the plebs by the Plebeian Assembly), they had the right to appeal a magistrate's decision (*provocatio*) through 'due process'. Their position was sacrosanct: to interfere with the act of a tribune could be punished by death. The ultimate check on constitutional powers (save the dictator), a tribune could veto (*intercessio*) any act by an assembly or a magistrate. However, the veto applied only to the act of

passing the law (not the legislation itself) and had to be carried out in person (like filibustering in the American Senate and the British House of Commons). The moment the tribune left (or was murdered or physically restrained), the measure could be passed. Tribunes' powers existed only within the city walls.

• Checks: tribunes could not veto a dictator. Their 'sacrosanct' status was declared but not always enforced.

The highest offices – consuls, censors and praetors – were elected by the Centuriate Assembly (Comitia Centuriata). Dictators were appointed by the consuls. Lower-level magistracies were elected by the Tribal Assembly (Comitia Tributa). Tribunes of the plebs were elected by the Plebeian Council (Concilium Plebis). To understand the elections, it is necessary to understand how these assemblies operated.

Assemblies

Comitia Centuriata (Centuriate Assembly)
The Comitia Centuriata was organized by military units (*centuries* – groups of 100 men), arranged in five classes based on wealth (generally landownership). The system cleverly aligned the greater military obligations with a voting majority in the assembly for Rome's wealthiest citizens (first-class citizens and *equites* (cavalrymen)). Of the 193 *centuries* in the Centuriate Assembly, 98 of the votes came from the first class. Upper classes voted first and once a majority was reached the vote ended (some *centuries* were dismissed before voting). This assembly elected senior state officials, declared war, concluded peace treaties, approved legislation and, before it was transferred to the courts, had a final say in cases of execution or exile.

Comitia Tributa (Tribal Assembly)
Open to all citizens, the Tribal Assembly was organized into thirty-five tribes (four urban and thirty-one rural). In turn, these tribes were organized geographically (unlike the Comitia Centuriata, which was organized by wealth), in a similar way to modern parliamentary constituencies, but these distinctions became less clear as tribe membership passed from father to son. Although votes were announced in advance, members of urban tribes had a better chance of attending them (though increased attendance did not increase the overall vote afforded to each tribe, which was one vote each). The order in which the tribes voted was also important, as the first tribe (*principum*) could sway successive voters. However, the order of voting was chosen 'randomly', by lot, so the process was less stratified than in the Centuriate Assembly, which was organized and voted in order, according to wealth. The presiding official was a consul or praetor, and this individual retained a great deal of power, calling the assembly and setting the agenda of each vote. There was none of the democratic

debate we see in modern equivalents (e.g. the House of Representatives and the House of Commons), merely a 'yes' or 'no' vote on a legislative, electoral or judicial issue. Although often called the 'people's assembly' by later sources, such as Livy, Cicero and Polybius, one should be careful about applying modern or even late republican terminology to this early–mid-republic assembly.

Concilium Plebis (Meeting of the Plebs)
This was the plebs' parliament, which voted, like the Comitia Tributa, in tribes or districts. It elected its own officers and formulated decrees for the plebs, which would later (278 BC) be made binding for the community as a whole.

The Senate
Originally an advisory body taken from Rome's 100 leading families, the Roman Senate initially retained an advisory role in the republic. It could pass decrees – *senatus consulta* – on social, political and military agendas, but though its advice was often followed, these decrees were not legally binding and they could be overruled by the assemblies. The Senate's evolution as an institution came directly as a result of Rome's growing empire. In times of war, its advice took on a new authority and its role in foreign policy afforded greater financial and administrative powers. Unlike other magistracies, Roman senators (mostly former praetors, consuls and censors) were not elected but appointed by consuls and censors, and the resulting membership was often elitist. Was the Senate ever meant to assume all the powers it assumed in the mid-late republic? Cicero thinks so: 'Our ancestors made the Senate the guardian, defender, the protector of the state, they wanted the magistrates to respect the authority of this order and to be, so to speak, the servants of this most weighty council' (*In Defence of Plancius* 65.137). However, senators such as Cicero were not inclined to underrate the powers they wielded.

Even using the most conservative dates – from *c.* 450 BC to the end of the first triumvirate (*c.* 59 BC) – the republic lasted for nearly 400 years. Few modern constitutions can claim such longevity (the US constitution is only 240 years old). The fact that a constitution laid out by a relatively small collection of agrarian communities continued to function for a vast empire attests to the functionality and flexibility of this document.

The Roman constitution in practice: Cincinnatus and Maelius

Just as American history textbooks abound with diagrams of the US constitutional branches, Roman literature has numerous dry, theoretical accounts of the Roman constitution. Both fail to capture what is arguably the most important part of a constitution: how it is applied and manipulated on a daily basis. Set in 439 BC, Livy's tale of the infamous Spurius Maelius (his first name means 'bastard') and the hero

Cincinnatus ('curly haired') (Livy, 4.13–14) reveals a continuing issue with checks and balances in the Roman constitution that was just as significant in Livy's time (see Chapter 1) as it was in the mid-fifth century BC. Cincinnatus was an established leader: appointed dictator in a war against the Sabines (458 BC), he won a decisive victory in just sixteen days and immediately stepped down (George Washington was named the 'American Cincinnatus'). Maelius, on the other hand, was a wealthy equestrian (second-class) upstart, who, realizing he had no chance of being elected consul without the support of a patrician Senate, courted popular support by giving free corn to the plebs. This act of generosity (which Livy acknowledges was not unworthy) was condemned, not in its own right, but because it set a bad precedent (see the Catiline conspiracy of 62 BC). The official in charge of providing corn to the plebs, Minucius, was not impressed with Maelius' goodwill (which infringed upon his exalted office and drove up the price of corn). Minucius approached the Senate with 'evidence' (in the form of rumours) of weapons stored at Maelius' house and tribunes betraying the people. After being berated by the Senate for their inaction, the consuls blamed the appeal laws (the tribune's *provocatio* and *intercessio*) for their lack of authority and called for 'a resolute man who was free from the net of legal controls'. Cincinnatus was unanimously approved as dictator and appointed Servilius as his master of the horse, who proceeded to the Forum the next day for a final showdown with Maelius.

> Maelius and his followers understood that it was against them that the force of so great an office was directed, but those who were ignorant of the plans to set up a kingship asked what outbreak of civil violence or what sudden outbreak of war had demanded the awesome appointment or a dictator or required Quinctius, a man in his eighties, to become the helmsman of the state. Servilius, master of the horse, was sent to Maelius by the dictator and said, 'The dictator summons you.' When Maelius, fearful, asked what he wanted, Servilius informed him that he must stand trial to face a charge that Minucius had brought before the Senate. Whereupon Maelius shrank back into the group of his supporters and at first looking all around sought to turn tail and escape. Eventually, when an attendant was ready to lead him off by order of the master of horse, he was snatched away by those surrounding him. As he fled he called upon the Roman plebs to protect him . . . While he was crying out Servilius pursued him and slew him. Covered in the victim's blood . . . Servilius announced to the dictator that Maelius, after being summoned, had thrust away the attendant and was inciting the mob when he received his due punishment. The dictator said, 'Congratulations, Caius Servilius, you have saved the Republic.' He announced that Maelius had been lawfully slain (even though he was innocent of the charge of aiming at kingship) on the grounds that he had been summoned by the master of horse and had failed to appear before the dictator.
>
> **(Trans. R. Garland)**

While the constitutional role of a Roman dictator clearly works and the republic is duly 'saved', there are a few cracks evident in the rose-tinted glass of the constitution, particularly with regard to due process. Was Maelius really a threat to the state? The only 'proof' appears to be the testimony of Minucius, a fellow patrician, who clearly had an axe to grind. There was no investigation or trial, but the consuls' complaint that they lacked proper powers seems to imply a death sentence (one of the few limits to their powers). Cincinnatus follows this episode with a rousing monologue that condemns Maelius for his pathetic aspirations: 'Spurius Maelius! . . . a rich corn dealer of humble birth – a man who thought he could purchase our liberty with a sack of flour, and that Rome, mistress of Italy, could be lured into servitude by throwing her a biscuit! . . . it is a monstrosity.' Even assuming Maelius' aspirations were as pathetic and misguided as Cincinnatus suggests, was his murder necessary? Moreover, does the master of the horse possess the powers of a dictator, for it is Servilius (not Cincinnatus) who murders a Roman citizen in the middle of the Forum, ignoring Maelius' plea for protection.

As a final act, Cincinnatus ordered the quaestors to liquidate Maelius' properties and hand over the proceeds to public funds, thus setting the most dangerous precedent of all: the murder of a Roman citizen without a trial followed by the confiscation of his property for public use. Cincinnatus' actions reveal a growing disparity between the citizen classes in Rome. If a citizen of Rome's second-highest class can be heckled off the political stage, what message does that send to everyone else? The fact that, on numerous occasions in the second and first centuries BC, Rome was nearly lured away from her liberty by similar 'biscuits', was not lost upon Livy. Although it is a single episode, the story of Maelius is an event that resonates throughout the republic, not to mention in a modern context, where the rights of the individual can be lost within a larger political machine.

LAW AND ORDER: ROMAN LAW AND THE STRUGGLE OF THE ORDERS

Laying down the law in Rome: the Twelve Tables

> Making laws so that liberty will be equal for all, from the highest to the lowest.
>
> **(Livy, 3.31)**

The class struggles which dominated the Roman republic were addressed in both the city's constitution and her laws, where 'due process' was defined. Although the constitution provided a framework of power, the Romans still lacked a formal and codified system of laws. The frequency of office change afforded a check on individuals, but it also created inconsistency in the practice and application of law. In a modern context, legal cases are often based on precedent. Not having an encoded law or permanent offices to employ it created inconsistencies in the Roman legal system, making it both capricious and arbitrary. Patrician legislators manipulated laws to suit their own needs (a problem that continues to plague legal practice). According to Livy (3.31), it was the plebs who called for a codified law to be decided by a council of plebs and patricians. This did not go down well with the patricians:

> The fathers ['*patres*'] did not scorn the notion but they declared that no one should propose a law unless he belonged to the ranks of the fathers. Since they were in accord about the laws and only disagreed about the proposer, they sent legates to Athens with orders to copy down the famous laws of Solon and get to know the institutions, the customs, and the laws of other Greek city-states.

> **(Trans. R. Garland)**

Although Rome sought a Greek template, the resulting product was distinctly Roman. Unlike the Greeks, who often selected an individual such as Solon in Athens (a man with the superior wisdom to leave the city as soon as his laws were in place), the Romans elected a decemvirate ('ten men') to define their laws. While the patricians succeeded in electing a solely patrician body of decemvirs, the subsequent disgrace of these men (there were episodes of rape, deceit and suicide) ultimately weakened the case for patrician moral superiority.

Inscribed in bronze and set up in public, the Twelve Tables were not so much a resource as a testament to the sacred and permanent power of the law. Sadly, the very popularity of these laws (Cicero records memorizing them as a boy (*De Legibus* 2.4, 23)) precluded them from being recorded elsewhere. The laws constituted a set of rules for public, private and political behaviour, and the concepts of landownership, *possessio* and *proprietas* (the modern precept 'possession is nine-tenths of the law' may have its roots here) were crucial, distinguishing between those who owned their own land (*possessio*) and those who had been granted the use of public land by the state (*proprietas*). Some laws, such as the ban on intermarriage between plebs and patricians or the stipulation that perjurers should be thrown from the Tarpeian rock, eventually lost their practical application. The laws demonstrate clear distinctions between class, age and gender. Stealing during the night was punishable by death, but during the day distinctions applied: a freedman would be flogged; a slave would be flogged and thrown over the Tarpeian rock; and if underage (before puberty), a youth would be flogged and required to make reparation. Distinctions between intentional and accidental murder and the right to remove a neighbour's overhanging tree survive today as the basis of European law.

Balance of powers? Theory and practice in Roman law

> Remember what I said at the beginning: unless a state maintains a balance of
> rights, duties and functions, so that state officials possess enough power,
> deliberations of the leading citizenry and enough authority, and the people
> enough freedom, it is not possible for it to remain stable.
>
> **(Cicero, *On the Republic* 2.30)**

Perhaps the most important distinction in understanding law, ancient as well as modern, is the division between legal theory and practice. Laws are often composed to represent a social ideology, but the extent to which these laws are employed in practice can vary. Note the 'legal' drinking age in America: how many university students consume their first alcoholic drink at twenty-one? Similarly, when legislation declares social equality, it does not necessarily make it so in reality (at least not immediately). The fact that many of Rome's laws were passed and recast suggests that some ideas, though set in law, were not successfully enforced. In this respect, laws can document both the aspirations and the realities of Roman legislation.

By the mid-fifth century BC, the tribunes of the plebs and the Twelve Tables had been employed to balance the system of power and the tensions between the classes. However, Aulus Gellius' (AD 120–150) account of the patrician Lucius Veratius, who goes around slapping free men and then paying them the fine (twenty-five small coins, as prescribed by the Twelve Tables, which had become a nominal sum indeed after centuries of inflation), illustrates the discrepancies that emerged between legal theory and practice, especially after a period of time had elapsed (*Attic Nights* 20.1.13).

In ancient Rome, as in the modern world, people of financial means often lived a less fettered existence. Declaring that all men are equal in the eyes of the law does not change the way they are treated overnight (though legal validation is a vital step in the process). A strength of the Roman legal system can be seen at the end of Gellius' account, when the praetors move to adjust the law. Perhaps the most important insight offered by laws is an ability to see the Roman constitution in action: to view the balance of powers and the vital process of check/checkmate in Roman politics.

Roman law in action: the tribune of the plebs

In 494 BC the plebs went on strike as a result of their continued dissatisfaction with the patricians' ruling powers (for many plebs, the transfer from a king to an oligarchy did not bring many advantages) and took a stand on the Aventine hill (Cicero, *On the Republic* 2.33). The resolution of this conflict was the *Lex Sacrata*, which gave tribunes their powers of veto and made them sacrosanct. The powers of the tribunes were somewhat less spectacular in practice. Two years later, a law was passed to penalize anyone who interfered with the act of a tribune (he would be fined, and put to death if he did not pay). This was reaffirmed in 449 BC: 'This was the third time the law was enacted since the expulsion of the kings. The cause of it being enacted so many times I take to be no other than this: that the power of a few was greater than the liberty of the plebs' (Livy, 10.9). These laws were meant to allow plebeians access to public offices, including the consulship, but this does not appear to have happened until the law was formally codified in 367 BC. Early lists of consuls, dictators and other office-holders confirm that the highest offices (established by the mid-fifth century BC) were not held by plebeians until later, with the first recorded pleb quaestor in 409, the first consul in 367, and the first censor in 351. Even then, Livy's 'equality for all' is dubious. The first plebian dictator, Gaius Marcius Rutulus (356 BC) was obstructed in every way by the patrician Senate during his military campaigns. According to Livy, this only increased his support among the broader populace, who voted him a triumph without the authorization of the Senate. In Livy's account 'the people' are probably the Comitia Tributa, although the Latin is somewhat ambiguous (Livy, 7.17–21). (One limitation of first-century BC accounts is that they tend to ascribe modern terms to more ancient practice. For the same reason that one should not assume that votes in Congress were the same in 1780 as they are today, readers should be careful of the way later sources employ popular terminology in accounts of the early republic.)

This extended period of conflict, aptly named 'the struggle of the orders', diminished only when Rome was threatened by foreign enemies, who took precedence over her internal social and political problems. It is not coincidental that compromises between patricians and plebs came after Rome had suffered significant defeats (e.g. the sack of Rome by the Gauls c. 390 BC), times when the patricians came to depend upon their plebeian clients. The sack of Rome (the severity of which is sometimes overstated) was not only destructive to the city's buildings and archives; it also inspired revolts from Etruscan, Latin, Samnite and Campanian allies. The fact that the city did 'bounce back' is a testament to its tenacity and resilience. However, Rome could not afford to fight numerous wars and adversaries with a 'house divided'. Her success in these wars, which helped to resolve social inequalities, also led Rome into conflict with Greek city-states to the south, which were more wealthy and sophisticated adversaries. Rome's combination of military success and social solidarity in the second half of the fourth century BC made her both a desirable ally and a formidable opponent.

THE ORIGINS OF EMPIRE: ROMAN WARFARE AND IMPERIALISM (281–121 BC)

Imperialism and the conquest of Italy (281–264 BC)

It is vital to consider Rome's foreign policies and what she intended to achieve as she expanded. Certainly, Rome's battles with her Etruscan, Latin and Samnite neighbours in the fourth and early third centuries BC might be seen as wars of survival, during which her very existence as a city was threatened. The defensive nature of Rome's battles in the these centuries is indicated by the construction of the Servian Wall, which dates from 378–350 BC and enclosed 426 hectacres (see Map 5, no. 16), an area roughly the same size as one of the Greek cities, such as Naples, Syracuse or Tarentum. Her urban population rose from an estimated 30,000 in the mid-fourth century to 60,000 (the estimated size of the Athenian citizen population under Pericles) by 300 BC, and to at least 90,000 by 270 BC. These increases in both population and interaction within the rest of Italy are evident in the building of two aqueducts, the *Aqua Appia* (*c.* 312 BC) and the *Aqua Anio Vetus* (272 BC), and the creation of the *Via Appia* (312 BC), a road which ran from Rome to Capua (twenty miles north of Naples) (see Map 5, no. 4A–B). Rome's first coins were minted in Naples (326 BC) and then in Rome in the early/mid-third century BC. The increased wealth of the city is evident in a number of monumental building projects dating to the mid-fourth century BC, which reflect a thriving economy and a broader global network. Four centuries after the city's foundation, Rome finally assumed the characteristics so often attributed to a thriving metropolis: roads, running water, monumental buildings and a bipartisan government.

Rome's greater security came at a cost, however. Her expansion was closely monitored by her neighbours and after the defeat of the Latin League in 338 BC, and successes against the Samnites in Campania, she had become a force to be reckoned with (though not necessarily respected) in Italy. This is particularly evident in Rome's first interactions with Greek armies under Pyrrhus, king of Epirus, a man who modelled himself on Alexander the Great, recruited by the Greek colony of Tarentum (see Map 2). Pyrrhus saw Italy as a 'wild west' ripe for the taking. The conflict, borne from Rome's involvement with Thurii (a neighbour of Tarentum), illustrates how military might is not tantamount to cultural supremacy. Dionysius of Halicarnassus (*Roman Antiquities* 19.5) records how, in 281 BC, a Roman legate, Postumius Megellus, who gave a speech at the theatre in Tarentum, was mocked by the crowd for his coarse Greek and then literally shat upon by the town drunk Philonides, nicknamed 'Kotule' (drinking cup). While this episode has probably been embellished, it is Tarentines and Pyrrhus who appear to possess the cultural and military superiority.

Rome's subsequent battles against Pyrrhus were a series of defeats resulting in significant losses for both parties. After the Battle of Ausculum (see Map 1) in 279 BC, Pyrrhus famously remarked, 'another such victory as this and we shall be lost' (Plutarch, *Life of Pyrrhus* 21.14) – hence the term 'a Pyrrhic victory'. Initially, the Romans were outmanoeuvred by diverse military tactics. Pyrrhus' forces included his elite Epirote troops, Rhodian slingers, archers, Thessalian cavalry, as well as Italian troops and exotic elephants, which were used to break up the infantry lines. However, Rome's large reserves of manpower, her leaders' ingenuity and the fact that her forces were based in Italy eventually proved decisive. The Romans devised numerous inventive solutions, including anti-elephant chariots and the use of flaming pigs (the pigs were covered in pitch and lit to scare the elephants – a tactic almost too bizarre to be invented by Dionysius (*Roman Antiquities* 20.1–3)). Pyrrhus was drawn into battle against Punic forces in Sicily and when he returned in 275 BC he was soundly thrashed by the Romans at Beneventum. He died a few years later – bashed in the head by a lady with a roof tile, according to Plutarch.

Rome's victory placed her on the world stage as a military and economic power. This was signified in the *Aes signatum* bronze ingots (the main currency in the Roman world at this time) depicting Epirus' elephants on one side and a Roman sow on the other (Figure 2.1). One would not generally assume that pig trumps elephant, but this imagery expressed pride in Rome's humble agrarian background and her ingenuity. These bars represent both the revenue these campaigns brought to Rome and how Romans illustrated their victories to a wider audience: through depictions of a savvy swine versus vanquished elephants.

The attitude of Romans to the people they defeated was enlightened and tactically sound. They refused to deal with conglomerate states such as the Latin League or the Etruscans as a whole. Each city was treated in accordance with its individual merits and behaviour, a policy which had the appearance of 'fairness' (setting important precedents for rewards and punishment) while also promoting a strategy of 'divide and conquer'. Some were granted Roman citizenship (some with voting rights, others without) and some were offered probationary citizenship; others had to relinquish territories (which would become *ager publicus* – 'public lands' – effectively breaking up the aristocratic powers of the local elite). The differing statuses of Italian cities were divisive and intermarriage between different cities was forbidden. All were required to provide manpower for the armies of Rome. Her soldiers were not given formal pay but they did receive the fruits of victory, public lands (often those confiscated from the enemy). Some of the defeated towns, such as Cosa and Aquilea (which means 'lookout'), were refounded as colonies, which could be seen as imperialism, but some scholars are inclined to treat this as defensive action, on the grounds that the colonies served as strategic outposts for protecting Roman settlements.

FIGURE 2.1   *Aes signatum* of pig and elephant, British Museum (reg. no. 1867,0212.2). This 'signed' bronze bar minted in Rome, probably after the victory at Beneventum in 275 BC, weighs 1.6 kilos (not exactly pocket money) and could be used to assess a Roman citizen's wealth. It was worth five asses so is often called 'quincussis'. Minted to convey the military victory of Roman forces against the Greek forces of Pyrrhus, the savvy swine not only represent Roman ingenuity against a larger and more established foe but also exemplify the economic benefits of military conquest. The Twelve Tables (*c.* 450 BC) set out bronze as a base for currency (e.g. ten asses = one sheep). Photo © Trustees of the British Museum.

The rise of the individual: Appius Claudius Caecus – pretty fly for a blind guy

In an environment where military victory had become a defining part of life, it was inevitable that some individuals, particularly generals, would gain prominence. The Claudii were one of six families (the other five were the Aemilli, Scipios, Valerii, Fabii and Manlii) who could trace their ancestry back to the start of the republic. Suetonius provides a history of the *Claudii* while tracing the ancestry of the emperor Tiberius (*Tiberius* 2), and Livy records members of the Claudian gens in the fifth century (including one of the infamous decemvirs of 450 BC). **Appius Claudius Caecus** ('the Blind'), however, is one of the first substantiated figures in Roman history. He is attested in both historical records and surviving monuments, such as the *Via Appia* and the *Aqua Appia*. An inscription, recarved in the first century AD, records his numerous contributions to Rome:

> Appius Claudius, son of Caius, Caecus, censor, consul twice, dictator, interrex three times, praetor twice, curule aedile twice, questor, tribune of the soldiers

three times. He captured several towns from the Samnites, routed an army of Sabines and Etruscans. He prevented peace being made with King Pyrrhus. In his censorship he paved the Appian Way and built an aqueduct for Rome. He built the temple of Bellona.

(CIL XI.1827)

Note that political offices come first and are listed in descending order, placing censor first (*before* dictator). These are followed by his military conquests in the Samnite and Italian wars, then by his refusal to surrender in the Pyrrhic Wars. His collection of offices and his public works, including a road, an aqueduct and a temple, were vast and expensive undertakings that demonstrate the power of a censor and the immense consolidation of authority within a single individual. It was a model that Augustus would mimic as a 'traditional' Roman leader. That his descendants (including Tiberius, the adopted son of Augustus) traced their careers back to Caecus illustrates a strength and a weakness in the Roman political system: Rome was never a democracy and its 'meritocracy' was often chosen from the same few families.

The Punic Wars (264–146 BC)

In 264 BC the Mamertines, Campanian mercenaries who had taken over Messana (modern-day Messina; see Map 1), sought Carthaginian aid against their Greek neighbours. However, their Carthaginian 'liberators' were not inclined to leave. Citing Campanian blood as specious grounds for allegiance, the Mamertines appealed to Rome. The Senate could not agree (Polybius suggests that they did not want to get involved), but Appius Claudius Caudex ('Blockhead' – grandson of Appius Claudius Caecus) took the issue to a citizens' assembly (probably the Comitia Tributa, although the sources do not specify), citing the rich booty of Sicily. The Romans did not declare war, but they sent a contingent to Sicily, a move that so surprised the Carthaginian commander that he retreated. This 'pre-emptive strike', designed to preclude a larger battle, is often viewed as an act of imperialism. However, as in the present, the battle cries of 'justice' and 'freedom' were often fronts for a different agenda.

Diodorus of Sicily, a historian who wrote at the end of the republic (200 years later), argued that Rome shielded the utterly godless Mamertine marauders not on account of good faith and pity but because her people wanted an excuse to take Sicily (Diodorus, 23.1.4). While Diodorus' assessment is an accurate reflection of Rome's imperial policy during his lifetime, it is not clear that the earlier Rome's motives were so grand, at least not initially: the disapproval of the Senate and the deployment of a small force suggest an interest in maintaining a buffer zone rather than a thirst for imperial conquest. Had either party known that this skirmish would result in three series of battles, totalling forty-two years of warfare over more than a century, leaving

300 cities in Libya and 700,000 people (according to Strabo: *Geography* 17.3) as a 'smoking heap of rubble', their approach might have been different.

Carthage, in North Africa (see Map 2), was a Phoenician colony, hence the Latin name 'Poenus' for a Carthaginian. The Phoenicians were a seafaring people and their legacy survives today in the Phoenician alphabet, which was adopted by most of the western world. The power of their navy was legendary. Originally said to be from Tyre, they colonized the coasts of North Africa, Spain, Sardinia and Corsica as well as western Sicily. Phoenicians traded in gold, ivory, bronze, tin, pottery, grain, perfumes and the purple dye used to mark a senator's toga. Their armies included Greek mercenaries and conscripts from their colonies. These diverse forces were formidable: Virgil, in addition to describing the ill-fated love affair between Aeneas and the Carthaginian Dido, explains that Carthage was 'opposite Italy and the mouth of the Tiber, rich in resources and especially severe in the pursuit of war' (*Aeneid* 1.13–14). Carthage's military supremacy was vital to the Romans. A foreign adversary was someone against whom Italy's varying factions could unite. The defeat of the Carthaginians, a long-respected military and economic power in the Mediterranean, would also enhance Rome's role in a global market, effectively moving her into the 'major league' of Mediterranean trade. Finally, the Carthaginians surrounded Italy to the west (Spain, Corsica and Sardinia) and the south (North Africa) while also maintaining allies in Greece and the east.

The First Punic War (264–241 BC) began on the rocky shores of Sicily, which were abandoned in favour of naval engagements off the island's northern coast. This decision favoured the Carthaginians and Rome suffered a number of beatings before she got her 'sea legs'. Yet again, Rome's large population, natural resources and ingenuity eventually granted her victory. According to Polybius (*Histories* 1.21–22), Rome built a navy of 100 quinqueremes ('five oars') with five levels of oars (triremes have three); these larger and heavier ships performed better in foul weather, though they were not as manoeuvrable as triremes. One account claims that Rome's navy was based on the model of a Carthaginian ship that washed ashore. The labelled parts allowed Romans to reassemble the ship like a dresser from IKEA. Before casting the Romans as ambitious cultural hackers, however, one must note the technical and tactical adaptations they employed, such as the Corvus ('Raven'). This new feature, described by Polybius (*Histories* 1.22–24) and depicted on a number of Roman coins (Figures 2.2a and b), was a one-metre-wide and eleven-metre-long plank with a sharp hook at the bottom that was embedded into an enemy ship. It allowed Rome's soldiers to make the most of their greatest strength – hand-to-hand fighting – while effectively disabling the enemy ship (diminishing the advantage of the skilled Carthaginian sailors). Despite some disadvantages (e.g. it could not be used in rough seas), it was a major factor in Rome's naval victory at Mylae in 260 BC. The successful Roman general **Gaius Duilius**, a *novus homo* ('new man'), returned to Rome as a

FIGURE 2.2a The *Aes grave* ('heavy' bronze) was large enough to fill the palm of one's hand and weighed a Roman pound (*libra*): initially 328 grams, later reduced to *c.* 275 grams (roughly 2.5 times the weight of an iPhone 5). This *Aes grave* (type RRC 35/1) was minted in Rome during the late third century BC (*c.* 225–217 BC) after Rome's naval victory over Carthage. It depicts the prow of a Roman ship, including the innovative Corvus and the fighting platform. The rather ungainly *Aes grave* eventually made way for smaller *As* coins. Photo © CNG Coins.

FIGURE 2.2b This bronze *As* (type RRC 85/2) from *c.* 211 BC, weighing 37 grams, was a fraction of the size of its predecessor (but still six times the weight of a US quarter or a British ten-pence piece). It records its weight and mint 'ROMA'. Later versions, minted in the second century BC (e.g. type RRC 196/1) weighed less (*c.* 19 grams). These lighter and more defined coin types show how the Punic Wars shaped Rome's military and economic policies. Photo © CNG Coins.

wealthy hero. He dedicated a victory temple to Janus (the god of beginnings and endings, war and peace, who looks forward and backwards in time in the Forum Holitorium (the vegetable market). He also erected a monument in the Roman Forum made from the prows of defeated ships called 'rostra'. His inscription (see website case study) records 13 sunken ships, 31 captured ships and 2,160,000 sesterces (a fortune at the time).

Both sides suffered heavy losses, but eventually Rome's superiority in numbers won out. In 241 BC, the Carthaginians sued for peace, withdrew from Sicily, and paid a heavy fine, which resulted in a mercenary revolt and the Roman annexation of Corsica and Sardinia. While the acquisition of Sicily could be seen as a justifiable outcome, Rome's annexation of the other two islands suggests a more expansionist foreign policy, and many historians consider it an act of foul play. The First Punic

War also did little to address the larger conflict between two emerging powers. The Carthaginians fortified their colonies in Spain and a new generation of generals was already in the making.

Who started the Second Punic War remains a subject of debate and the fact that the majority of our sources are Roman does not help. In a battle between two aggressors, it is often difficult as well as misleading to point the finger of blame. Livy weaves tales of a ferocious young Hannibal, who, being taught to hate Rome by his father Hamilcar Barca, mercilously raided the town of a Roman ally. The truth of the matter is more elusive. Hannibal's sack of the city of Saguntum in Spain is often cited as an act of aggression, though the city was outside Rome's boundary, and Hannibal did not attack until he had permission from Carthage (behaviour that does not bespeak a war-hungry marauder). Hannibal's bold aggression was not in taking Saguntum but in attempting the impossible: a crossing of the Alps into Italy with tens of thousands of infantry, cavalry, baggage trains and elephants. Livy describes Hannibal and his men (and presumably their elephants) traversing steep inclines, hanging on to shrubbery and blasting walls of solid rock with fire and raw red wine. Despite losing a large number of men (it is said he lost half his army –18,000 infantry and 2000 horsemen – on the way), Hannibal entered Italy with the element of surprise and won a series of battles in 218–217 BC in northern Italy (see Map 2).

Hannibal was an excellent strategist who seldom fought the same general twice: Publius Cornileus Scipio barely escaped his first encounter with the Carthaginian (the Battle of Ticinus), Tiberius Sempronius' army was destroyed (two-thirds of his men were killed) while crossing an icy river at Trebia, and General Flaminus was cut off from Rome. Hannibal's army had Numidian cavalry and Spanish soldiers, the likes of which many Romans had not met before. Although many of his men perished in the Alps crossing, he reinforced his forces with Gauls and northern Italians, who were persuaded to join him by the merciful treatment of Rome's traitors and the harsh punishments imposed on loyalists. At the end of these campaigns, Hannibal was a mere fifty miles from Rome.

A vengeful and bloodthirsty general would surely have marched on the city (there are many who wonder why Hannibal did not). Livy (22.58) believed that Hannibal's aim was the restoration of *dignitas* (self-respect) and *imperium* (power or, perhaps, domination). If his goal was Rome's complete capitulation, his course in invading southern Italy makes sense. The swift conversion of the northern Italians led Hannibal to believe that southern Italy would be easily swayed, too. After the disaster at Trasimene, the Senate appointed a dictator, Quintus Fabius Maximus Verrucosus Cunctator ('the Warty Delayor'), five times consul and two times dictator, who argued against a large confrontation with Hannibal, preferring guerrilla warfare tactics. After he stepped down as dictator, the two consuls Varro and Aemilius Paullus proposed a large-scale battle to the anxious assemblies. The resulting **Battle of**

Cannae in 216 BC would be the city's most famous defeat (see Map 2). Nearly 90,000 soldiers, headed by Varro and Aemilius Paullus themselves, outnumbered Hannibal's army, but as the central lines of Carthaginian forces broke, the Romans rushed in (as fools do). Hannibal held the outer edges of the lines and used his cavalry to encircle around the Roman army's rear until it was utterly surrounded: 'The Romans held out, but their outer ranks were continually struck down, with the remaining circle of soldiers huddling together in a contracting circle, until they were finally killed where they stood' (Polybius, *Histories* 3.116). Polybius (*Histories* 3.117) puts the number killed at 70,000, while Livy (22.59) estimates 50,000, including 80 of Rome's 300 senators and 29 of her 48 military tribunes. This is not only the worst defeat recorded in Roman history; it is on par with the worst defeats in terms of battle casualties in the modern world, including the Battle of Gettysburg and the first day of the Battle of the Somme. 'No other nation in the world could have suffered so tremendous a series of disasters and not have been overwhelmed' (Livy, 22.54).

Although many of her allies defected, Rome continued with remarkable tenacity, and when the treasury was empty, her citizens and remaining allies gave their own money and other resources. Debts were cancelled and many men were freed for military service. For the next fourteen years, Hannibal ravaged southern Italy and the Romans fought to free it, while also fighting in Spain. Publius Cornelius Scipio (the elder) was sent with his brother Gnaeus to Spain, where they both died in successful battles (211 BC), leaving two vital legacies: an army that had adapted to Spanish- and Carthaginian-style techniques and a general who had come to understand Hannibal's tactics – P. Cornelius Scipio (the younger).

The Battle of Zama (201 BC)

P. Cornelius Scipio (soon to be known as 'Africanus'), often called 'Scipio the Elder', was an A-list Roman celebrity and a bit of a wild card. Not unlike Alexander the Great, his first military success, a charge to save his father at the Battle of Ticinus, marked him out at the tender age of eighteen. He witnessed the terrible defeat at Cannae and, according to Livy (22.53), stormed into the Senate to demand they not capitulate to Carthage. Although barely twenty, he was given joint command of the survivors of Cannae with Appius Claudius Pulcher ('the Pretty': great grandson of Appius Claudius Caecus 'the Blind'). He stood for quaestorship and was unanimously elected years before he was legally eligible to do so. At twenty-four he took up the command of the army in Spain (left vacant by the deaths of his father and uncle in 211 BC). His personal life was a public relations dream: he married Aemilia Paula, daughter of the consul Aemilius Paullus, who had died at Cannae. Their daughter Cornelia would go on to become the mother of the famed Gracchi.

After being elected consul in 205 BC at the age of thirty-one, Scipio took a few leaves from Hannibal's book of strategy. First, he took the formation of an army into his own hands: although he could not levy an army for the state, he was allowed to enlist volunteers and accept donations of money or materials from the allies. The fact that the Roman people were prepared to bend their constitution to give Scipio the power to recruit his own army and collect resources illustrates both their faith in him and their desperation. This policy would set a dangerous precedent, the full implications of which were not immediately evident. Like Hannibal had done over a decade earlier, Scipio forced a confrontation on the enemy's home front, taking his army to Africa. He then undermined Carthage's alliances with her neighbours (as Hannibal had done with respect to Rome's in Italy), gaining the support of the Numidian king, Masinissa. Finally, Scipio leapt into battle at Zama, forcing Hannibal's hand. It seemed that Hannibal had finally met his match (Figure 2.3).

Hannibal fought well, placing mercenaries in his front lines, keeping his veterans at the back and deploying his war elephants. But Scipio (having been at Ticinus and Cannae) anticipated this and in addition to utilizing traps and javelin throwers, he placed his troops in small units called *hastati* with gaps that could be opened, like curtains, to let the elephants pass through. Livy (30.33) points to the contrast between the unity of the Roman force and the disarray of the Carthaginian army in the call to arms: 'Hannibal was addressing his Carthaginian contingent and the various national leaders . . . mainly through interpreters . . . when the horns and trumpeters on the Roman side blasted and so momentous a cry arose that the elephants panicked and turned back into their own men.' This passage, typical of Livy's florid style, suggests that the Romans' cohesion played a fundamental role in their victory. Masinissa's Numidian cavalry (fighting for Scipio) prevailed but then dispersed behind the lines without returning to fight. The Roman forces, as at Cannae, were drawn into the Carthaginian centre. It looked as though history might repeat itself, but then Masinissa's cavalry finally re-emerged and Hannibal's men were surrounded.

Hannibal escaped Carthage to rally more forces but found that his city, unlike Rome, had no men left. By 201 BC, a peace treaty had been forced on Carthage. In it, the city agreed to hand over all but ten of her longboats and pledged to pay a sum of 10,000 talents over the next 150 years. These terms, negotiated by Scipio, were kind in comparison with what the Senate had demanded (some senators had wanted Carthage razed to the ground). Hannibal survived as a talented but defeated figure, reminiscent of Napoleon or Robert E. Lee. Tales of his character have been the subject of numerous debates: some criticize his love of gold and blood, while others paint him as an 'ideal' general, such as Ulysses S. Grant – an unassuming man who quartered, fought and ate with his troops. Two facts are agreed: Rome's victory would not have been worthy of legend without Hannibal as an adversary; and, exaggerations aside, the Carthaginian general was a bold and brilliant tactician whose battle tactics are still used as models in military academies today.

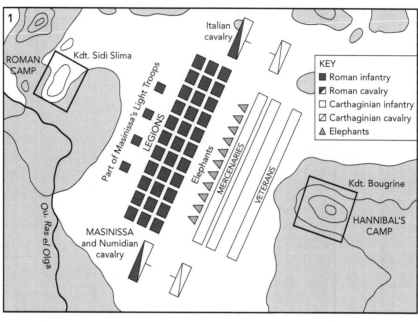

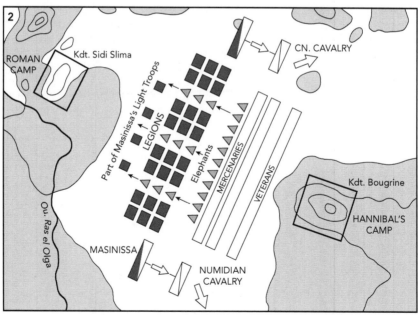

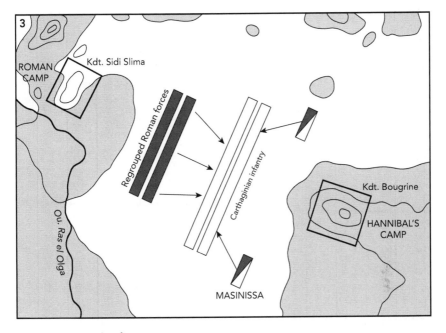

FIGURE 2.3 Battle of Zama
1   This plan depicts the initial advance of Scipio's troops: the arrangement of Roman
    troops into flexible *hastati* as well as the intended advance of the Numidian cavalry.
2   The *hastati* split and the elephants charge between the lines. The Italian cavalry and
    the Numidians under Masinissa drive off the Carthaginian cavalry.
3   Despite the lessons learned at Cannae, one can still see the Roman centre being
    drawn into the centre of Hannibal's line, which could have been disastrous, if not for
    the return of Masinissa's cavalry.

ROME IN THE SECOND CENTURY BC: THE VIRTUES AND VICES OF GLOBALIZATION

> An unprecedented achievement, that the Roman state extended its domination
> over nearly all of the inhabited world in less than 53 years.
>
> **(Polybius, *Histories* 1.1)**

> Scipio, voted the agnomen 'Africanus' for his military success, returned to Rome
> in an unparalleled triumph, bringing 123,000 pounds of silver and giving 400 asses
> to his soldiers. The Numidian Masinissa was given magnificent honours (crown,
> curule chair, and an ivory sceptre): the signs of kingship that were so adamantly
> rejected by Romans centuries earlier.
>
> **(Livy, 30.45)**

Appian (*Punic Wars* 66), a Greek historian from Alexandria who wrote in the first century AD, provides a vivid description of the procession:

> Everyone in the procession wore crowns, trumpeters and wagons weighed down with spoils led the advance. Towers portraying captured cities and pictures illustrating the campaigns were brought forward; then gold and silver . . . after them white oxen, Numidian elephants and captive Carthaginian and Numidian Leaders . . . Scipio wore a golden crown with precious jewels . . . a purple toga entwined with golden stars. He carried an ivory sceptre and a laurel branch . . . a symbol of Roman victory.

To a Roman audience, the fruits of war were material wealth, slaves, exotic goods and a global market for trade. However, each of these fruits of war bore a vice. For Appian, whose seminal work was an account of Rome's civil wars in the first century BC, there was a link between Scipio Africanus (a man with immense financial, political and military power) and the individuals who would tear Rome asunder over a century later. Scipio returned not only as a successful general but in the guise of a king who paid his own army. While Rome celebrated, the rest of Italy lay in ruins, ravaged by war or suffering through lack of manpower. Rome had no standing army and Scipio's soldiers would need those 400 asses, as many of their farms were now defunct and being sold cheaply to wealthy merchants and aristocrats. The disenfranchised farmers who poured into the city found inflated prices (due to the influx of material wealth) and low wages (due to the arrival of slaves). Once the pomp and circumstance of Scipio's procession faded, what remained was a widening gap between the haves and have-nots. As Rome punished allies who had been disloyal, many of her loyal allies began to feel that their contributions had gone unrecognized.

For a nation with the military power and resources to conquer Greece and Africa, it is telling that fifty years elapsed between Rome's victories and the annexation of these areas as provinces. A province was defined as a territory outside Italy belonging to the Roman people and governed by a Roman official. Though they were subject to taxes, provinces generally did not have the privileges that were offered to Rome's allies. The collection of taxes in the provinces (by private contractors called *publiciani*) became a vital source of revenue with numerous political consequences. Former praetors or consuls (*propraetor, proconsul*) were 'called forward' (*prorogatio*) to serve as provincial governors. In addition to waging wars and accepting gifts, these governors were granted *imperium* to rule as they saw fit. Each appointment (later extended to five years) was an opportunity to enrich oneself (then, as now, running for public office was a costly endeavour) and each also offered temporary immunity from indictment for one's acts in office. The Senate, which allocated both the governorships and provincial revenues, found itself in control of vast financial resources as well as a number of political careers.

In the first half of the second century BC, Rome favoured client kingdoms, which were known as *socii et amici* ('allies and friends'), over the annexation of provinces. While few would deny Rome's aim of increasing her wealth, the nature of her desire was one of immediate gratification: 'friends with benefits' rather than committed long-term relationships. Clients paid no taxes but provided troops and in return would receive Roman diplomatic and military support (often merely the threat of Roman intervention would suffice). The increasing global respect for Rome's power led to ever more pleas for intervention. Like America in the early twentieth century, efforts to stay out of foreign affairs were overcome by the causes of 'liberty' and 'freedom'. The ensuing interventions should not necessarily be seen as Roman aggression. A series of Macedonian Wars (215–148 BC; see Map 2) began when Philip V of Macedon offered support to Carthage in the Second Punic War. Rome responded by forging alliances with some Greek city-states. In 197 BC Rome invaded Macedon in support of those Greek allies (which she would not have had were it not for Philip's aggression). After a series of victories, Rome demonstrated her power at the Isthmian Games of 196 BC by 'freeing' a series of Greek city-states (Livy, 32.32), in the hope that they would prosper, trade and stop bickering. Sadly, this did not happen. After nearly seventy years of war against Macedon, Rome decided to annex the whole area as a province, a decision her Greek allies did not accept. When Rome was attacked by the Achaean League (her former 'liberated' allies), she withdrew their freedom: Achaea was incorporated into the province of Macedonia and the city of Corinth was razed to the ground in 146 BC as an example to the others.

Meanwhile, Carthage appeared to be recovering. Plutarch (*Cato* XXVII) has a lovely yarn about how the elder Cato dropped a Libyan fig on the floor of the Senate and, as those around him admired its lusciousness, noted that it had come from a prosperous place not three days' sailing away. For Cato, who habitually ended his speeches in the Senate with '*Carthago delenda est*' ('Carthage must be destroyed'), this was cause enough. While a fig is hardly a weapon of mass destruction, the episode illustrates distrust of a former enemy – a theme that is surely familiar to modern audiences. The Third Punic War, if one can call it that, was a three-year siege in which the city of Carthage held out heroically against Rome. Polybius (*Histories* 38.5) records the words of Scipio Aemilianus (the adopted grandson of Scipio Africanus): 'I shudder to think that the same order may one day be given for Rome.' Rome's utter destruction of the city (it was burned and its 50,000 survivors were sold into slavery) does not suggest a nation motivated by thoughts of immediate colonization. Carthage was finally colonized 100 years later, under Julius Caesar.

Rome's change in foreign policy may have been motivated by greed, but it is unlikely that this was the sole cause. By the mid-second century BC, Rome was already a global empire in an economic sense. Her squabbling client kingdoms were a diplomatic burden on Rome, which lacked the legal authority to enforce the resolutions. Carthage (146 BC) and Macedon (147 BC) both appear to have been cases where control rather than fear prompted Rome's annexation. In light of recent events, it may be foolhardy to assume that Rome entered into African and eastern affairs with a clear 'exit strategy' or intentions to remain for a protracted period. Political power remains an entity that it is easier to capture than to control.

Hellenization in Rome: remaining Roman, becoming Greek?

While Rome was exporting troops, she was importing slaves, booty and Greek culture. Scipio Africanus' procession of wealth and foreign booty was mimicked again and again as Roman generals returned from foreign campaigns with statues, gold and the enslaved *glitterati* of the eastern world (including the historian Polybius). Livy (40.5) records a Macedonian prince (an ally of Rome) who was mocked at his own court: 'they ridiculed the appearance of the city, which had not yet been beautified in either its public or its private places'. Greece provided the model for a successful culture, with its symbols of wealth and power recognized (and respected) across the Mediterranean. Rome's attempts to copy certain elements of Greek culture are often described as Hellenization, but one has to be careful with words like this and (later) Romanization, which imply either a 'one-way' transfer of culture or the adoption of an ideology through material culture. In the same way as buying a hamburger at McDonald's does not make a person a capitalist, adopting certain elements of a culture is not tantamount to adopting its ideology. The vital distinction lies in examining both what is adopted by a foreign culture and how those elements are used.

For example, Roman victory temples (vowed by a general after success in battle) were popular features in Rome in the third and second centuries BC. Unlike the passing triumphal procession, each victory temple, located along the *Via Triumphalis* (the Triumphal Route), offered a permanent memorial to an individual and a way to incorporate his victory into the monumental landscape of Rome. In this respect, a victory temple was more of a monument than a functioning temple, but it retained a religious element by representing the divine intervention of a B-list deity (often of a military nature, such as Hercules Victor or Spes (Hope)), attesting to the pre-ordained destiny of Roman conquest. By the mid-second century BC, some of these temples were being made from imported Greek marble and/or carved by Greek architects. The Temple of Hercules Victor (Figures 2.4 and 2.5; see Map 5, no 5) was probably dedicated by Lucius Mummius Achaicus, a *novus homo* and victor in the Achaean Wars (144 BC). His victory is monumentalized by a round, Greek, 'tholos'-style temple carved in white pentelic Greek marble with Corinthian columns (perhaps

FIGURE 2.4 Temple of Hercules Victor. The oldest surviving marble building in Rome, this temple has survived primarily because it was converted into a Christian church. Of the surviving columns, some are Cararra (Italian marble, possible later replacements) and others are white Greek pentelic marble. The use of the Corinthian order, not overwhelmingly popular in Rome at this time, could be a reference to Lucius Mummius, whom many believe to be the dedicator of the temple, and who conquered the city of Corinth in 146 BC. Photo by author.

reflecting Mummius' defeat of Corinth). However, while Greek materials, architecture and technicians were employed, the concept of a victory temple was entirely Roman, and the function of these elements as *spolia* (fruits of war) served a distinctly Roman purpose. In contrast to the fine white pentelic marble and the beautiful rendering of the column capitals, the surviving dedication (Figure 2.5), carved in Roman travertine, is poorly chiselled in leaning, lopsided letters and employs dubious syntax (assuming it belongs to this temple; it was not found in context).

Two main sources on Hellenization, often considered the founding fathers of Roman history, are Marcus Porcius Cato (234–149 BC), a successful general of the Punic Wars, *novus homo* and champion of 'traditional' Roman values, and Polybius, a Greek aristocrat, who was captured and deported to Rome in 167 BC. That men such as these rose to respectability and fame demonstrates fundamental changes in the attitudes of Roman society. Although their audiences, intentions and perspectives

FIGURE 2.5 Inscription of L. Mummius (*CIL* 1(2).626). This dedication records the career of Lucius Mummius, the first known *novus homo* of a plebeian family to receive a military agnomen – 'Achaicus' – for his victories in Greece. Though the agnomen is not recorded, Mummius uses larger letters at the top and bottom of the text to emphasize his name, his office (consul), his dedication to Hercules Victor, and his military triumph (implicit in the title 'Imperator', which will later be attributed only to Rome's emperors). Vatican Museums, Pio-Clementine Museum. Photo © Vatican Museums.

were different – Cato wrote in Latin for a traditional Roman elite and Polybius wrote in Greek to explain the Roman constitution to the Greek world – both came to similar conclusions about the Hellenization of Rome.

Cato, nicknamed *Censorius*, was a quintessential Roman censor. Having risen to military office through success and competence, he advocated the virtues of a hard-working and productive meritocracy. When asked how it was that a bunch of nobodies had statues in Rome while he had none, he famously replied: 'I would much rather have men ask why I have no statue than why I have one' (Plutarch, *Cato the Elder* 19.4). He did not object to Greek literature or its material culture: during his time in office he constructed a Greek basilica ('king's chamber') called the Basilica Porcia, adopting a Greek structure and allying it with a slightly different function and ideology. Rather, it was Rome's increasing attachment to wealth and Greek luxuries that alarmed Cato. Appian's *Civil Wars* (1.28) records how Cato pulled down an almost completed theatre on the grounds that the project would cause further acrimony and that becoming accustomed to Greek luxuries was not in the Romans' public interest. He also won the enmity of every wealthy woman in Rome when he fought against the repeal of the *Lex Oppia* (see Chapter 6), a law passed in the aftermath of Cannae, which forbade Roman women from owning or displaying a certain amount of gold and commodity items. Cato feared that the increasing role of wealth and the power of wealthy individuals to curry favour would corrupt society as a whole, claiming, '[It] is the surest sign of deterioration in the republic when pretty boys fetch more than fields, and jars of caviar more than ploughmen' (Polybius, *Histories* 31.25.). This comment is not just a statement of value but a canny economic observation: Rome's farms and ploughmen were her products and exports, while slaves and caviar were foreign imports. The moment Rome's need for exports outstripped her ability to produce, Rome would have not only a social problem but an economic disaster.

Cato did not ask of others what he could not do himself, and to reaffirm his agrarian values he wrote a treatise on farming, extolling 'traditional farming' (perhaps ignoring the fact that an elite audience who required a handbook on farming or managing slaves was already far removed from Rome's traditional agrarian beginnings). Although his homespun, penny-pinching nationalism was often ridiculed (not unlike the 'rail splitter' Abraham Lincoln), Cato's concern that Romans (particularly those in positions of power) were losing touch with urban and agrarian workers was well founded. He recognized that if the Senate failed to support a broader populace, the people would find a champion elsewhere: among the wealthy generals against whom he so often railed.

Polybius, as a Greek, had few concerns that Rome would ever become 'Hellenized'. Although he claims to be writing for posterity and a Roman audience (*Histories* 30.22), most historians agree that his primary audience (suggested by the language, style and cultural assumptions of his work) were his fellow Greeks, to whom he sought to explain their Roman masters. His period as a tutor to one of Rome's most prestigious families (the Scipio Aemilli) gave him an unusual perspective on the events he described. In the Greek historical tradition of Herodotus and Thucydides, Polybius travelled extensively, interviewing veterans and examining treaties and archives. In his mind, the Romans were comparable to the Spartans in their severe military ways and their constitution, and these cultural differences were far too ingrained to be overcome. He illustrates this beautifully in an account of Lucius Anicius, a praetor celebrating a victory of the Illyrians, who employed Greek actors to put on a play inside a circus (which would have been like staging a ballet in

Wembley Stadium). After a while, the increasingly bored Roman audience requested a bit more 'excitement':

> At first they [the performers] did not know what to do, then one of the lictors showed them how to make themselves into two contingents, facing each other and coming against one another as though they were in battle. The fluteplayers caught on at once, and, taking on a movement to the beat of their own savage tune, [made] a scene of utter chaos . . . When a chorus member, whose clothes were closely tied, turned round suddenly and raised his hands, like a boxer in the face of the approaching fluteplayer, the audience applauded and roared with delight.
>
> **(Polybius, *Histories* 30.14)**

This story, told with an irrepressible smirk, illustrates how 'the cut and paste' model of cultural transmission fails on application. You can take the Roman out of the circus, but you cannot take the circus out of the Roman. Indeed, the fact that the theatre was constructed inside an existing circus seems to be a deliberate statement about the nature of Hellenic culture in Rome: it is always viewed within a Roman framework.

By the mid-second century BC the sight of a triumphant general bringing vast wealth into Rome had become familiar, as had lavish games put on to impress the public. However, when all the fanfare had finished, it was the Senate, a few wealthy generals and a rising class of savvy market entrepreneurs called *negotiatores* (many of them slave-traders) who retained most of the profits. Less and less of the fruits of war trickled down to the Italian soldiers, who continued to lose their farms and/or livelihoods and increasingly resented the fact that their military service did not secure them full voting rights in Rome. While distinctions between patrician and plebeian became less important, the consolidation of wealth and political offices among a few families – who called themselves *nobiles* or *optimates* ('the best') – was viewed with increasing anger by the rest of the populace: *the populares*.

THE GRACCHI AND THE AGRARIAN CRISIS

Tiberius (168–133 BC) **and Gaius** (159–121 BC) **Gracchus** were not social under-dogs: their father was a famous consul, and their mother Cornelia was a Scipio who had turned down an offer of marriage from an Egyptian king (see Chapter 6). These would prove to be unusual antecedents for two politicians whose economic policies and championing of the poor would shake the foundations of the republic. Both men began with successful military careers, and Plutarch (*Tiberius* IX) claims that the root of Tiberius' sympathy for the poor lay in what he witnessed in Etruria as quaestor:

The wild beasts that roam over Italy have every one of them a cave or lair to lurk in; but the men who fight and die for Italy enjoy nothing but the common air and light; with their wives and children they wander around homeless . . . they fight and die to keep others in the lap of luxury, and though they are styled as conqueror of the world, they cannot claim a single clump of grass as their own.

He paints a picture of a desperate world where, after extended military service abroad, some soldiers returned to find their neglected farms already sold to large aristocratic landowners who employed slaves. While archaeological evidence in Italy does not necessarily support the massive socio-economic changes implied in this passage (which was written hundreds of years after the event), one should be equally careful about dismissing a literary source on the basis of archaeological evidence alone. The nature of longer-term military campaigns on foreign soil must have had ramifications at home. Just as in a modern context, larger businesses with cheaper labour may have outpriced smaller local businesses, making agrarian living more competitive. The influx of wealth, inflation and foreign goods would also have played a role. Even if the change were not as dramatic as Plutarch suggests, there is probably at least a kernel of truth in what he describes.

One may ask what happened to all the land Rome conquered in Italy, Spain, Africa and Greece. The confiscated lands, called *latifundia*, had been lent in large parcels to a few individuals, many of whom eventually ceased to pay rent. An increasing number of slave revolts demonstrated the double-edged sword of slave labour and senators began to discuss the reallocation of land, but the subject met fierce resistance from a competitive urban elite, who made Cato's concerns about the corruption of wealth seem almost prophetic. The Gracchi brothers and their immediate family (which included the Claudii) sought to address this situation. It is worth considering whether their support of the popular cause was genuine or merely a means of furthering their own political agenda; or, indeed, whether they were motivated by a combination of the two. Connected to the Aemilii, the Scipios and the Claudii, Tiberius and Gaius were well aware of the struggles between senatorial families; one could say they lived in the eye of the storm.

In 133 BC, after being elected tribune of the plebs, Tiberius proposed the *Lex Sempronia Agraria*, which upheld an earlier law limiting possession of public lands to 500 iugera (1 iugera = *c.* 0.65 acres), reaffirming the distinction between borrowed and owned lands (originally outlined in the Twelve Tables; *possessio* versus *proprietas*). As a compromise, those 500 iugera would be theirs to keep, rent free, in perpetuity. The surplus lands would be distributed, in packs of 30 iugera (*c.* 18 acres), to the landless. This plan served three purposes: it gave land to disenfranchised veterans; it increased the number of eligible (landowning) citizen-soldiers; and it removed a population of angry dissidents from Rome. The proposal seemed fair, but for landowners who had come to think of public land as theirs (many of whom were senators), it was somewhat less rosy. The distribution of lands by three men (*triumviri*), who could parcel it out as they saw fit, caused particular controversy. In an effort to avoid a confrontation with the Senate, Tiberius took the proposal straight to the Concilium Plebis. He was opposed by his co-tribune, Marcus Octavius. While consul versus tribune battles were regular features of Roman politics, the opposition of a fellow tribune was a constitutional stalemate. Tiberius responded by shutting the markets and the treasury, then asking the Concilium Plebis to vote his co-tribune out of office for trying to obstruct the people's vote. M. Octavius was removed, the law was passed, and Tiberius, his brother Gaius and his father-in-law Appius Claudius were appointed triumvirs. The 'family affair' of triumvirs did little to undermine the Senate's accusation that Tiberius' agenda was self-motivated. The battle may have been won, but the war had just begun.

The Senate-approved budget left the triumvirate with very little money. Tiberius responded by asking for funds from the recently annexed province of Asia, noting that the allocation of provincial revenues should be under the jurisdiction of the people, not the Senate. Opposing his plan would have set the Senate against the people, so the Senate acceded, but from this moment onwards Tiberius was a marked man. To save himself from retribution, he tried to run for office again on a more liberal programme. When attempts to stop his re-election failed, some senators and the *pontifex maximus* (who was meant to be a symbol of religious respect and authority; see Chapter 5) beat Tiberius to death on the steps of the Capitol with cudgels. The inviolability of the tribune clearly remained a constitutional grey area in practice. The bodies of Tiberius and his supporters were thrown in the Tiber, and many others would be murdered and exiled subsequently, none of them convicted by trial. The Senate claimed that Tiberius had sought kingship and was a threat to the state (not unlike the charges laid against Maelius), but this does not explain why due process was subverted. Against the wishes of a consul, the Senate took it upon itself to assume the powers of dictator 'for the protection of the state'. Is a threat to the power of the Senate the same as a threat to the republic? From this moment onwards, the distinction between the two would be fiercely debated.

Tiberius' land reforms survived his murder and an estimated 75,000 smaller landholdings were created, a figure that is supported by aerial photographs of land centuriation and by inscriptions, which record the land parcels. Nearly a decade after his brother's assassination, Gaius Gracchus returned to Rome, was elected tribune of the plebs, and then re-elected. A passionate orator, Gaius' reforms went even farther than his brother's, and though they had a clear public benefit, they also curtailed the Senate's powers. Gaius suggested the inclusion of *equites* (members of Rome's second class) on juries, particularly in extortion trials, where provincial officials were tried by senatorial juries (the same men who had appointed them). In reaction to his brother's murder, Gaius sought to prohibit murder of a Roman citizen without the approval of the people. His most liberal proposal was the suggestion that voting rights should be given to all Latins. However, Gaius lost his third tribunal election and the consul Opimius began repealing his laws. A confrontation ensued and Opimius' herald was killed. When summoned to face the consul, Gaius (like Maelius) doubted he would receive a fair trial, so he fled to the Aventine, like his plebeian predecessors. Opimius went to the Senate, which passed a *senatus consultum ultimum* decree; this provided moral backing for senior officials to act 'for the preservation of the state'. Gaius knew his cause was lost, and at his own request one of his slaves stabbed him to death.

Many scholars, including Cicero, trace the fraying of the republic to these events, which established the ultimate power struggle between the Senate and the people of Rome. In the city itself, this was the beginning of civic bloodshed and rule by the sword: 'From this time onwards, right was crushed by might, the most powerful now took precedence in the state, and disputes of the citizens, which were once resolved with friendly compromises, were now settled by arms' (Cicero, *Velleius Paterculus* 2.3.3). Wars were started not for good reasons but on the basis of the profits that might be obtained. While responsibility for this sea change is not necessarily theirs, the Gracchi brothers certainly represent a watershed in Roman politics.

Their legislation highlighted links between agrarian and military problems at home as well as in the administration of the provinces. In particular, the Gracchi drew attention to the powers accumulated by the Senate through their jurisdiction of Rome's provinces. Although this authority began as an extension of its role in foreign relations, a sound diplomatic policy that allowed a long-standing governmental body to forge lasting relationships with foreign nations, the long-term ramifications were not considered. There was no check on the emerging senatorial powers in the system. Gaius' legislation to prevent the murder of a Roman citizen without the approval of the Roman people was an attempt to forge a 'check' on the Senate's growing power. The Senate's response, the *senatus consultum ultimum*, claimed the powers of a dictator without election or consultation with any branch of government. Constitutionally, there was only one possible check to either of these factions: a dictator. It should not come as a surprise, therefore, that a number of dictators emerged in the twilight of the republic in the following century.

THE TWILIGHT OF THE ROMAN REPUBLIC: ADMINISTERING AN EMPIRE (121–60 BC)

In 150 years Rome had gone from a city that was mocked for its simple bronze ingots and tufa temples, a culture that was shat upon by Greek colonies in southern Italy, to a global power minting coins throughout the Mediteranean. Similarly, Rome's literary traditions had moved from Latin translations of Greek works (Gnaeus Naevius in 270 BC) to a Greek author (Polybius) extolling the Roman constitution to his fellow Greeks. In addition to a broader empire, Italy and her economy had been transformed from a group of local citizen-run farms to a collection of large estates, worked mainly by slaves. As Rome became a metropolis of international slaves, wealthy tycoons and treasure-laden generals, the disparity between those who had fought in the wars and those who had benefited most from them became more stark. The *optimates* were dominated by a successively smaller number of Roman families, who shared both patrician and plebeian posts between themselves, leaving the balance of power in the hands of fewer and fewer individuals. The struggle of the orders took a new shape as these few elite families with a traditional agenda were increasingly challenged by the *populares*.

MARIUS AND THE REFORMATION OF THE ROMAN ARMY (157–86 BC)

The Roman army had been transformed from a collection of Roman citizen-farmers fighting for a single season to an international, full-time force that employed soldiers and tactics from across the Mediterranean. Roman soldiers fought for the security of an empire that provided cheap grain, slaves and commercial opportunities for the same entrepreneurs who would purchase their defunct farms. The recruitment and loyalty of these men lay increasingly in the hands of any general who promised booty and glory. The republic's insouciance towards its disenfranchised veterans only served to strengthen the bond between a general and his army. While the allocation of land to veterans was a step forward, there were no guarantees in the political turbulence that followed the Gracchi crisis. In the figure of Gaius Marius, a humble soldier from Arpinum in Latium, the *populares* found an advocate who offered a different solution to the agrarian crisis: the reformation of the Roman army. Although there is some debate over which reforms he actually proposed (a great many are attributed to him), his meteoric rise to power reveals the growing tensions between the *optimate* and *populare* factions.

Marius began by serving two *optimate* generals – Scipio Aemilianus (in Spain) and Quintus Metellus (in Africa). He was thirty-seven when elected quaestor, followed by a praetorship at forty-one, but despite gaining repeated victories for Metellus, the fifty-year-old Marius was not given leave to return to Rome for another election, allegedly because Metellus wanted him to wait until his own twenty-year-old son was ready for office. This episode illustrates the growing disparity in the application of Rome's standards. The republic no longer appeared to be Cato's meritocracy but an aristocracy that cherry-picked electoral candidates. Marius boldly chose to step away from his *optimate* support and run for a consulship in 108 BC, which polarized the class struggles in Rome. The historian and orator Sallust (86–35 BC), who was born in the year of Marius' death, provides an account of his election and his public support:

> The general's [Metellus'] noble rank, which had previously been a distinction, became a source of unpopularity, while Marius' humble origin afforded him greater favour . . . More than this, the spin-doctoring magistrates were exploiting the feelings of the people, in every assembly accusing Metellus of treason and exaggerating Marius' virtues. Eventually, the crowds were so excited that all the artisans and farmers, whose prosperity and livelihood depended upon manual labour, abandoned their toils and came to Marius, treating their own needs as less important than his success. As a result, the *optimates* were defeated and after an interval of many years the consulship was given to a 'new man'.
>
> **(Sallust, *Jugurthine War* 73)**

Sallust, a former governor of Africa and a senator, may be biased, but his account shows a fragmented social and political environment, in which both sides felt that undue influence was being exerted. While the people's support for Marius may have been merited by his successes and his 'ideal general' behaviour of dining, sleeping and lodging with his troops (Plutarch, *Marius* 7), it was undoubtedly enhanced by the fact that he was a *novus homo* underdog.

Marius' military reforms of the Roman army created a permanent standing army. Abandoning the outdated and exclusive landowning enlistments, he recruited volunteers from the urban poor with promises of glory, booty and a permanent job. Other changes included the creation of a more diverse infantry, which allowed for the use of a broader spectrum of weapons and skills. He also simplified the army's supplies, creating *muli Marianum* ('Marian mules'), men who would carry all their own supplies and armour, thereby reducing the need for the unwieldy baggage trains that had often slowed down the army in the past. A new javelin (*pilum*) designed to break upon impact (so that it could not be reused by the enemy) is also attributed to Marius. He was elected again in 104 BC, and *in absentia* from 103 to 101, to serve as consul and war leader against the Gallic tribes. While the Senate baulked at the continued re-election of an absent consul, the situation was the product of growing social acrimony: Rome had suffered defeat when the *optimate* Caepio had refused to follow the orders of M. Manlius, a consul and *novus homo*. Rome's social struggles, dangerous in the capital, were lethal on the battlefield.

Marius, without doubt, was an excellent general and a true advocate of the Roman people. Sadly, he was not a skilled politician. Plutarch's account (*Marius* XXVIII) depicts a man who was noted for bravery in war quivering in the face of a shouting assembly:

> He tried to sway the people with flattering attentions, and appeased the masses to gain popularity, thus demeaning the dignity and nobility of his high office as well as his own person . . . In addressing a political drama or a rambunctious crowd, his ambition made him tremulous, and that steadfast solidarity that he displayed in battle abandoned him when he approached the popular assemblies.

This aspect of his character also emerges in his shady political behaviour. Elected consul for the sixth time in 100 BC, Marius allied himself with the tribune Saturninus, who attached proposals for giving land in North Africa to Marius' veterans to popular legislation. The *optimates* utilized a number of constitutional loopholes (e.g. noting bad omens, such as the sound of thunder) to prevent the people's assembly (by which the sources probably mean the Comitia Tributa) from meeting. With no constitutional check on the Senate's growing power, Marius employed the only resource he had left: his army, which intervened on his behalf.

The unforeseen consequence of allowing Marius to recruit and train an army of volunteers was a collection of soldiers whose livelihood and loyalty lay not with Rome, but with their general. While one can see the seeds of this in the victory procession of Scipio Africanus, the men who followed him had families and farms and a stake in the Roman republic. By contrast, Marius' soldiers (like America's colonists) had little to lose by challenging a government that benefited from their labour but offered little in return.

Saturninus attempted to rig the consular elections and was prosecuted (the latter was far less common than the former). Then the Senate issued a *senatus consultum ultimum*, forcing Marius (and his army) to turn against his principal supporter 'for the protection of the state'. Saturninus and his cronies were taken to the Senate for a 'fair trial', but an angry mob pulled the tiles off the roof and lynched them. ('Mob' is an interesting term for a group that probably contained a number of *optimates*.) Having thrown due process (along with a number of roof tiles) out of the window, the Senate repealed all of Saturninus' legislation, including the allocation of lands to Marius' veterans. Marius went into exile and the senators hailed their victory, forgetting, as careless people do, that they had just disenfranchised a large part of the Roman army.

Marius waited for the chance of a triumphant return. His moment came when Rome's allies in central Italy, who had stood steadfastly against Hannibal, saw that their voters' rights might be shelved. After many attempts at negotiation, they reluctantly declared war. In the *Phillipics*, a series of speeches in which Cicero speaks out against Mark Antony, he describes a meeting between the Roman consul Gnaeus Pompeius Strabo and the rebel commander Publius Vettius Scato. When the consul asks how he ought to address the commander, Scato replies, 'As a friend at heart, but by necessity an enemy' (*Phillipics* 12.27). Initially, the rebels claimed a number of successes, taking Rome by surprise. The engagements were brutal, and the generals who served in these wars – including Pompey, Catiline and Cicero – were profoundly shaped by them. Everntually, the rebels were outmanned and outgunned, but with defeat came victory: many of the rebel cities attained Roman citizenship; local constitutions were altered to allow citizens to serve both locally and in Rome; and Latin was at last adopted as the official language of Italy.

Meanwhile, in the east, Rome confronted a new enemy. Corruption, overtaxation by tax syndicates (*publiciani*) and extortion by provincial governors had created numerous enemies in the Roman province of Asia. Unsurprisingly, then, many cities accepted when King Mithridates of Pontus offered freedom from Rome; but some 80,000 Roman citizens were slaughtered, too. Sulla, a consul in 88 BC, was appointed to command the Roman counter-attack, a campaign which promised almost limitless booty. Marius, aware of a ripe opportunity for personal enrichment, made another dodgy alliance, this time with the tribune Sulpicius Rufus, who proposed popular legislation with an addendum to transfer command of the Asia campaign to Marius. Sulla was understandably livid. His six legions at Nola were like cats in a corner and they behaved predictably. After the recent tumult of the civil wars, Marius did not expect an outright assault by Sulla. However, although many of the latter's generals refused to march on Rome and his men nearly broke, he took the city and prevailed upon the Senate to declare Marius and his supporters 'enemies of the state' and to repeal Sulpicius' legislation. Only Sulpicius was killed; Marius escaped to Africa with his veterans and Sulla launched his campaign in Asia.

Marius made one last bid for power with the consul Cinna the following year, marching on Rome with a motley army of 'volunteers' (many of them were slaves from the countryside), persuaded to join up with promises of freedom, booty and glory. The bloodshed he brought upon Rome tainted his legacy and, having been elected to his seventh consulship in 86 BC, he died on 13 January of drink and delirium, according to Plutarch.

However, while Marius is often accused of undermining the principles of the republic, he was far surpassed in this by his successor: Sulla.

SULLA FELIX (138–78 BC) AND HIS CONSTITUTIONAL REFORMS

Although Sulla's first march on Rome in 88 BC had come as a surprise, the growing loyalty of Rome's soldiers to their generals and their isolation from republican institutions (such as the Senate) had been evolving for a century. Sulla, who married into the Metelli (a key *optimate* family), offered the Senate a general who was loyal to their agenda, so long as they supported him. It seemed like a match made in heaven, but it provided only an immediate solution to an immediate problem (his military appointment). The underlying division between the political factions remained. When his campaign in the east was completed (in 83 BC), Sulla returned to Rome to fight the opposition raised by the consuls Gn. Papirus Carbo and Marius Junior. He was joined in Brundisium by two young men who had a good sense of where the wind was blowing: Marcus Licinius Crassus (aged thirty-two) and Gnaeus Pompeius (aged twenty-three). Sulla marched on the city for the second time and, having defeated the opposition, exhumed Marius' remains, which he scattered in rage.

The living did not fare much better. Sulla's solution to the balance of power problem in Rome was to decree a victor and decimate the opposition. In 82 BC the Senate voted him the title Felix ('Lucky'), perhaps to imply divine intervention, and named him dictator, legitimizing his quest to destroy the popular opposition. Sulla thanked them by purging the Senate and the elite through proscription lists. If your name was on one of the lists, you could be legally killed by anyone (giving all Sulla's supporters the power of the master of the horse). While the sources vary on the extent of the slaughter, at least 500 people – including forty sentators – seem to have been killed in this way. Sometimes the wrong name was inscribed on a list, meaning a person was killed 'in error'. Following the example of Cincinnatus, Sulla confiscated the lands of the murdered individuals for 'public use' (although they were usually passed on to his cronies). The Senate (originally numbering 300), which had been depleted by both the recent wars and the proscription lists, was now filled with 450 new members of Sulla's choosing. Membership was for life, so the legacy of Sulla's cronyism survived long after his own demise. He imbued the Senate with great power, especially in *quaestiones* (jury courts), for whom he established seven permanent courts. He also increased the number of quaestors and praetors. He did not, however, increase the number of consuls, which created a bottleneck of elite competition on the top rungs of the *cursus honorum*. Finally, he stripped the veto from the tribunes of the plebs, debarred them from standing from any other office, and made them submit their voting agenda to the Senate for approval.

Were Sulla's reforms constitutional? It is difficult to see what he did as an interpretation (rather than a redrafting) of the Roman constitution. While many would have cast Sulla in the role of king, he thwarted everyone by retiring from public life three years later. His solution to the power struggle was to create a clear chain of command in the Senate, which was checked by Sulla himself. Upon his demise, no successor emerged. Sulla was a man of few regrets, but one was his failure to proscribe the teenage nephew of Marius – Julius Caesar – in whom he saw 'many a Marius' (Suetonius, *Caesar* 1).

THE LAST DAYS OF THE REPUBLIC (79–60 BC): CRASSUS, POMPEY, CAESAR AND CICERO

The men who would define the end of the republic were all in their twenties when Sulla died, but whether their roles were cast by then is debatable. The three men who would form the first triumvirate, the wealthy Marcus Licinius Crassus (*c.* 115–53 BC), the military genius Gnaeus Pompeius (106–48 BC; known as the 'Young Butcher' under Sulla and usually as 'Pompey' in English) and the wily Julius Caesar (100–44 BC), had been pieces on Sulla's chessboard but no decisive moves had yet been made. **Marcus Tullius Cicero** (106–43 BC), a *novus homo*, came to prominence in the months before Sulla died, when he bravely defended a man called Roscius against a charge of parricide that had been filed by one of Sulla's favourite freedmen. Roscius was acquitted on the grounds that others had a greater motive for murder, and Cicero's speech in the trial (*Pro Roscio Amerino* XXX) is known for coining the legal maxim *Cui bono* ('Who stood to gain?'). Regardless of the role Sulla may have played in setting the political stage, it would be a decade before these men assumed leading roles in Roman politics.

For Crassus and Pompey, 70 BC marked their year as co-consuls. The men who had joined Sulla in Brundisium thirteen years earlier vied for military success. Pompey famously stole a triumph from Crassus after the suppression of Spartacus' slave rebellion in 71 BC (Crassus was awarded a mere *ovatio*). By then, many of Sulla's reforms were being overturned (including the one that required Pompey to be a senator and/or at least forty-two before he could run for consul). Sulla may have blocked the elective path of a politician, but he neglected to check the path of military advancement for a general. Pompey and Crassus reinstated the powers of the tribune and a proposal to reinstate *equites* as jurors on the *quaestiones* courts was circulating. Caesar (now thirty) was elected as a quaestor and during his service in Spain he saw a statue of Alexander the Great, sadly noting the discrepancy between himself and a man who had conquered half the globe before his thirtieth birthday (Suetonius, *Caesar* 7). Even ten years after Sulla's demise, it seemed highly doubtful that these three men might form an alliance.

Roman law and administration: Cicero, *In Verrem*, and the extortion courts of Rome

For Cicero, 70 BC proved a vital moment in his career as he prosecuted a provincial governor in one of the *quaestiones perpetuae* (extortion courts). The case reveals both the rising political star of Cicero and the corrupt machinations of political life in the late republic. First, Gaius Verres, former governor of Sicily, was clearly guilty and did little to hide his vast accumulation of wealth. One of Sulla's cronies, he was of undistinguished birth and was not favoured by the aristocrats, which made him an ideal adversary for Cicero: the young lawyer's prosecution of this particular senator would give him prestige but would probably not make too many enemies among the Senate's *optimates* (whom he desperately hoped to join). Only a small fraction of the extortion cases ever resulted in a conviction, suggesting that the Senate was not regulating itself effectively. This led to a suggestion that two-thirds of the jurors on these courts should be *equites*, rather than senators, a proposal that was predictably rejected by the Senate. Cicero skilfully used this to his advantage during the trial.

Verres' defence was elaborate and well constructed. He hired the best orator, Quintus Hortensius Hortalus, who was standing for consul that year. In January 70 BC, at the arraignment, Verres also tried to get Q. Caecilius Niger (his quaestor in Sicily) appointed as attorney for the prosecution. When this failed, he called upon the help of the powerful Metelli family. Two members of that family were standing for election that year – L. Caecilius Metellus (also for consul) and M. Caecilius Metellus (for praetor of the extortion courts). Their cousin, another Metelli, stood as co-council for Hortensius. Their plan was to delay the proceedings until they were elected to office in the summer. The trial date was originally set for May, but another extortion case was to be prosecuted first (by yet another Metelli), and so Verres' trial was delayed until 5 August, after the elections. Hortensius and the two Metelli won their elections and then set about intimidating the Sicilian witnesses (Cicero, *In Verrem* 1.27). Roman holidays ran from 16 August to 18 September, and Cicero's eloquence seemed to assure that his delayed prosecution case would last at least until they began, which would leave the defence over a month to prepare its response and spin out the trial until Hortensius and the Metelli took office in the new year.

To Verres' and Hortensius' surprise, Cicero's first speech (*In Verrem* 1) was remarkably brief. Rather than detailing specific crimes, he addressed the senators as friends, exposing the machinations behind the execution of the trial and urging them to act in the interests of justice if they wanted to keep their roles as jurors during extortion trials: 'This is a trial in which you will be passing a verdict on the defendant, but the Roman people will also be passing a verdict upon you. This case will determine whether it is possible, when a jury consists of senators, for a very guilty but very rich man to be convicted' (*In Verrem* 1.46). Cicero's short address meant the defence team had little to respond to and forced a counter-statement from an unprepared Hortensius. At one point, the cornered orator exclaimed, 'I don't understand these riddles'. Cicero replied, 'Well, you ought to – after all, you've got a sphinx in your house' (Quintillian, *Institutio Oratoriae* 6.3.98), alluding to one of the exotic 'gifts' Hortensius had received from Verres. Embarrassed by the damning evidence, Verres stopped attending the trial and by the time the case resumed in September he had fled into exile.

Cicero's prosecution marked the young lawyer out for greatness and exposed the seedy underbelly of Sulla's unchecked aristocracy in the Senate. The Sicilians were offered meagre compensation, but the guilty verdict offered hope to provincials and aspiring new men. The doors of opportunity and justice now seemed to be open again, despite Sulla's attempts to close them.

The events leading up to the first triumvirate (67–60 BC)

The administration of a large empire continued to plague the Roman republic. Pirates in the Mediterranean threatened Roman markets and citizens, for whom they showed little respect. Caesar claimed to have been captured on his way to Rhodes and held for forty days, awaiting a ransom. He swore to his captors that he would find and crucify them and he duly kept his promise, although he mercifully slit their throats before hanging them on the crosses (Suetonius, *Caesar* 4). A solution to the pirate problem was proposed in 67 BC in the form of an extraordinary military command that offered unprecedented authority (a proconsulship with powers throughout the Mediterranean and twenty legates) and resources (1000 ships) to a man of proven military acumen: Pompey. Amid senatorial opposition, Pompey found an ally in Cicero (who was elected praetor that year). His command of 'zone defence' in the Mediterranean was successful and he was awarded another massive campaign (66–63 BC) in Asia Minor. As a general, Pompey was unrivalled. Although his portrait (Figure 2.6) presents him as a cheerful, rather portly chap, he was an astute politician, 'more of a fox than a lion'.

Meanwhile, in Rome, Crassus was elected censor and was courting popular support, offering citizenship in Cisalpine Gaul and attempting to annex Egypt as a province. However, his co-censor objected to these proposals and both men tendered their resignations. In 64 BC a number of interesting characters arose in the elections for public office. Julius Caesar ran for *pontifex maximus* against two more experienced candidates who lacked the financial resources of Caesar's patron: Crassus. The consular elections set two patricians from old families – L. Sergius Catilina (Catiline) and G. Antonius Hybrida – against Cicero, the *novus homo*, who emerged clearly in first place. The deprivations of Sulla continued to haunt the city and a case challenging the constitutional force of the *senatus consultum ultimum* was brought against G. Rabirius for his actions against Saturninus (thirty-six years earlier). The case never reached completion, but it expressed strong public disapproval of the murder of Roman citizens without trial.

Further discontent was added to this turbulent environment when Catiline lost a second election (for the consulship in 62 BC). Bankrupt and disillusioned, he desperately appealed to the *populares*, campaigning for cancellation of debts and redistribution of land (Figure 2.7). Like Maelius before him, Catiline saw that he would not be elected by legitimate means and he appeared to be collecting arms and fomenting rebellion. This put Cicero in a difficult position: he was not dictator with

FIGURE 2.6 Life-size bust of Pompey (a first-century copy of a contemporary likeness). Although his hair is styled after Alexander the Great, this portrait, with a wrinkled forehead, raised brows and the ghost of a smile, portays a rounder, stockier and more approachable-looking man. Photo © Ny Carlsberg Glyptotek, Copenhagen.

powers to protect the state and his co-consul was a former ally of Catiline. In attacking a member of an *optimate* family, Cicero was well aware of his *novus homo* status and the fact that the evidence (mostly rumour) could implicate a number of *optimate* families. So he waited until he had definitive proof in the form of letters from the conspirators of a Gallic faction (November 63 BC) and then took decisive action. His proposed solution, a *senatus consultum ultimum*, was passed to sanction the murder of the conspirators. Caesar argued eloquently against the murder of the conspirators

FIGURE 2.7 Terracotta bowl carrying an election slogan. This bowl, now on display at the Museo Epigrafico in Rome, was filled with food and handed out to voters as part of election propaganda. The bowl (*CIL* VI. 40905) records Marcus Porcius Cato (a descendant of Cato the Elder), who ran (in 63 BC) for the office of tribune of the plebs, which he held in 62 BC (assuming that this bowl and another, recording the name of Cataline, were not inscribed at a later date by an enterprising antiquarian). Photo © Ministero dei Beni e delle Attività Culturali e del Turismo – Soprintendenza Speciale per i Beni Archeologici di Roma.

without a trial, and while Cato the Younger and many senators hailed Cicero as 'saviour of the republic' for his swift and decisive action, many *populares* condemned the decree and the circumvention of due process.

Caesar spent 62 BC recovering debts in Spain as quaestor (with financial support from Crassus), then stayed on as governor, conquering local tribes. For these latter victories he was hailed 'Imperator' by his troops and voted a triumph by the Senate. Cicero, perhaps unwisely, chose to stay in Rome, providing a constant reminder of his controversial actions. Pompey, who had kept out of the recent political drama, returned triumphantly to Italy, where he disbanded his army.

Just eighteen months before the formation of the first triumvirate, there was little to suggest its imminent arrival. The common denominator between Caesar, Pompey and Crassus in 60 BC was Cato the Younger, who (like his ancestor) fought to check the rising powers of wealthy generals. Although Rome's most accomplished generals – Caesar (Crassus' man) and Pompey (Crassus' enemy) – should have been at loggerheads, both were thwarted by the Senate. Cato persuaded the senators to deny Caesar's request to register *in absentia* for the upcoming consular elections, forcing him to forgo his triumph (a general could not enter the city before ritually returning the *fasces*). When Caesar's consulship ended, the Senate allocated the smallest provincial settlement, 'policing the forests and tracks of Italy', to him. Pompey's efforts to give his veterans land had stalled in 61 and 60 BC. For all the faith he had shown by disbanding his army, he was still treated with mistrust by the Senate. Finally, Crassus, who had negotiated bids for tax collection in Asia during his censorship, argued for a remittance on behalf of a tax syndicate that could not make its payments. Although the default of a tax syndicate would have disastrous effects on trade in general and a number of Roman businessmen in particular, Cato blocked the proposed remittance.

The Senate's efforts to control Caesar, Pompey and Crassus unwittingly created an incentive for their alliance. This is documented in a letter from Cicero to his friend Atticus (*Ad Atticus* 2.3), written in late 60 BC, which relates his meeting with a friend of Caesar, who promised that Caesar would bow to Cicero's and Pompey's advice: 'this path offers the following boons: a close connection with Pompey, with Caesar as well (should I desire it), a return to popularity with my enemies, peace with the people and serenity in my old age'. Cicero felt that he was the mastermind of the new alliance. Pooling their resources, with Caesar as an intermediary, Crassus and Pompey reconciled and formed a formidable team. Cicero was asked to join them, but refused. Only a few months later, in another letter, he describes the alliance he had championed to his friend as 'the most odious, disgraceful and infamous regime that ever existed' (*Ad Atticus* 2.19).

Historians will continue to debate whether Cicero could have saved the republic by reconciling the 'three-headed monster' (commonly referred to as the first triumvirate) with the Senate. The informal 'gentleman's agreement' was neither official nor constitutional, but (in all fairness) neither was the *senatus consultum ultimum*. The imbalance in Rome's constitutional powers created by the city's expansion and consolidated by Sulla (who also gave the office of dictator a permanently negative connotation) was never rectified by subsequent reforms. The inability of the popular assemblies to check the Senate's power and Rome's increasing reliance on individuals to achieve an end illustrate that Romans of the late republic had already taken irrevocable steps towards monarchy.

FURTHER READING

* indicates sourcebook

Beard, M. and Crawford, M., *Rome in the Late Republic*, Duckworth, 2002 (new edition).

Crawford, M., *The Roman Republic*, Fontana, 1992 (2nd revised edition); Harvard University Press, 1993 (2nd edition).

Eckstein, A.M., *Rome Enters the Greek East*, Oxford, 2008.

Flower, H.I. (ed.), *The Cambridge Companion to the Roman Republic*, Cambridge University Press, 2004.

Garland, R., *Hannibal: Ancients in Action*, Bristol Classics Press, 2010.

Goldsworthy, A., *The Fall of Carthage: The Punic Wars, 265–146 BC*, Cassell, 2003.

Holland, T., *Rubicon: The Triumph and Tragedy of the Roman Republic*, Abacus, 2004 (new edition); *Rubicon: The Last Years of the Roman Republic*, Doubleday, 2005 (new edition).

Keaveney, A., *Sulla: The Last Republican*, Routledge, 2005 (revised edition).

Mouritsen, H., *Plebs and Politics in the Late Roman Republic*, Cambridge University Press, 2001.

Patterson, J.R., *Political Life in the City of Rome*, Bristol University Press, 2000.

Rosenstein, N. and Morstein-Marx, R. (eds), *A Companion to the Roman Republic*, Blackwell, 2010 (new edition).

Roselaar, S.T., *Public Land in the Roman Republic*, Oxford University Press, 2012.

*Sherk, R. (ed.), *Rome and the Greek East to the Death of Augustus*, Cambridge University Press, 1984.

Shotter, D., *The Fall of the Roman Republic*, Routledge, 2005 (2nd edition).

Syme, R., *The Roman Revolution*, Oxford University Press, 2002 (reissue).

Wiedemann, T.J., *Cicero and the End of the Roman Republic*, Classical World Series, 2013.

Wiseman, T.P., *Roman Political Life, 90 BC–AD 69*, Exeter University Press, 1985.

For an illustrated guide to republican coinage see: http://andrewmccabe.ancients.info.

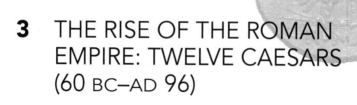

3 THE RISE OF THE ROMAN EMPIRE: TWELVE CAESARS (60 BC–AD 96)

SOURCES ON THE TWELVE CAESARS

The tale of Rome's transition from republic to empire is recorded by two famous Roman historians: P. Cornelius Tacitus (AD 56–after 117) and C. Suetonius Tranquillus (AD 69–c. 140) (see Chapter 8). The period in which they lived and wrote is often referred to as the 'Silver Age' of literature (the 'Golden Age' being the late republic). Both men, friends of the letter-writer Pliny the Younger, served under the emperors Trajan and Hadrian and were born outside of Italy (Tacitus hailed from Cisapline Gaul or Gallia Narbonensis and Suetonius from Algeria), demonstrating the decidedly cosmopolitan fabric of the Roman empire. Although they were contemporaries, the two men had distinct approaches to history and their accounts read like different sections of the same newspaper: Tacitus from the 'politics' pages, and Suetonius from the 'lifestyle' pages. Tacitus' *Histories* (published AD 104 and covering the 'year of four emperors' and the Flavians) and his *Annals* (published in AD 117 and covering the death of Augustus to Nero) employ an empire-wide lens to provide a detailed, year-by-year account of Rome's political history with subtle moral undertones. Suetonius, who published his *De Vita Caesaris* (often translated as 'The Twelve Caesars') in AD 119, focuses on physical descriptions and rowdy escapades in the imperial court. Writing at a time when a series of emperors – Nerva (AD 96–98), Trajan (AD 98–117) and Hadrian (AD 117–131) – were promoted on the basis of merit, both men consider whether family dynasties work as an institution. Both come to similar conclusions about the emperors: all of them (albeit some less so than others) are greedy, lascivious tyrants (excepting the three most recent ones, listed above, who are not recorded by either historian). Inheritance does not appear to alleviate the problem.

Each account assesses different aspects of imperial rule while providing a check on the other. Suetonius, who investigates imperial character through the development of the emperor as an individual, begins with the life of Julius Caesar (*c.* 85 BC). Tacitus' account, which examines the formalization and legitimacy of imperial power, starts with the death of Augustus and the transference of formally recognized powers to his Julio-Claudian heirs.

> The preceding period of 820 years, dating from the foundation of Rome, has found many historians. So long as republican history was their theme, they wrote with equal eloquence of style and independence of outlook. But when the Battle of Actium had been fought and the interests of peace demanded the concentration of power in the hands of one man, this great line of classical historians came to an end. Truth, too, suffered in more ways than one. To an understandable ignorance of policy, which now lay outside public control, was in due course added a passion for flattery, or else a hatred of autocrats. Thus neither school bothered about posterity, for the one was bitterly alienated and the other deeply committed. But whereas the reader can easily discount the bias of the time-serving historian, detraction and spite find a ready audience. Adulation bears the ugly taint of subservience, but malice gives the false impression of being independent. My official career owed its beginnings to Vespasian, its progress to Titus, and its further advancement to Domitian. I have no wish to deny this. But partiality and hatred towards any man are equally inappropriate in a writer who claims to be honest and reliable.
>
> **(Tacitus, *Histories* 1.1; trans. Kenneth Wellesley)**

While Caesar is a founding father for the image of the emperor (hence Suetonius' inclusion of him), he was not an emperor in legal or political terms and the transfer of his wealth and legacy to Octavian did not include political offices (hence Tacitus' exclusion of him). Equally, 'Caesar' was not an official title when Octavian adopted it, merely a family name that reaffirmed his legitimacy as a rightful heir. This practice, adopted by subsequent heirs, included the name Augustus as well, which then became part of the imperial titles.

Despite differences in approach, Tacitus and Suetonius were both writing in response to the most popular and prevalent mode of history in the ancient world: public monuments. We cannot hope to understand their accounts without considering the version of history presented by Rome's monuments, statues and coins. These objects provided a visual narrative that, unlike written accounts, was presented to a broader audience of individuals on a more permanent medium. The accounts of Tacitus and Suetonius often contradict material evidence, such as Augustus' inscribed account of his life, the *Res Gestae Divi Augusti*, and his Prima Porta statue (see Figure 3.4 below), which depicts a frail and middle-aged Augustus sporting giant biceps and a six-pack. Written works provide a check both on each other and on the imperial family's propaganda machine, whose monuments often survive in greater numbers than historical accounts. To develop an understanding of Rome's first emperors, one must compare and reconcile the varying illustrations of their characters from the material and historical sources. Although this chapter is subtitled 'Twelve Caesars', it employs a combination of historical accounts and material evidence to reconstruct an image of imperial Rome. The format is designed to reflect the evidence, focusing on specific emperors who ruled for more extensive periods and paying less attention to more transitional figures. Basic names, dates and offices held for each emperor can be found on the Roman Emperors web resource.

THE FIRST TRIUMVIRATE (60–48 BC)

Rome's movement towards monarchy was a product of many factors, crucial among which were the consolidation of power in the hands of generals, the prevalence of bribery in elections, and the increasing dominance of the Senate. The success of the first triumvirate (an unofficial alliance) between Caesar (100–44 BC), Pompey (106–48 BC) and Crassus (115–53 BC) was immediately evident in the election of Caesar as consul in 59 BC. Often referred to as a 'double bribery', this election saw both Crassus (supporting the popular candidate Caesar) and the incorruptible Cato (supporting the *optimate* candidate, his son-in-law Capurnius Bibulus, as co-consul) blatantly resort to bribery to protect their political interests. The fact that buying votes had become the *modus operandi* for both factions illustrates how corrupted the process had become. When Caesar approached the Senate with a proposal for land distribution, Cato and his *optimate* colleagues rejected both the bill itself and the very concept of land redistribution. Cicero (106–43 BC) – who observed that his colleague Cato the Younger 'speaks in the Senate as though he were living in Plato's republic, instead of Romulus' cesspool' (*Ad Atticus* 21.8) – was increasingly isolated from his *optimate* friends, who continued to ignore popular issues.

Denied by the Senate, Caesar turned to the 'popular assembly' (probably the Comitia Tributa), but his co-consul Bibulus kept calling off the meetings on account of 'bad omens'. In times of crisis, Rome was meant to appoint a dictator, but the two consuls had to agree; in this case, that meant a political stalemate was inevitable. On the day of the scheduled vote, chaos unfolded: Bibulus' *fasces* (the symbol of his power as consul) were smashed and something worse than mud was slung in his face. A tribune who tried to veto the proceedings was thrown from the platform. From this point onwards, Suetonius tells us that Caesar did as he wished and 'it became a joke to sign bogus documents executed during the consulship of Julius and Caesar rather than during the consulship of Bibulus and Caesar' (Suetonius, *Caesar* 20). Having passed his land reform, Caesar made the senators take an oath to support it (perhaps to prevent them from repealing it later). He passed three vital pieces of legislation: forgiving the debts of Crassus' tax syndicate in Asia; arranging land settlements for Pompey's veteran soldiers in the east; and regulating the conduct of provincial governors. Regardless of how it was obtained, the sole consulship of Caesar showed how much could be accomplished by a single individual without bipartisan acrimony.

After a successful but controversial year in office, Caesar arranged a five-year appointment in Gaul (which would conveniently prevent him from being indicted for any acts he committed during his recent consulship). The triumvirate sealed their bonds with marriage: Pompey married Caesar's daughter Julia (his fourth wife); and Caesar married Calpurnia (whose father would be consul the following year, along with Pompey's friend Aulus Galbinus). The triumvirate was renewed in 56 BC when Pompey and Crassus were elected consuls. Then they took rich provinces in Spain and Syria, respectively, for five years and extended Caesar's command in Gaul.

Caesar's successful campaigns in Gaul, which were reported to Rome in his own written commentaries, *De Bello Gallico*, kept him both popular and distant from crises at home. In 51 BC he enjoyed a major victory against Vercingetorix, the Arvernian chief, at the Battle of Alesia (see Map 4), despite being outnumbered nearly four to one. Caesar's own account of this battle is detailed, long-winded and not particularly gripping, while later ones, such as that of Lucius Annaeus Florus (fl. *c.* 130 AD) – *Abridgements of All the Wars for 700 Years* – underestimates his achievement, omitting the simultaneous attack of another Gallic force of 250,000 infantry and 8000 cavalry, whom Caesar also managed to rout. The mighty city of Alesia, garrisoned by 80,000 troops, was defended by its walls, its fortress and sheer river banks on both sides. Caesar invested it with an earth wall, a fence of stakes and a moat into which he diverted water from the river. His wall was topped by a massive parapet and eighteen towers were built into it. First he starved out the inhabitants. Then, when they dared to sally forth, he cut them down at the wall and fence, finally forcing them to surrender.

Some scholars trace Caesar's commitment to world domination back to his military success in Gaul; however, these wars were a dangerous game. Brave almost to a fault, Caesar (according to his own accounts; see Chapter 8) dashed recklessly into the front lines of battle and was nearly killed on numerous occasions. Apart from enriching him and his reputation, his campaigns in Gaul did not provide a great deal for Rome, other than the annexation of Gaul itself, which was divided into three areas – Aquitania, Lugdunensis (Lyon) and Belgica (see Map 4) – creating a border with the Rhine, a buffer zone between Italy and Germany. Perhaps the most significant aspect of the campaigns was the integration of Celtic and Roman societies, resulting in both a powerful cultural hybrid and the roots of the modern nation of France.

TROUBLE IN PARADISE: THE COLLAPSE OF THE FIRST TRIUMVIRATE

Dispersed across an empire, the ties that bound the triumvirate started to weaken: Pompey's wife Julia (Caesar's daughter) died in 54 BC and Crassus died on campaign in Syria in 53 BC. The following year, Pompey was sole consul after a nasty episode between rival gangs resulted in the death of Clodius, whose supporters accidentally burned down the Senate with his funeral pyre. With Crassus gone, Pompey began to distance himself from Caesar. He sought to remove the protection provincial governorships had traditionally afforded to former office-holders, knowing that Caesar would soon return to Rome as a private citizen, and could be tried for the events of his consulship. A further snub was Pompey's rejection of Octavia (Octavian's sister) as a wife in favour of forging an alliance with the Metelli family by marrying Cornelia Metella.

In 50 BC, amid growing tensions between Caesar and Pompey, Marcus Scribonius Curio, a tribune and agent of Caesar, suggested a compromise: both leaders should disband their armies. The Senate was overwhelmingly in favour but twenty-odd dissidents (including Pompey) 'arranged' a tribune's veto. When Marcus Antonius (Marc Antony; 83–30 BC) made the same proposal in 49 BC, bringing with him a signed acceptance from Caesar, the consuls blocked the vote and a new motion was tabled to declare Caesar an enemy of the state. Antony used his tribune's veto but was warned to leave Rome when the Senate passed a *senatus consultum ultimum* declaring Caesar an enemy of the state.

ALEA IACTA EST: 'THE DIE IS CAST'

Caesar's subsequent march on Rome could be seen as an act of war on his own country. However, his well-known phrase 'the die is cast' (Suetonius, *Caesar* 33), spoken as he crossed the Rubicon river (see Map 1), suggests a different interpretation of events. The Senate's decree left Caesar with few viable options. By using the passive voice ('is cast' implies an action taken by someone else) and the metaphor of the die, which even today exemplifies the precarious nature of fate, Caesar emphasizes his reluctance to act as an aggressor (like Aeneas; see Chapter 1). He is acting simply on the hand he has been dealt: the die was cast by a few gambling politicians in Rome, but the consequences would fall upon the Roman people. As it happens, the Romans did learn from the past and when news of Caesar's approaching army reached them, Pompey decided to leave the city and engage Caesar in the provinces, preventing Italy from becoming at battlefield. After successfully defeating Pompey's forces in Spain, Caesar moved to Greece in 48 BC, where Pompey was well connected. While Caesar could count on a loyal army at the Battle of Pharsalus (Epirus; see Map 4), Pompey had to contend with nervous soldiers and anxious *optimate* senators, who urged him into battle against his better judgement. The result was a disastrous defeat for Pompey's forces. He fled to Egypt, where he was embraced by a number of men with knives.

Caesar's victory at Pharsalus was a muted one, however: when Roman fights Roman, everyone stands to lose. Separating himself from the legacy of Marius or Sulla, Caesar offered clemency to all (soldiers and senators) who had fought against him. He went to Egypt, where an ambitious young Cleopatra VIII welcomed him with the exceptional 'red carpet' treatment of having herself delivered to his camp wrapped only in rug. She managed to convince Caesar that she was the rightful heir to Egypt's throne and then gave him a son (and heir to the Egyptian throne) named Caesarion. Roman sources present conflicting images of Cleopatra – from an empty-headed temptress obsessed with luxury to a manipulative Lady Macbeth who would do anything to protect her country (see Figure 3.3 below). These images, the products of Augustan propaganda, are difficult to reconcile, but the latter seems more convincing than the former. On his way back to Rome, Caesar stopped in Asia Minor to anihiliate Pharnaces, where he coined the phrase '*Veni Vidi Vici*' ('I came, I saw, I conquered').

HAIL CAESAR!

> Caesar was the only sober man who ever tried to wreck the constitution.
>
> **(Attributed to Cato in Suetonius, *Caesar* 53)**

In his absence and during a time of crisis, Caesar was appointed dictator, an appointment that was regularly renewed until he assumed the role for life. Between his military campaigns against stalwart Pompeians in Africa and Spain from 48 to 44 BC, Caesar planned reforms in Rome: from her calendar to her public buildings, including the port at Ostia. He removed tax syndicates in Asia and encouraged the resettlement of Romans in provinces, offering citizenship to a number of provincials (which allowed men like Tacitus and Suetonius to achieve higher social status). Caesar's actions and pardons won gratitude but not loyalty. The Senate, in particular, bided its time, voting Caesar more and more privileges and honours, including such 'excessive honours' as an uninterrupted consulship, dictator for life, censor and the title *pater patriae* ('father of his country'). He was given honours 'too great for a mortal man' (according to Suetonius, *Caesar* 76–79), including a golden throne in the Senate, temple altars and a statue among the gods; a month on the Roman calendar was even named in his honour. His acceptance of the military title 'Imperator', which would eventually come to mean emperor, gave him the official *imperium* power over life and death not only on campaign but within the city of Rome.

One day, when the Senate came to Caesar's new forum, where he had suggested the senators should meet (their new Senate house was still under construction), he did not stand to greet them (Suetonius, *Caesar* LXXVII). Though this incident was later blamed on an irritable bowel, his lack of respect caused anger and accusations that Caesar wanted to be king. Caesar's refusal of kingly honours when Antony tried to crown him at the Lupercalia festival (Suetonius, *Caesar* 79) was too little and too late to stem the growing tide of resentment.

Did Caesar have kingly aspirations or merely a long-standing dislike of the Senate? The physical description of Caesar in Suetonius, which sets him out as 'tall, well built, fair, with a broad face and keen dark eyes' (Suetonius, *Caesar* 45), is not at odds with his portrait. Suetonius' amusing commentary on Caesar's baldness and his epic comb over, also evident in his portrait, mockingly suggests that Caesar's love of the laurel crown was not necessarily due to what it represented, but to what it hid (Figure 3.1). Regardless of the good he accomplished, Caesar's appropriation of public funds, his personal appointment of officials and generals, and his general insouciance towards republican traditions were too much for many proud senators. On the Ides of March 44 BC, dozens of senators stabbed him during a meeting of the Senate that was taking place in a hall adjoining the Theatre of Pompey (see Chapter 7; Map 5, no. 6). It was said that Caesar fell, ironically, at the foot of Pompey's colossal statue.

In Shakespeare's *Julius Caesar* (3.2), the proud Brutus justifies his participation in the assassination: 'As Caesar loved me, I weep for him; as he was fortunate, I rejoice at it; as he was valiant, I honour him; as he was ambitious, I slew him.' The judgement of history is that Caesar's driving ambition and energy led him to enact too many changes too quickly, without showing proper respect or consideration for the traditions and constitutional practices that he was sweeping away. While they were willing to subvert a dysfunctional constitution, the people were not prepared to remove it entirely. The role of a dictator was to govern the republic with the aim of restoring it. As it became clear that restoration was not on Caesar's agenda he lost his usefulness and the office of dictator in the republic became defunct.

Coins minted at the time, depicting Brutus on one side and the cap of liberty with two swords on the other (Figure 3.2), suggest that the murder was legitimized by the state. It was not. Literary sources concur in painting Caesar's assassination as an unpopular event, which only served to increase his fame and respect among the people. As we enter an age of imperial propaganda, it is important to remember that Roman coins had a political as well as an economic function, representing the agenda of the person who commissioned them. They did not necessarily reflect popular belief just because they were made for public consumption.

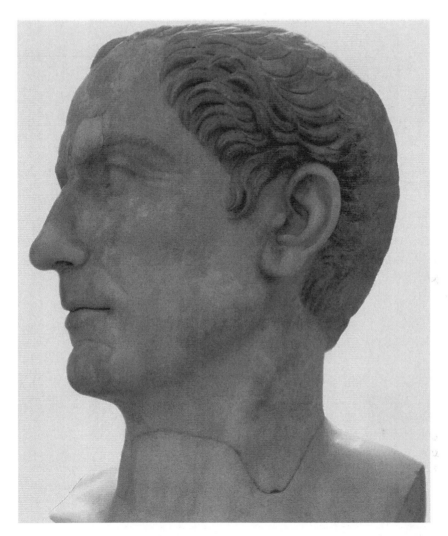

FIGURE 3.1 Bust of Caesar (side view) from the era of Trajan, now in the National Archaeological Museum, Naples. From this perspective one can see his strong aquiline features, the short crop styling which Augustus would adopt, as well as the comb-forward style Caesar used to cover his receding hairline. Photo © VRoma: Barbara McManus.

One of Caesar's most impressive legacies was not just the wealth he passed on to his heir Octavian, but the fact that his will was ratified. Although the cost of pardoning his enemies had been high, Caesar's clemency had been a shrewd political move. To dispose of him and his legacy, the Senate would have to declare him an enemy of the state, repealing or nullifying all his acts. Therefore, many senators and

FIGURE 3.2 'Ides of March' denarius, minted in 43–42 BC. Depicting Brutus' head on one side (recorded in the text as 'BRUT IMP') and the liberty cap with two daggers and the text 'EID MAR' on the other side, this coin clearly refers to Caesar's assassination as a liberation. The small silver coin (3.6 grams) was minted by his magistrate L. Plaetorius Cestianus 'on-the-go' in a moving mint that travelled with Brutus in northern Greece. It shows the growing importance of imagery for a leader, especially on coinage, that will become common practice for emperors during the empire. In 2011 one of these coins sold for $546,250, among the highest prices ever paid for a coin. Photo © CNG Coins.

officials who had been promoted or elected during his reign found themselves in an awkward position. Antony obtained Caesar's will from the Vestal Virgins, then made his intended gifts to the Roman people (including three gold pieces a head) public knowledge. In this way Caesar had one final victory: his will and acts were ratified by a sheepish Senate. His funeral was a public event, and a wax effigy of his body with all the stab wounds was shown to a rioting mob of mourners while Antony gave a stirring eulogy (Suetonius, *Caesar* 84). Although his murderers (Brutus and Cassius) were not prosecuted, they left Rome after the funeral mourners attempted to torch their homes.

THE RISE OF AUGUSTUS AND THE SECOND TRIUMVIRATE (44–31 BC)

Gaius Octavianus – Caesar's heir and, according to some sources, his adopted son – was eighteen when his uncle died. It was late April 44 BC when he arrived in Rome. By then, Marc Antony and Marcus Aemlius Lepidus (91–13 BC), who had been Caesar's chief assistants, had assumed control over the state and Caesar's fortune. Octavian, although blatantly marking his status by taking the name 'Caesar', was not yet ready to confront Antony. Cicero, who was attacking Antony with a series of orations that would be his undoing, happily took Octavian under his wing, hoping to ally the young man with the Senate. His true feelings about Octavian, however, are recorded in one of his personal letters: 'the young man should be complimented, honoured and got rid of' (*Ad Familiares* 11.21). Cicero woefully underestimated Octavian, whom he sent out with two consuls to defeat Antony in 43 BC. Both consuls were killed and Octavian, though victorious, chose not to pursue Antony. Instead, the young Caesar returned to Rome with eight legions and 'suggested' that he be made consul. He was nineteen years old.

As consul, Octavian ratified the *triumviri reipublicae constituendae* (the 'second triumvirate'), a formal, legal, five-year appointment empowering Antony, Lepidus and Octavian himself to 'restore' the Roman constitution. This included powers to enact laws (without the Senate's approval), exercise jurisdiction (without appeal) and nominate magistrates. They also divvied up the provinces and legions between themselves (though these allocations would change after Philippi). Elections were still held and there was formal consultation with the Senate, giving the appearance of a republic 'under construction' but not yet vanquished. This illusion was undercut by Sullan-style proscriptions, which included death and confiscation of property for at least 150 knights (*equites*) and 150 senators, including the noble Cicero, whose head and hands were cut off and sent to Rome (Appian, *Civil Wars* 4.2). In 42 BC Julius Caesar was deified and a comet streaking across the sky was taken to be his soul and called the *sidus Juli*. In October of that year, the triumvirs sought to avenge him at the Battle of Philippi (in Greece) against Brutus and Cassius. Antony remained the clear front runner and military strategist: while he crushed Cassius' forces, Octavian's men were routed by Brutus and the young heir was found hiding in a bog three days after the battle (Pliny the Elder, *Natural History* 7.46).

Following his victory at Philippi, Antony stayed in the east to continue Caesar's Parthian campaign, collecting booty, prestige and mistresses (including Cleopatra) as he went. Lepidus headed to Africa; and Octavian was saddled with the task of piecing Italy back together and tackling Sextus Pompey (Pompey's son), who, acting as the Jack Sparrow of the Mediterranean, was causing a grain crisis in Rome. Challenged by Antony's supporters in his attempts to gain land settlements for his veterans, Octavian laid siege to Perusia (modern-day Perugia) against Antony's brother Lucius and Antony's wife Fulvia. Slingshots from the siege (41–40 BC), found embedded in the walls, record jaunty epithets about their targets: 'Open wide Octavian [with a picture of a phallus]' and 'Bend over Baldy Lucius and Fulvia, I'm coming in' (*CIL* 11.6721.10 and 14). Although Lucius and Fulvia were 'allowed' to escape, they both died in suspicious circumstances at the end of the year. Octavian and Antony tried to resolve their differences in Brundisium in the autumn of 40 BC; and Antony, now in need of a wife, married Octavia, Octavian's sister.

Despite initial failures, Octavian's admiral Marcus Vispsanius Agrippa, a childhood friend of humble origins, succeeded in defeating Pompey's heir, Sextus Pompey, off the coast of Sicily. These naval engagements (38–36 BC) cast Octavian in the role of Caesar's natural successor. In the wake of this success, Lepidus tried to assume control of Sicily, but he was outmanoeuvred by Octavian, who persuaded Lepidus' soldiers to desert. From this point, Lepidus was out of the picture, and a battle of images and ideology between the young, abstemious Octavian in the west and the wealthy playboy Antony in the east could begin. Despite their political differences, the divide between Octavian and Antony was blamed on a woman. As Antony sent Octavia back to Rome and sued for divorce, it became clear that he had chosen Cleopatra over her and Alexandria over his duties to Rome.

Octavian, who seems to have been chronically underestimated by all of his enemies, used the opportunity to paint Antony as a pathetic captive of the Egyptian queen, spinning the conflict not as a civil war but as an ideological battle against Egypt and the corruption of eastern culture. Returning to Alexandria (rather than Rome) for the triumph of his eastern victories and minting coins depicting himself and Cleopatra (Figure 3.3), Antony facilitated Octavian's case against the Egyptian queen, whose

FIGURE 3.3 Denarius of Antony and Cleopatra (32 BC), Alexandria Mint (type RRC 543/1). With portraits of Antony and Cleopatra (who are not terribly dissimilar in appearance) on either side, this small silver coin (3.5 grams) presents the two rulers on equal ground. Although the portraits are not conventionally flattering, they show a keen understanding of what is acceptable on coins. Antony is shown bare-headed with his victory over Armenia recorded in the text ('ANTONI ARMENIA DEVICTA') and signified by the Armenian crown depicted on his back. This links him with Cleopatra, who wears a crown as queen, and the text records her as 'queen of kings and of the children of kings'. She is subtly linked to Antony's victory by the depiction of a prow at her chest. It was not permissible for a woman to be associated with a military victory or for a Roman man to wear a crown, but Antony and Cleopatra walk a fine line by linking their roles and images. Photo © CNG Coins.

son Caesarion had the only other claim to be Julius Caesar's rightful heir. In 31 BC, the Romans yet again chose a Greek site, Actium (Epirus; see Map 4), for their final showdown. Agrippa's naval aptitude won the day and Cleopatra fled the scene, leaving Antony to commit suicide. Rather than face the prospect of marching through Rome in chains, the wily Cleopatra had a basket of figs hiding two asps delivered to her, then placed the snakes on her breasts to bite and kill her. Caesarion was murdered, and a triumphant Octavian returned to Rome, now effectively in charge of the Roman world.

AUGUSTUS: RESTORER OF THE REPUBLIC? (27 BC–AD 14)

> Twice, Augustus seriously considered restoring the republic ... ultimately, however, he decided not to do so.
>
> **(Suetonius, *Augustus* 28)**

The events that immediately followed the Battle of Actium forced Octavian to assemble his powers into an acceptable constitutional form and to depart from Caesar's legacy, avoiding suggestions of a return to a monarchy (or a dictatorship) that had caused so much trouble in the past. He achieved this gradually over a number of years in a manner that did not appear to undermine the authority of the Senate as a consultative body. Octavian – who had previously gone by the name Gaius Caesar, or *divi filius* ('son of a god') – accepted the name 'Augustus' in 27 BC and launched a media campaign to record his 'restorations' of law, order, religion, peace and public buildings. While continuing to hold successive consulships, in 27 BC he formally resigned all the special powers he had been granted, but in return accepted for ten years the strategic provinces of Cilicia, Cyprus, Gaul, Spain and Syria, for which troops were required. Augustus' own version of the process was incorporated into one of the statements engraved on bronze tablets at the entrance to the family mausoleum which he built in the Campus Martius (see Map 5, no. 1): 'During my sixth and seventh consulates [28 and 27 BC], when I had put down the civil wars and was universally acknowledged to be in complete control, I transferred the management of affairs of state to the Senate and the Roman people' (*Res Gestae Divi Augusti* 34).

At this time Augustus was confirmed as divine successor to the pharaohs in Egypt. The subjugation of Egypt to the Roman people was monumentalized by Augustus in 10 BC with two giant (200-ton) obelisks, shipped from Alexandria, which were set up in the spina of the Circus Maximus (Map 5, no. 3) and as the pointer of a giant sundial in the Campus Martius. These Egyptian monuments were rededicated to the Roman sun god (Sol) and were integrated, like the country they represented, into a Roman monumental world. Augustus balanced this image of foreign war with an Altar of Peace (*Ara Pacis*), dedicated on the east side of the obelisk in the following year (see Map 5, no. 7). This monument, commissioned by the Senate, depicts peace, prosperity and the security of the Roman family in a series of beautiful reliefs that show processional scenes with men, women and children (many of whom are modelled on members of the Augustus' family; see Figure 6.7). Augustus also promoted individuals, such as Marcus Agrippa, to whom he gave responsibility for a number of vital public building projects (such as the baths in the Campus Martius). Promoting a man of humble origins made Augustus' Rome look like a meritocracy. While he remained *primus inter pares*, 'first among equals', Augustus' monumental scheme in the Campus Martius, which combined an obelisk for the Roman people, the Senate's Altar of Peace, his own mausoleum and Agrippa's baths, created a beautiful illusion of unity and the balance of power among officials in the republic.

In 23 BC, because of illness, he gave up his claim to hold the office of consul for life. This was a diplomatically sound move, as it opened up to others an additional chance of honour, and in its place he was granted for life the privileges of a tribune of the people, with powers to apply a veto and to present matters direct to the popular assemblies. It may seem like semantics, but Augustus' method of retaining the official titles of the republic (being voted the powers of a tribune and a consul) and consulting with the Senate were important distinctions between himself and Julius Caesar, and it served to maintain the semblance of a republic. In reality, Augustus' reforms were not all that they were cracked up to be. From the turn of the century, only emperors or members of the imperial family would be allowed to undertake major public works in Rome. There was much foreign war during Augustus' 'reign of peace', and his rigid social classifications (such as the *Lex Julia Theatralis*; see Chapter 7) would define and divide Roman society even at public events. His 'restorations' of old monuments were sometimes merely excuses to move or redecorate (such as a series of old statues of Rome's greatest men (*summi viri*) he 'restored' and moved into his new forum, where they became part of his monument).

Augustus' public image is at odds with his physical description in Suetonius (*Augustus* 79), for although he is regarded as 'remarkably handsome', with 'clear bright eyes', we are also told that he could not care less about his hair, that his body was 'marked with blemishes', that he sometimes limped (80), and that he suffered from a fragile constitution and ill-health on a number of occasions (82). When we compare this account to his image in public portraits, such as the famous Prima Porta statue (*c.* 20 BC; Figure 3.4), certain discrepancies arise. The middle-aged Augustus has the body of an Olympic athlete, wears a large military chestplate (cuirass) and sports perfectly coiffed hair (Augustus is identified by a distinct 'crab claw' arrangement of locks on his forehead in his portraits).

FIGURE 3.4 Prima Porta statue of Augustus. This marble statue, probably a copy of a bronze original, was discovered in the nineteenth century at a villa outside of Rome associated with Livia. Dated to 20 BC, it depicts, at the centre of the breastplate, the peaceful return of the Roman standards (lost by Crassus in Syria). And, like the *Ara Pacis* and Augustus' *Res Gestae*, it implies a peace without bloody warfare, and the dawning of a new era in Rome. The idealism is also evident in the portrait of Augustus, who (by now forty years old and notoriously frail in constitution) is represented in the body of a young athlete with a youthful face. In a world without plastic surgery, the Romans still found a way to ascribe surreal beauty to their celebrities. Vatican, New Wing. © 2014. Photo Scala, Florence.

Augustus' reign lasted over forty years and gave the western world the term 'Augustan' to denote an age of glittering literary achievement. Though the boundaries of the Roman empire had not yet reached their widest extent, Augustus consolidated them by reorganizing and strengthening the army, and removing it from Italy to patrol the provinces. He remodelled the civil service, largely rebuilt parts of Rome itself and appointed 3500 firemen under a chief fire officer to guard against conflagration. After a century of civil war and strife, Augustus gave the Roman people four decades without civil wars, a capital city of marble, and a new concept of what it meant to be Roman in a growing empire. He died in the family house at Nola in Campania at the age of seventy-six.

While accomplishing the seemingly impossible in so many ways, one of his greatest difficulties was producing a viable successor. Married three times, his only child was a daughter (Julia) by his second wife. He had, however, taken the precaution, after several earlier attempts to do so had been aborted by deaths, of nominating a successor – his stepson Tiberius – to whom the year before his death he had granted a form of power of attorney over affairs of state.

TIBERIUS (AD 14–37)

Though Tiberius had been groomed by Augustus as his successor, he was only fourth choice after Agrippa, husband of Augustus' only child Julia, and their sons, Gaius and Lucius, all three of whom died in the lifetime of Augustus. Thus, to an already diffident nature was added a sense of inferiority. On Agrippa's death (13 BC), Augustus compelled Tiberius to divorce his wife Vipsania and become Julia's third husband. Julia was notorious for her affairs, which are recorded by a number of ancient sources. In 6 BC, during his five-year term as the equivalent of chief tribune of the people, a highly influential role (until then performed by Augustus himself), Tiberius retired to Rhodes. This may have been related to Augustus' promotion of his grandsons (and true blood relatives) Gaius and Lucius, and/or the behaviour of Julia. Certainly, by the time he returned in AD 2, Julia had been banished by her father for adultery. In AD 4, after the deaths of Lucius (AD 2) and Gaius (early AD 4), Tiberius was adopted by Augustus and sent to command the imperial armies, all based outside Italy. From then until Augustus' death, which happened while Tiberius was travelling, he hardly had occasion to visit Rome.

Tiberius was summoned back not by the Senate but by his elderly mother, Livia, widow of Augustus. The circumstances of her marriage were bizarre, whatever interpretation is put on them. It is said that Livia's first husband was forced to divorce her and that she married Augustus when she was six months pregnant with Tiberius' younger brother, Drusus. Augustus had just divorced his own second wife, Scribonia, because he was 'sick of her perpetual bitching' (Suetonius, *Augustus* 62) on the very day she gave birth to their only child. Livia had been sixteen when Tiberius was born; now in her seventies, she was a matriarch and she wanted a share in ruling the country. Tiberius would have none of that, but Tacitus reports that, in order to secure his position, he had Agrippa Postumus, the last surviving grandson of Augustus, starved to death on the prison island to which he had been exiled for his antisocial behaviour. According to Suetonius, this could have been done without Tiberius' knowledge on instructions left by Augustus or by Livia acting in Augustus' name. (Tacitus likes to paint imperial women as poisoners and Lady Macbeth types, whispering foul words and ambition into the ears of men.)

Tiberius was fifty-five when he came to power. Despite being well groomed for office, he had an uneasy relationship with the Senate. He never accepted some of the titles voted to Augustus (e.g *pater patriae* – 'father of his country') and his attempts to relinquish certain powers met with resentment:

> Tiberius happened to say that although he was not equal to the whole burden of the state, he would undertake the charge of whatever part of it might be entrusted to him. Thereupon Asinius Gallus said, 'I ask you, Caesar, what part of the state do you wish to have entrusted to you?'
>
> **(Tacitus, *Annales* 1)**

Although Suetonius describes him as an attractive, healthy man (*Tiberius* 68) and a learned scholar, whether he was cut out to be emperor is a separate question.

Several years of intrigue and counter-intrigue followed, as candidates to succeed Tiberius (and their wives or mothers on their behalf) jockeyed for position or were jockeyed completely out of the way, as happened to Drusus, the emperor's only son. Tiberius probably played no part in any of this, but merely sensing what was going on unsettled him and further contributed to his indecision in matters of government. When Drusus died in AD 23, a grieving Tiberius began to lean heavily on Lucius Aelius Sejanus (d. AD 31), the prefect of the imperial guard. Sejanus became his friend (there was little reason for Tiberius to trust the imperial family) and asked for the hand of Drusus' widow (a request that was refused). In AD 26, in his late sixties, Tiberius, always happiest when away from Rome, retired to his holiday mansion on the island of Capri, never to return to the city. However, he could still exercise power from a distance, and wrote a letter to the Senate expressing his suspicions of his old friend. Sejanus was executed and his corpse dragged through the streets before being thrown into the Tiber. His family and many of his cronies suffered the same fate. The treatment of his children casts an especially chilling light on the workings of the Roman penal system:

> Though the fury of the people was quieting down and many had been pacified by the earlier executions, it was then decided to attend to the two surviving children of Sejanus. They were therefore taken to jail, the boy realizing what was in store for them, the girl so innocent that she kept asking what she had done, crying that she would do nothing wrong again and that surely a gentle spanking would be enough this time. The archivists of the time record that because there was no legal precedent for the execution of a virgin, the hangman had intercourse with her beside the noose. The pair were then strangled and their bodies, young as they were, thrown on the steps by the Capitol.
>
> **(Tacitus, *Annals* 5.9)**

Tacitus, who suggests that Tiberius' retirement home was a den of iniquity, notes that he left for it 'with only a few companions: a former consul [and] . . . a Roman knight of the higher rank . . . the rest being intellectuals, mainly Greek, whose conversation he enjoyed' (*Annals* 4.58).

Tiberius' last years were still fraught with morbid mistrust, reports of flagrant and more discreet family adulteries, and a continual narrowing down, by natural and unnatural death, of candidates for the succession. Whether Tiberius, who was seventy-eight, died naturally or was murdered is uncertain, but by then the field had been reduced to just two: his grandson Tiberius Gemellus (*c.* AD 20–37), who was suspected by many (including Tiberius) of being the offspring of his mother's affair with Sejanus; and his last surviving great-nephew, Gaius Caesar, now twenty-four, nicknamed *Caligula* ('Little Boots') after the miniature army boots he had worn as a child. With typical vacillation to the last, Tiberius named them joint heirs. Suetonius records that, upon hearing of his death in Rome, the crowds shouted, 'To the Tiber with Tiberius' (*Tiberius* 75).

CALIGULA (AD 37–41)

The question as to who would succeed Tiberius was resolved easily enough. Naevius Cordus Sutorius Macro (d. AD 38), a former chief of the fire service in Rome and now commander of the imperial guard in succession to Sejanus, had met Caligula in Capri, and they got on well together. Despite some family tension (some accounts blame Tiberius for the murder of Caligula's father Germanicus, and the deaths of his mother and five siblings), when Macro proposed Caligula's name to the Senate as emperor, there was no objection. Perhaps more importantly, the role of the imperial guard in nominating the emperor had now been established. At first, it seemed that the choice was correct, for Caligula was everything a young and charismatic ruler should be – generous to the public (and to the imperial guard), genuinely interested (though inexperienced) in matters of government, sensible, witty and just. He recalled many political exiles and dropped the charges against them, and banished all male prostitutes. He formally adopted his cousin, Tiberius Gemellus, and appointed his uncle Claudius (his dead father's younger brother) to be, with him, consul *suffectus* in AD 37 (*suffectus* in this context means 'deputy' or 'substitute'). Julius Caesar had instituted the procedure whereby an elected consul was invited or required to stand down during his term of office in favour of a suffect consul. Especially when emperors appropriated for themselves successive consulships (a policy begun by Augustus), this device was subsequently used to increase the number of men qualified for the most senior administrative or military posts in the provinces of the empire.

Six months into his reign, Caligula fell ill. When he recovered, the citizens of Rome found they were living in a nightmare. According to Suetonius, Caligula had since childhood suffered from epilepsy, known in Roman times as the 'parliamentary disease', since it was regarded as an especially bad omen if anyone had a seizure while public business was being conducted. (Caligula's distant cousin Julius Caesar probably suffered from what is now recognized as late-onset epilepsy.) This, or some other ailment, violently affected Caligula's mental state and he became irrational, with delusions of not only grandeur but divinity. His physical description in Suetonius hints at anomalies, depicting him as freakishly tall, spindly and pallid, with a sunken, glowering forehead, a hairy body and a balding head: 'He was by nature ugly, but he made himself even more so by practising gruesome faces in the mirror' (*Caligula* 50). Depictions of Caligula are sometimes said to 'reflect the madness within', but this is often prejudicial. His portraits show a young and handsome man, for obvious reasons: it would be suicidal for an artist to create an ugly official portrait for a notoriously volatile emperor.

In the wake of his illness, Caligula showed no respect for political, military, economic, religious or social practices. He was the antithesis of Augustus' school of leadership. He put Tiberius Gemellus and Macro to death without trial. He made his favourite horse consul. He claimed a very successful battle against the English Channel after firing artillery into the sea and sending his men to collect shells on the beach as the spoils of war (*Caligula* 46). Perhaps he just had an excellent sense of humour? His extravagance knew no bounds, and he introduced heavy taxation to help balance his personal expenditure.

In such an atmosphere, executions and displays of sheer blood lust were commonplace, and conspiracies and plots proliferated. Finally the inevitable happened: one of the plots succeeded. Caligula was assassinated by members of his imperial guard: the imperial guard giveth, the imperial guard taketh away. Caligula had been emperor for less than four years at the time of his death. He had four wives, three of them married during his imperial reign (the last, Caesonia, and their daughter Julia were murdered at the same time as the emperor himself), and, according to

Suetonius, he committed incest with each of his three sisters (*Caligula* 24). It was going to be fairly difficult for the notion of dynastic succession to 'bounce back' after this emperor.

CLAUDIUS (AD 41–54)

After their assassination of Caligula, members of the imperial guard, who were systematically sacking the palace, found his uncle Claudius cowering behind a curtain. Instead of killing him too, they pushed him into a litter and carried him off to their camp. There he was made an offer: to be the imperial guard's nominee for emperor. Obviously feeling that to be emperor was a fate not quite as bad as immediate death, Claudius cemented the deal by promising a special bonus in return for their support, thus creating a precedent which future aspirants would have to follow. In the absence of any other obvious candidates, the Senate confirmed the choice of the imperial guard.

Claudius was fifty years old, a scholar, being the author of historical works in both Latin and Greek (though none has survived) and the inventor of three new letters of the alphabet, which have come down to us in inscriptions. However, he had no experience of administration or government. Indeed, his unsuitability as a candidate may explain why, unlike so many other members of the imperial family, Claudius had not been murdered during or immediately after Caligula's reign.

In the accounts of ancient historians, Claudius comes across as a mishmash of conflicting characteristics: absent-minded, hesitant, muddled, determined, cruel (by proxy), intuitive, wise and dominated by his wife and his personal staff of freedmen. He was probably all of these. Suetonius' description is hardly flattering, saying he was handsome and dignified as long as he sat or laid down, but his legs shook when he walked, he laughed maniacally, stammered and sometimes foamed at the mouth when annoyed (*Claudius* 30–31). In portraits he tends to look a bit like Augustus' ugly cousin, with a large, wrinkled forehead, prominent ears and a large upper lip (Figure 3.5). If his choice of women was disastrous, there are countless instances of this particular failing on the part of prominent public figures. And he may, with sound reasoning, have preferred the advice of educated and trained executives from abroad to that of potentially suspect aristocratic senators, even if some of those executives did use their influence to their own financial advantage. His was a thoroughly sound if not glittering reign, which lasted almost fourteen years.

Claudius revived the office of censor, which had fallen into disuse, and took on the job himself, introducing into the Senate several chiefs from Gaul as new members. With the help of his personal staff, he reorganized and rationalized the financial affairs of the state and the empire, setting aside a separate fund for the emperor's private

FIGURE 3.5 Portrait of Claudius. Now in the National Archaeological Museum, Naples, this first-century AD head of Claudius sports the *corona civica* (civic crown of oak leaves), worn by both Augustus and many subsequent prominent figures, including Napoleon. While maintaining the short-cropped Augustan hair, Claudius' forehead is wider, his ears more prominent, his eyes closer together and his brow wrinkled. Photo © VRoma: Barbara McManus.

household expenses. He repaired roads, restored aqueducts (see Figure 7.9) and supervised the supply of grain (which was mostly imported from Africa and Egypt). Encouraging importers to build up stocks against the winter months and times of famine, Claudius offered to insure them against losses on the open sea, an unusual provision in ancient times. To make unloading easier and to relieve congestion on the Tiber, he carried out a scheme originally proposed by Julius Caesar – the construction of a new port at Ostia (see Map 1). Unfortunately, it was built to the north of the mouth of the Tiber, with a channel connecting the two, which meant that the prevailing current from the sea deposited in the harbour accumulations of silt brought down by the river (this problem was later resolved by the emperors Nero and Trajan).

Claudius' most far-reaching initiative was a successful full-scale invasion of Britain, after reconnaissance by the expedition's leader, Aulus Plautius. Britain, a potentially hostile and possibly united nation just beyond the boundary of the existing empire, presented a threat that could no longer be ignored by Rome. Claudius, for so long the butt of family jokes, wanted military glory, and here was a chance for him to get it. The force which sailed in AD 43 was a formidable one, even by Roman standards. Whether Plautius had instructions to call on Claudius if he got into difficulties or simply to invite him over to preside at the kill is not clear. He did get into difficulties, however. The only surviving account of the campaign is by Cassius Dio of Nicaea, governor of Africa and then Dalmatia, writing in Greek at the beginning of the third century AD:

> Shortly afterwards Togodumnus [son of the British king Cunobellinus (Cymbeline), who died between AD 40 and 43] was killed, but the Britons, far from giving up, were all the more united now in a determination to avenge his death. Plautius, unwilling to advance any farther, consolidated the territory he had gained and sent for Claudius . . . When he received the message, Claudius handed over the administration of affairs at home and abroad . . . and then himself took the field . . .
>
> Assuming command, he crossed the river, engaged the barbarians, who had rallied together at his approach, defeated them, and took Camelodunum [Colchester], Cunobellinus' capital. Then he put down many other tribes, defeating them or accepting their surrender, and was hailed *imperator* numerous times, which was against the rules, for no one could receive this honour more than once in the same campaign . . . He confiscated the tribes' weapons, which he handed over to Plautius with orders to subdue the rest. He then returned to Rome, sending news of his victory ahead with his sons-in-law, Magnus and Silanus. When the Senate heard about his achievement, it granted him the title of Britannicus and authorized him to celebrate a triumph.

(Roman History, 60.21)

Claudius was in Britain for just sixteen days. Plautius followed up the advantage gained, and was from AD 44 to 47 governor of this newest province of the Roman empire. When Caratacus (brother of Togodumnus) was finally captured and brought to Rome in chains, the emperor pardoned him and his family.

Claudius' victory in Britain gave him military clout as well as the agnomen 'Britannicus', which was reflected in monuments across the empire, from coins and the Arch of Claudius in Rome to a relief in the Sebasteion at Aphrodisias (Turkey), which depicts a triumphant Claudius standing over the defeated figure of Britannia gripping her hair. Despite his lack of charm or good looks, Claudius' political, military and economic projects set him out as the most successful heir of Augustus.

Claudius was married four times and, in spite of his physical disadvantages, he was more successful than any of his imperial predecessors in fathering progeny (if less lucky in love). At his succession, he was on his third wife, his distant cousin Valeria Messalina, who three weeks later presented him with a son (afterwards known as Britannicus, the title having been conferred on him by a grateful, or perhaps astonished, Senate at the same time as it awarded Claudius the same honour). Eventually Messalina was discovered too many times *in flagrante delicto* and in AD 48, at the age of twenty-four, she was duly disposed of by traditional Roman methods. Speculation was rife as to who would be the next imperial consort. It turned out to be Agrippina, Caligula's sister and Claudius' own niece. To marry her, Claudius had to have a law enacted permitting such unions. Agrippina already had a teenage son from a former marriage, later known as Nero. She persuaded Claudius to adopt him and to give him his own daughter Octavia in marriage. Then, according to Tacitus, she poisoned him. In death, as in life, Claudius was ridiculed by the aristocratic elite. The Stoic philosopher Lucius Annaeus Seneca (AD 4–65; see Chapter 8) composed a lampoon of the former emperor entitled the *Apocolocyntosis* ('Pumpkinification') *of Divine Claudius*. Whether Seneca himself would do a better job as ruler was about to be tested.

NERO (AD 54–68)

Nero was artistic, sporty, brutal, weak, sensual, erratic, extravagant, sadistic, bisexual – and latterly almost certainly deranged. He was sixteen when his mother secured for him the office of emperor by engineering his presentation to the troops as a candidate and by promising the imperial guard what was now the customary bonus. Shortly afterwards, the only other possible contender, Claudius' son Britannicus, was removed from the race, probably by poison.

During the early years of his reign, Nero was kept in hand by his tutor Seneca and Sextus Africanus Burrus, praetorian prefect, both of whom attempted to restrain the young ruler and control his mother Agrippina's attempts to exert influence. In AD 58, Nero took Poppaea, the wife of his partner in debauchery, Marcus Salvius Otho (whom he dispatched to be governor of Lusitania), as his mistress. Agrippina sided with Nero's wife, Octavia. Nero retaliated, according to Suetonius, with a grotesque and abortive series of attempts on his mother's life, including three by poison and one by engineering (the ceiling above her bed was rigged to collapse while she was asleep). Finally (and here the accounts of Suetonius and Tacitus agree), he had a collapsible boat constructed, which was designed to deposit Agrippina in the Bay of Naples. It did, but she swam ashore. In AD 59 Nero finally resorted to more conventional means: he sent a man round to his mother's house to club and stab her to death.

Nero celebrated by redoubling his bouts of excessive licentiousness and by creating two new festivals of chariot-racing, athletics and musical contests, which gave him further opportunities to demonstrate in public his talent for singing while accompanying himself on the lyre. No one was allowed to leave the auditorium while he was performing, for whatever reason. Suetonius writes of women giving birth during a Nero recital, and of men pretending to die and being carried out as if to burial. Burrus actually did die in AD 62 and soon after Seneca retired, leaving Nero subject to corrupt advisers who indulged his passions for sport, music and rowdy parties, during which he and his guests publicly performed sexual acts of unimaginable ingenuity. Having divorced Octavia in AD 62, he had her executed on a trumped-up charge of adultery, then married Poppaea, by now divorced and pregnant with his child. But then he killed her, too: Suetonius says he kicked her to death when she complained about his coming home late from the races. In AD 65 there was a conspiracy to assassinate him. When it was discovered, there was terrible retribution in which both Seneca and his nephew, the poet Lucan, died. There were no trials: anyone Nero suspected or disliked was sent a note ordering them to commit suicide. Gaius Petronius, a satyric novelist and former 'fashion guru', died in this manner in AD 66 (see Chapter 8), as did did countless senators, noblemen and generals.

In AD 64 fire had ravaged Rome for six days. According to Tacitus, who was nine years old at the time, of the fourteen districts of the city, 'four were undamaged, three were utterly destroyed, and in the other seven there remained only a few mangled and half-burned traces of houses' (*Annals* 15.40). This was the famous occasion when Nero was said to have 'fiddled while Rome burned'. Suetonius has him singing from a tower overlooking the conflagration. Cassius Dio records that he climbed the palace roof from which there was the best overall view of the fire and, assuming the garb of a lyre-player, sang 'The Capture of Troy' (*Roman History* 60.18). Tacitus has a similar story: 'At the very time that Rome burned, he mounted his private stage and, reflecting present disasters in ancient calamities, sang about the destruction of Troy,' but he is careful to qualify this as 'an unauthenticated report' (*Annals* 15.39).

Such reports, however, made people suspicious of the genuine relief measures that Nero initiated. His appropriation of a vast tract of land razed by the fire between the Palatine and Esquiline hills for his *Domus Aurea* ('Golden Palace') only added to suspicions of foul play. The vast luxury complex (with two different kinds of running water), set in rambling pleasure gardens designed for Nero's amusement, was blatantly built in the faces of the Roman people. It did not matter that he had residential areas in the city rebuilt at his own expense to a proper grid pattern with broad streets and open spaces.

Nero found scapegoats in the members of the latest religious sect, Christianity, whose adherents were rounded up and torn to death by dogs or crucified in public spectacles. The killings went on throughout the day and into the night, when more victims were burned to death to serve as street lighting, while Nero mingled with the crowds in his personal chariot.

He represented himself wearing the crown of the Sun god Sol. His coinage depicts him growing more corpulent (up to three chins) as time progresses, and his hair is represented in an increasingly elaborate 'Elvis' style in portraits and on coins. Suetonius (*Nero* 1) describes him as a dandy, 'pretty rather than handsome', with chicken legs, a pot belly, a dreadful acne and body odour, robed often in a dressing gown with a brightly coloured scarf and no shoes. Nero's sexual proclivities, his public performances, his proposed abolition of taxes and his excessive personal expenditure, as well as his willingness to be worshipped as a living god, set him out as the antithesis of Augustus in social, political, economic and religious matters.

In AD 68 one of the governors in Gaul, Gaius Julius Vindex, withdrew his oath of allegiance to the emperor and encouraged the governor of northern and eastern Spain, Servius Sulpicius Galba, a hardened veteran of seventy-one, to do the same. The revolutionary army was suppressed by legions who marched in from Germany, and Vindex committed suicide. Galba, however, informed the Senate that he was available to head a government and waited. The Senate, relieved that someone was prepared to take personal responsibility, not only declared Nero a public enemy but sentenced him to death by flogging. Nero thought of fleeing, dithered, then killed himself with the help of his secretary. Such was the end of the Julio-Claudian dynasty.

THE YEAR OF FOUR EMPERORS (SUMMER AD 68–WINTER AD 69)

The senators confirmed that Galba, the sole surviving descendant of an ancient patrician family and the former governor of Spain, was their choice to succeed Nero. However, though Nero died in the summer, Galba did not arrive in Rome until October. The tradition of appointing emperors outside of Rome had begun. Confident in the support of the Senate, he took the title Caesar but refused to pay the now-traditional bonus to the imperial guard. On 2 January AD 69 the troops in Lower and Upper Germany proclaimed Aulus Vitellius as their emperor. Meanwhile, Marcus Salvius Otho (former husband of Poppaea) returned to Rome from Luisitania and was disappointed at Galba's wholly unqualified choice of a successor and co-ruler: Marcus

Piso Licinianus. Otho reverted to the time-honoured tradition of bribing the imperial guard, persuading them to proclaim him emperor on 15 January. The troops then marched on the city and hacked Galba and Piso to death.

Otho immediately declared war on Vitellius and charged out to meet him in northern Italy, but he was outflanked and committed suicide in April. Vitellius, by far the most corpulent of Rome's emperors, arrived in the city in mid-July and instantly began celebrating with extravagant entertaining and gambling. He refused the title of Caesar but assumed the office of *pontifex maximus*, an interesting choice for a man who, 'while a sacrifice was in progress, thought nothing of snatching lumps of meat or cake off the altar, almost out of the sacred fire, and bolting them down' (Suetonius, *Vitellius* 13).

Meanwhile, in Judaea, the forces of the eastern Mediterranean had proclaimed yet another candidate – Vespasian – emperor on 1 July (before Vitellius had set foot in Rome). Otho's former supporters in the Danube had also offered support to Vespasian. The man who controlled Rome's bread basket (Egypt) bided his time while the Danube forces attacked the imperial army at Cremona in northern Italy and then marched on Rome. Vitellius was caught and tortured to death on 24 December, at which point Rome acclaimed her fourth emperor that year.

It is unclear who actually ran Rome from July to October AD 68, from April to July AD 69, and from December AD 69 to October AD 70, three periods when there was no emperor in the city. The events of these months illustrate a fundamental change in power structure of the Roman empire – from a Rome-based operation involving the Senate and the imperial guard to an empire-wide economic and military network of individuals who possessed the power to overturn the state. One can also see how, despite a century of imperial rule, Rome had not yet developed a clear process or definition of imperial powers. Both of these issues would be addressed by the new emperor Vespasian, who would prove to be one of Rome's best imperial figures.

VESPASIAN (AD 69–79) AND THE FLAVIAN DYNASTY

If a temporary return to a dynastic succession can be said to represent a constitutional change for the better, then sanity and internal peace were for a time restored with the appointment of Vespasian. He was almost sixty-one when he arrived back in Rome in October AD 70, but he was still fit and active, and he had two sons, Titus (aged twenty-nine) and Domitian (nineteen). Titus remained in Judaea to continue the campaign against the Jews, who had precipitated the First Jewish War in AD 66 by revolting against the consistent malpractices and insensitivity of the Roman administration. This he did with undoubted, if misguided, skill and panache, taking Jerusalem in September AD 70. On Titus' return to Rome in AD 71, Vespasian formally made him his associate in government, granting him the title of Caesar and appointing him commander of the imperial guard, a sound move given the role that body had played in altering the balance of power.

The triumph from the Judaean Wars brought vast wealth to the empire. The party lasted thirty days and included not only foreign booty but art plundered from Nero's private collection. What Nero had taken for himself, Vespasian now restored to the Roman people in the form of a Temple of Peace, in the Forum, which was quite possibly Rome's first combined mall and museum. Perhaps Rome's greatest public building, the Colosseum (Map 5, no. 9), was also built on the site of Nero's private gardens and dedicated from the booty of the Judaean Wars. Vespasian personally began the restoration of the city, collecting the first basket of rubble and carrying it on his shoulders (Suetonius, *Vespasian* 8). A man willing to get his hands dirty with manual labour could not have been more distinct from the pampered figure of Nero. These projects drew attention away from the excess and civil strife that followed Nero's reign by drawing a deliberate parallel between Vespasian and Augustus as restorers of Rome.

Vespasian was a man of equestrian birth: his father was a tax-collector, and his elder brother had served as consul *suffectus*. He was a professional soldier who had served with distinction as a legionary commander under Aulus Plautius in Britain. It was this that led to his own appointment as consul *suffectus* in AD 51 and later to his appointment as governor of Africa, before Nero sent him to Judaea. A practical army man, Vespasian had neither the time nor the inclination for an extravagant life, and he was a brilliant and tireless administrator. Under his rule a clear outline of imperial powers was created in the form of the *Lex Imperio Vespasiani*. The granting of these powers, by both the Senate and the people of Rome, also made it clear how legitimate power was conferred (despite the rather dodgy methods used to obtain it). The title 'Imperator' also clearly came to mean emperor as this time, even when it was taken by one who was not a blood heir of Augustus. In addition to legitimizing imperial rule, Vespasian restored 3000 bronze tablets containing the laws and decrees of the city; so, like Augustus, he could be seen as the restorer of law and order as well as public buildings. Also like Augustus, he refused a number of the titles that were awarded to him.

His prudence, though criticized by his contemporaries, was of great value. For instance, he imposed a tax on public urine bins, which were often used by urban tanners and launderers. When questioned by Titus on the 'dignity' of taxing piss, Vespasian famously replied, 'Money has no smell' (Suetonius, *Vespasian* 23). This comment is still remembered fondly by Italians, whose slang term for a public urinal is *Vespasiani*. Equally humble, if one is to go by portraiture, were Vespasian's looks (Figure 3.6): he is depicted bald, heavily wrinkled, with a prominent nose and a large forehead. Suetonius is unusually silent on the matter of his appearance, though he captures his wry sense of humour quite well.

FIGURE 3.6 A contemporary likeness of Vespasian. Even the loss of the nose cannot detract from the impression of a strong and tough but inherently kindly man, with laughter lines around his eyes. Photo © Ny Carlsberg Glyptotek, Copenhagen.

Vespasian displayed unusual insight and sense in other areas, too. Though the destruction of Jerusalem and the retaliation against the Jews were carried out with unnecessary severity, and restrictions were placed on certain practices, the Jews were excused Caesar-worship. And, in AD 71, Vespasian instituted the first salaried public professorship, appointing Quintilian (c. AD 40–c. AD 100) to a chair of literature and rhetoric. He also exempted doctors and teachers of grammar and rhetoric from paying taxes and from having troops billeted in their homes. Under Vespasian, a new class of professional civil servants was created, drawn largely from the business community. Military considerations largely dictated his extending the empire into northern England and Wales, and parts of southern Scotland, while advances were also made in Germany between the Rhine and the Danube. Moreover, he extended Latin rights to all native communities in Spain (which would produce two excellent emperors in the coming decades).

Vespasian died of natural causes, joking and with great dignity, according to Suetonius, in the family home in the Sabine mountains. On this occasion there were no doubts or worries about the succession. Lovingly mocked as a penny-pincher until the very end, Suetonius (*Vespasian* 19) records an actor at his funeral who, dressed in his funerary mask and miming his gestures, shouted, 'How much will this cost?' When he heard the price (100,000 sesterces), he replied, 'Here's a thousand, just pitch my body in the Tiber.'

TITUS (AD 79–81)

Despite a century of imperial dynastic rule, Titus had the distinction of being the first biological son to succeed his father as emperor. Thirty-nine years of age when he came to power, Titus had already enjoyed a spectacular military career, including a triumph after his capture of Jerusalem in 70 AD. He also had administrative experience as a prefect of the praetorian guard, imperial envoy to the Senate, and holder of seven consulships during Vespasian's reign. After the tumult that had preceded his father's accession, Titus' succession must have seemed like a cake walk, though some had reservations. As a young man, Titus had been dangerously like Nero in his charm, intellect, lavish ways and sexual appetite and proclivities. He was twice married and had a passionate affair with the Jewish princess Berenice (twelve years his senior), daughter of King Herod Agrippa, while he was in Judaea. He even brought her back to Rome. It is not clear how this news was received by her three husbands (one of whom was her uncle Herod, king of Chalcis). The pressure of public opinion in Rome, combined with anti-Semitism, eventually prevailed, and Titus sent her home.

Suetonius describes Titus as gifted, both physically and mentally, with a handsome face to boot, only slightly undermined by his diminutive height and 'small pot belly'. He lived long enough to demonstrate that he had some talent for government, but not long enough for any judgement to be made as to how effective a ruler he would have been. Yet, curiously, we have more tangible evidence from his reign of just over two years than from those of many emperors who ruled for much longer.

The Arch of Titus (Figure 3.7), celebrating his triumph over the Jews, still stands in Rome, across from the Colosseum (Map 5, no. 9), originally known as the Flavian Amphitheatre. Begun in AD 72 on the site of Nero's *Domus Aurea*, the building was finished in AD 80. Oval in shape, almost 200 metres long and over 150 metres wide, it housed an arena roughly 75 by 50 metres and could seat some 45,000 spectators. It was the first amphitheatre to be built entirely of stone, and its three tiers of arches, each of a different architectural order, surmounted by pilaster and a deep cornice, provided a model for Renaissance architects. Today tourists daydream and eat pizzas where, in the time of Titus and his successors, men and wild beasts were slaughtered

FIGURE 3.7 The arch of Titus, fifteen metres high and twelve metres wide, was, according to the inscription, erected by the Senate and the people of Rome (commonly abbreviated as SPQR: *Senatus populusque Romani*) to commemorate the deified Titus. It was not finished by Domitian, but probably completed by Trajan. Located at the eastern entrance to the Roman Forum on the triumphal route (*Via Triumphalis*) and adjacent to the Colosseum, the arch commemorated Titus' victory over Judaea, with interior reliefs depicting a triumphal procession of a chariot and the victorious soldiers carrying booty from the east, including a giant menorah from the great Temple of Jerusalem. Photo © Michael Wrench.

to please the Roman public. He also dedicated a large monumental bathing complex with libraries, shops, malls and a gym, supplied with water from the newly restored aqueducts (his works are recorded on the monumental gate at Porta Maggiore (Map 5, no. 8); see Figure 7.9).

While Titus' reign bore some of Rome's most spectacular monuments, it also saw incredible disasters: the eruption of Mount Vesuvius in August AD 79 and a fire in Rome the following year. We have an eyewitness account of the former by Pliny the Younger (*c.* 61–*c.* 112; see Chapter 8), who wrote to Tacitus:

To us at a distance, it was not clear which mountain was belching out the cloud, but it was later discovered to be Vesuvius. In form and shape the column of smoke was like a tremendous pine tree, for at the top of its great height it branched out into several skeins. I assume that a sudden burst of wind had carried it upwards and then dropped, leaving it motionless, and that its own weight then spread it outwards. It was sometimes white, sometimes heavy and mottled, as it would be if it had lifted up amounts of earth and ashes.

(Pliny the Younger, *Letters* 6.16)

Within an hour or so Pompeii and Herculaneum, among several other towns and villages in the area, were engulfed. Many of the survivors managed to escape with the help of the fleet stationed at Misenum, where Pliny was staying.

Although he had been emperor for only a few weeks, Titus immediately announced a state of emergency, set up a relief fund for the homeless (to which was diverted the property of any victims who died intestate), offered practical assistance in rehousing survivors, and appointed a team of commissioners to administer the disaster area. The red-hot ash and lava destroyed everything in its path, but when it cooled it preserved the final moments of its victims and their homes for modern generations of students and scholars.

Titus was just forty when he died suddenly. Some people suspected that it was the work of his younger brother, Domitian, who had made numerous attempts on his brother's life, all of which had been forgiven. Suetonius' account of Vespasian's passing, which was the subject of jokes (by others and himself), is an interesting foil for his record of the death of Titus, where he depicts a nation in mourning, with the senators who had criticized the emperor in life eulogizing him in death (Suetonius, *Titus* 2). Perhaps they knew what was coming.

DOMITIAN (AD 81–96)

By all accounts, Domitian was a thoroughly nasty person, but a reasonably effective ruler. First Vespasian then Titus had kept him from playing any part in the administration, perhaps to avoid any further suggestions of nepotism, or simply because they felt he did not have the necessary qualities. The public offices he did hold (including five terms as consul *suffectus*) were honorary, and this no doubt soured him. So when supreme power came his way, he accepted and gloried in it, arrogating the office of censor (to which he was elected for life in AD 85) and preferring to be known as 'our master, our god' (Suetonius, *Domitian* 13).

Under the Flavian emperors, the economy of the empire was rationalized to the extent that expenditure could be projected. Dependent kingdoms became provinces of the empire. Rome and her aristocracy took further strides towards cosmopolitanism. Domitian's contribution was to help these processes through efficient administration, combined with a refreshing pedantry – he insisted on spectators at public games dressing properly in togas – and a meanness that verged on the neurotic. He was particularly rigorous in exacting from the Jews the tax per head that was statutory throughout the empire. The historian Flavius Josephus (AD 37–c. 100), who was Jewish, suggests that it was imposed by Domitian in return for allowing them to practise their own faith. Many Christians were made to pay the tax too, on the grounds that they were Jews masquerading as something else. Suetonius records that Domitian was present in court when a ninety-year-old man was publicly examined to ascertain whether he was circumcised.

Domitian was often unsure when handling measures that required initiative. He attempted to resolve the problem of the Italian 'wine lake' by forbidding any new vines to be planted and ordering the destruction of vineyards on the other side of the Alps. Though he was popular with the army – he raised their pay, the first emperor to do so since Augustus – and had a successful campaign in Germany in AD 83, a few years later he led his troops into battle against a force of German tribes who were merely creating a diversion on the Danube and was heavily defeated.

Under Domitian, the number of executions rocketed. He used a vague charge of *maiestas* (treason) to justify all manner of persecutions and killings: 'A woman was tried and executed for undressing in front of a painting of Domitian' (Cassius Dio, *Roman History* 67.14.2). In the wholesale slaughter of AD 95, Manius Acilius Glabrio (consul in AD 91) and Flavius Clemens (consul that year with Domitian, husband of Domitian's great-niece, and father of two boys whom Domitian had adopted) both perished.

Conspiracies, real and imaginary, abounded, but Domitian's murder was not political. It was engineered by his wife, Domitia, whom he had exiled but with whom he had since reconciled. He was stabbed by a steward, ironically while reading the report of yet another fictitious plot. This marked the end of the Flavian dynasty. The Senate, no doubt relieved that none of its members was openly involved in the assassination, was at last in a position to make its own choice of ruler. A respected lawyer, Marcus Cocceius Nerva (AD 32–98), consul in AD 71 and 90, was nominated to take over the government. This would prove to be a decision of great significance.

The report of Domitian's death at the end of Suetonius' *Twelve Caesars* is a clear contrast to those of his predecessors: the Senate assailed him with insults and struck down his statues with glee; the people were apathetic; and his loyal army called for revenge (Suetonius, *Domitian* 23). Domitian was denied a state funeral, and his name was obliterated from all public records and monuments, a process known as *damnatio memoriae*. While erasure did physically remove a name (and it was carried out across the empire), that name was not necessarily forgotten (the titles that remained would have made identification easy). An ugly scar was left on the stone as a permanent reminder of a person's infamy (Figure 3.8). As it turns out, there is something worse than being forgotten: being remembered ignominiously for ever.

FIGURE 3.8 Image of *damnatio memoriae* on a base honouring the imperial cult temple of the Flavian family at Ephesus. Now at the museum in Selcuk, Turkey. Domitian's name (line 2) and his agnomen Germanicus (line 4) were erased, and the base was reinscribed to honour the Flavians (*Theoi Vespasiani*). Photo by author.

FURTHER READING

* indicates sourcebook

Alston, R., *Aspects of Roman History, AD 14–117*, Routledge, 1998.

Barrett, A.A., *Caligula: The Corruption of Power*, Routledge, 1993.

Boyle, A.J. and Dominik, W.J. (eds), *Flavian Rome: Culture, Image, Text*, Brill, 2003.

Eck, W., *The Age of Augustus*, Blackwell, 2000.

Gelzer, M., *Caesar: Politician and Statesman*, trans. Peter Needham, Harvard University Press, 2006 (new edition).

Griffin, M.T., *Nero: The End of a Dynasty*, Routledge, 1987.

Kamm, A., *Julius Caesar: A Life*, Routledge, 2006.

Koortbojian, M., *The Divinization of Caesar and Augustus*, Cambridge University Press, 2013.

Levick, B., *Claudius*, Routledge, 1993 (reissue).

Levick, B., *Tiberius the Politician*, Routledge, 1999.

Levick, B., *Vespasian*, Routledge, 2005 (new edition).

*Lewis, N. and Reinhold, M., *Roman Civilization: A Sourcebook*, vol. 1: *The Roman Republic and the Principate of Augustus*; vol. 2: *The Empire*, Columbia University Press, 1990 (3rd revised edition).

Millar, F., *Government, Society and Culture in the Roman Empire*, Chapel Hill, 2004.

Morgan, G., *69 AD: The Year of Four Emperors*, Oxford University Press, 2006.

Potter, D. (ed.), *A Companion to the Roman Empire*, Blackwell, 2006.

Sumi, G., *Ceremony and Power: Performing Politics in Rome between the Republic and Empire*, University of Michigan Press, 2005.

4 THE ROMAN EMPIRE: ZENITH AND DECLINE (AD 96–330)

Despite a number of disasters, particularly involving the succession of young and inexperienced rulers in the Julio-Claudian and Flavian dynasties, dynastic succession remained both an aspiration and a popular model for Roman emperors. The saving grace, however, was that able men from outside Rome were now able to make their way to the very top from modest beginnings, and, if allowed to reign without internal upheaval, could do so with as much insight and flair as any of the 'Twelve Caesars'. In some respects, the period known as the 'five good emperors' (AD 96–180) represented a return to the meritocracy of Cato's republic, with emperors promoted on the basis of experience and success, rather than birth. It was a time when Domitia Lucilla Minor, the daughter of a wealthy family of brickmakers (the Domiti), whose bricks have been found in some of Rome's greatest monuments (the Colosseum, the Pantheon and the markets of Trajan), could become the mother of the emperor Marcus Aurelius. Of Antoninus and Marcus Aurelius, who consecutively ruled the empire from AD 138 to 180, Edward Gibbon wrote: 'Their united reigns are possibly the only period in history in which the happiness of a great people was the sole object of government' (*The History of the Decline and Fall of the Roman Empire*, 1.3). By 'great people', Gibbon meant the Roman empire, and this was the period when the way was prepared for full rights for all Rome's citizens. Municipal governments were operating in the provinces, and where they proved effective and acted within the laws and customs of Rome, they were allowed to work without much hindrance. Over a third of the Senate itself came from the provinces, albeit chosen by the emperor, not the electorate.

MAKING THE EMPIRE WORK

To govern from the centre an empire of such geographical and cultural diversity, while also attending to threats from outside its boundaries, required tactical understanding and favourable circumstances. Becoming Roman did not mean trying to make everyone speak Latin and worship Roman gods; particularly in the Hellenized eastern half of the empire, Greek remained the spoken and written language (in addition to a number of others, such as Punic, Palmyrene and Aramaic). It was rather a fusion of central and local governments and of common cultural interests, where culture and religious practice travelled both east to west and west to east (see Chapter 5).

The procedure for establishing guidelines for the administration of a province probably changed little in principle from republican to imperial times. In the light of a report from a special commission, a law, usually bearing the name of the general who had brought about the establishment of the province, was enacted. This created administrative and judicial districts, defined and regulated the status and privileges of their inhabitants, established a tax system, laid down rules for the administration of justice, with due account being taken of existing facilities, and set out arrangements for the supervision, creation and amendment of local government by urban or rural authorities. None of this, however, could prevent, under the republican system, unsuitable governors being appointed and then acquitted of wrongdoing, or indeed blameless governors being prosecuted for political or personal reasons.

One significant change did occur, though: provincials now had more reason to trust their masters, and to benefit from this trust. One man was now at the top, with permanent responsibility for running the machinery of empire, and most of the governors were personally answerable to him. In cases of alleged maladministration, judgement was handed down by the emperor himself, by judges appointed by him, or by the Senate (which was under his supervision). Governors were also paid a fixed salary. An imperial civil service was established, mainly to administer the provinces. Communication was improved by road-building and the imperial postal system. Roman citizenship was becoming faster and easier for provincials to attain. Municipal institutions were founded in provincial towns, and special commissioners were appointed by the emperor to attend to the needs of impoverished or backward provinces. Provincial self-government was not on the agenda, however. The provincial council, representing all parts of a province, met once a year and had the right to deliberate on local affairs and make representations to the emperor or governor. The letters of Pliny the Younger, written during his time as governor of Bithynia and Pontus (north-western Turkey) to the emperor Trajan, record the intricacies of provincial administration and reveal the central role the emperor played in this system. The weakening of the role of emperor, which became an increasingly transient office in the third century, would affect not only the situation in Rome but the political, military and economic stability of the empire as a whole.

The principal functions of the provinces were to supply Rome with taxes and grain, the military with food and supplies, and the civil service and armies of the empire with cash. Beyond this, it was up to local initiatives how far the infusion of Roman culture and mores trickled down along with the benefits of education, status and wealth that accrued to some. The surviving remains of buildings in former provinces of the empire (such as the Pont du Gard and the theatre at Palmyra) testify to the prosperity that could be engendered by the 'Roman peace', even if many are of amphitheatres, living reminders of that unique but fatal Roman cultural contribution to mankind – the gladiatorial games. On those too far away from the centre of things, however, Rome made little impact.

SOURCES: CASSIUS DIO, AMMIANUS AND THE *HISTORIA AUGUSTA*

Despite the fact that two of Rome's most famous historians (Tacitus and Suetonius) lived during this period, neither chose to record the events of his own lifetime. However, Cassius Dio (AD 150–235), a Roman historian from Asia Minor, who was both a consul and a governor in Africa and Dalmatia, wrote a history of Rome (in Greek) from its foundation to AD 229. By sheer infelicity, only twenty-seven of the original eighty books (documenting the end of the republic and the years AD 217–220) survive, though he is quoted in a number of other sources. The Greek historian Appian (fl. AD 160) also wrote a history, surviving in only a few books covering the mid-republic. The remainder of our sources were written significantly later: Ammianus Marcellinus (c. AD 330–c. AD 395) wrote a continuation of the histories of Tacitus in thirty-one books, of which we have eighteen, covering the years AD 353–378. The only imperial biographies we have are in the *Historia Augusta*, often translated as 'Imperial Lives', from Hadrian (AD 117) to Numerianus (AD 284). This appears to be the work of several authors (or a forgery) and both its date and its veracity are considered dubious. However, this salacious account of Rome's later emperors – who levied taxes on male and female prostitutes to pay for the restoration of theatres and circuses (where the latter plied their trade) – does reflect the social, political and financial dissolution of the empire in the third century AD.

THE 'FIVE GOOD EMPERORS' (AD 96–180)

When, for the first time, the Senate made its own choice of emperor and appointed Nerva to succeed Domitian, its members ensured that equal perspicacity would attend the selection of his four successors. All four came from families which had long before settled out of Italy: those of Trajan, Hadrian and Marcus Aurelius in Spain, and that of Antoninus in Gaul. Nerva was sixty-five when he was pitchforked into supreme power, but, like a number of stop-gap rulers in more recent times, he performed wisely and courageously. He instituted alimentary schemes to help the urban poor, and made loans available to landowners, the interest on which went to support the children of needy families. He vowed publicly that he would never execute a member of the Senate, and stuck to his promise, even when the senator Calpurnius Crassus was found guilty of conspiracy against him. He not only assured himself of the support of the military by adopting as his son and joint ruler the distinguished commander in Upper Germany Marcus Ulpius Traianus (Trajan), but set an important precedent by nominating him as his successor.

Trajan, who was born in Italica, near Seville, in AD 52, became emperor in AD 98 and immediately proved he was a man of considerable discretion. He demonstrated this by establishing that the Senate would always be kept informed about what was going on, and that the sovereign right to rule was compatible with freedom for those who were ruled. That he was a brilliant general is clear from his military exploits, but he was also a good person to work for, as is evident in the correspondence between him and Pliny the Younger. Pliny frequently asks for advice on matters which are outside his immediate experience, notably his uncertainty about the status of Christians. During the second century AD Christians were persecuted for their beliefs, largely because these did not allow them to give the statutory reverence to the images of the gods and the emperor, and because their act of worship transgressed Trajan's edict forbidding meetings of secret societies. To the government, the Christians' behaviour was civil disobedience; to the Christians, Trajan's edict suppressed their freedom of worship. Pliny, as governor of Bithynia in AD 111, was so exercised by the anomalies on both sides that he wrote to Trajan to ask for guidance. Trajan replied:

> The actions you have taken, my dear Pliny, in investigating the cases of those brought before you as Christians, are correct. It is impossible to lay down a general rule which can apply to particular cases. Do not go looking for Christians. If they are brought before you and the charge is proven, they must be punished; with the proviso that if someone denies they are Christian and gives proof of it, by offering reverence to our gods, they shall be acquitted on the grounds of repentance even if they have previously incurred suspicion. Anonymous written accusations shall be disregarded as evidence. They set a bad example which is contrary to the spirit of our times.
>
> **(Pliny the Younger, _Letters_ 10.97)**

Trajan exercised less discretion in his choice of military campaigns, though they brought him considerable glory. After the triumphal procession with which he celebrated his final victory over the Dacians in AD 106, and the annexation of their territory, there were 123 days of public games, gladiatorial contests and a new scheme to provide food for poor Romans (see Chapter 6). His victories were monumentalized in large-scale projects that included public markets and Trajan's Forum (Map 5, no. 10), which also included law courts (like that of Augustus), war booty (like Vespasian's Temple of Peace), libraries and a monumental column (see Figures 9.1 and 9.2). He subdued the troublesome Parthians, who occupied the rugged desert south of the Caspian Sea, with notable victories between AD 114 and 116, conquering Mesopotamia and capturing both Babylon and Ctesiphon, capital of the Parthian empire. He fell ill on his way back to Rome in AD 117, having left his forty-one-year-old chief of staff, Publius Aelius Hadrianus (Hadrian), his ward since the age of ten, in charge. Later generations were so impressed by Trajan's achievements that in the late fourth century, when the empire had changed out of all recognition, new emperors were installed with the invocation, 'May he be luckier than Augustus and better than Trajan.'

Hadrian claimed that Trajan had adopted him on his deathbed: in any case he had already been acclaimed as emperor by the army in the east, and the Senate had little choice but to confirm him in the post or risk civil war. In the face of widespread revolts in the regions Trajan had conquered, Hadrian abandoned the recent acquisitions in the east and settled down to restore general order throughout the empire and consolidate the administration at home. Before he reached Rome in AD 118, four senior state officials, all Trajan's men, were executed with the acquiescence of the Senate, allegedly for plotting Hadrian's assassination. Hadrian disclaimed any responsibility for their deaths, but his relations with the Senate were permanently soured.

It may have been this uneasy situation at home which determined him to spend the years AD 121–125, 128–132 and 134–136 (half of his rule) tirelessly travelling around the vast confines of the empire, where he established boundary lines (see Chapter 8). The wall in Britain which bears his name, and of which portions still survive, is a monument to and a reminder of the role he assumed as ruler of an empire. His energy was inexhaustible, and he was always approachable.

Hadrian was a man of exceptional ability and wide learning. Enamoured of Greek culture, he adopted a fashionable beard and spent his life as a patron of the arts (especially architecture), literature (he was also a poet) and education. His artistic temperament, however, also included a jealous temper. According to Cassius Dio (69.3–6), Hadrian had Trajan's architect, Apollodorus of Damascus, murdered after he critiqued a number of the new emperor's plans. Apollodorus allegedly told him to go and 'draw pumpkins' (Hadrian, as is clear from the Pantheon (see Figure 7.5), loved a large dome) and noted that the statues for his temple to Roma and Amor (set back to back to reinforce the palindrome visually) would bump their heads on the domed ceiling if they stood to leave the building.

Hadrian's relationship with his wife Vibia Sabina, Trajan's great-niece, was also difficult: they had no children and she was said to have orchestrated a miscarriage rather than bear a monster like her husband. This acrimony may well have been prompted by Hadrian's open attachment to his beautiful Bithynian boy toy Antinous. While such behaviour was accepted in ancient Greek culture, it was regarded more sceptically in ancient Rome, especially when, upon Antinous' mysterious death in the Nile (probably by suicide) in AD 130, Hadrian displayed inconsolable grief. A new city of Antinopolis was founded beside the Nile, statues and obelisks were raised, and Antinous was declared a god. This deification, with its Graeco-Egyptian cult and festivals, while not unusual in the east, scandalized the Roman establishment. Hadrian also provoked the Jews into a renewed revolt by forbidding circumcision and proposing a shrine to Jupiter on the site of the ancient Jewish Temple in Jerusalem. The uprising, led by Simon Bar Kochba (d. AD 135) in AD 132, was surprisingly effective, and was put down only after Hadrian transferred Sextus Julius Severus, governor of Britain, to the Judaean front. If the account of Cassius Dio is accurate, in order to stop the threat of further war, the Roman army destroyed 50 Jewish fortresses and 985 villages, and killed 580,000 men. The remains of Jerusalem were ploughed into the ground, and a new city, Aelia Capitolina, was built on the site. Jews were forbidden to enter on pain of death. There was now an idol of Jupiter and a statue of Hadrian on horseback where the inner sanctuary of the Temple, the 'Holy of Holies', had been. The province of Judaea was renamed Syria Palaestina – or Palestine.

Just before he died in AD 138, Hadrian adopted the eminent senator Antoninus, then in his early fifties, and restricted the choice of Antoninus' successor to Lucius Verus (AD 130–169) or Antoninus' nephew Marcus Aurelius Antoninus (b. AD 121). The latter, an active devotee of Stoic philosophy (see Chapter 5), believed in the universal brotherhood and equality of man and insisted that equal imperial rights should be vested in his rival candidate, and these were duly (albeit largely nominally) exercised by Verus until his death in AD 169. On Hadrian's own death, the Senate, still harbouring resentment about the executions at the beginning of his reign, refused to ratify his deification. Antoninus, however, argued so persistently that the decision was overturned, and in recognition of his efforts he himself was awarded the surname 'Pius'.

It was perhaps because Hadrian left the administration in such good order that Antoninus' twenty-three-year reign was remarkable for its lack of incident. With the reports of Hadrian's globe-trotting missions available to him, he was able to spend most of his time at the centre of government in Rome. He did, however, make two adjustments to the empire's frontiers: the eastern boundary of Upper Germany was advanced and strengthened; and in Britain a fortified turf wall, thirty-seven miles long, was built right across the country from the river Clyde to the Forth, some way north of Hadrian's Wall. Though this Antonine Wall, built by the second, sixth and twentieth legions, appears to have been abandoned, and perhaps dismantled, in about AD 165, Hadrian's Wall stood firm until about AD 400, when the Romans withdrew from Britain. Coins minted in Antoninus' reign are the first to depict Britannia (Figure 4.1).

It appears Antoninus fully justified the honorific Pius, as he dedicated a temple to the divine Hadrian, Hadrian's Mausoleum (which survives as Castel St Angelo in Rome), as well as a temple to his wife Faustina, who was deified after her death. Unlike those of most other emperors, even Antoninus' death was calm and dignified. It is described in the *Historia Augusta*:

> Though he died in his seventy-fifth year, his loss was treated as though he were still a young man. His death was said to have happened like this: having eaten too much Alpine cheese at dinner, he was sick in the night and had a fever the next day. The morning after that, recognizing that he was getting worse, in the presence of the prefects he entrusted the state and responsibility for his daughter to Marcus [Aurelius], and gave instructions that the gold statue of Fortune which traditionally stood in the emperor's bedroom should be handed over to him. Then he gave the password of 'equanimity' to the officer of the watch, turned over as if going to sleep, and died . . . The Senate deified him; everyone vied with everyone else in singing his praises. All, however, were agreed on his dedication, humanity, intellect and goodness.
>
> **(*Historia Augusta*: Antoninus Pius, 12–13)**

FIGURE 4.1   Bronze sestertius from the reign of Antonius Pius, AD 141–143 (type RIC 742). The obverse depicts the bearded Antoninus Pius with a laureate head. On the reverse Britannia holds a military standard in her right hand and cradles a spear in her left arm while leaning on a round shield set on rock. The first image of Britannia to appear on a coin, it inspired a bronze farthing minted by Charles II in 1672, and it is now on the British fifty-pence piece. Photo © CNG Coins.

By contrast, the 'philosopher emperor' Marcus Aurelius spent a large portion of his rule in the field at the head of his armies, fighting two dangerous Germanic tribes, the Marcomanni and Quadi. The earlier part of his reign, from AD 161 to 166, was occupied with wars against the Parthians, successfully conducted by Verus with the help of his generals, but his army brought back from the east the most virulent plague (probably smallpox) of the Roman era, which spread throughout the empire. In AD 169 the Marcomanni and Quadi crossed the Danube, broke through the frontier defences, and penetrated into Italy as far as Aquileia, which they subjected to a frightening siege. The two emperors rushed north with an army into which slaves had been drafted, such were the ravages of the eastern campaign and the plague. Verus died. Marcus carried his body back to Rome, then set off to resume the northern war, which would preoccupy him for the rest of his rule.

In AD 175, Avidius Cassius, governor of Syria with additional responsibility for the entire eastern region, was proclaimed emperor on a false report of Marcus' death. He was, however, murdered by staff loyal to Marcus, who had set out to challenge him in person. The emperor returned home via Alexandria and Athens, where he endowed chairs of philosophy. Back in Rome, he celebrated a triumph and named his fifteen-year-old son Commodus joint ruler. There were further risings of the Marcomanni and other tribes in AD 178, so Marcus returned to the northern front, taking Commodus with him. Marcus died there on campaign at the age of fifty-nine, having impressed upon Commodus that he should continue the war, whose end seemed to be in sight. Instead, Commodus made a kind of peace of convenience, and returned to the comforts of Rome.

Marcus Aurelius left to posterity the triumphal column (Figure 4.2) in Rome which bears his name, records of his victories over the Marcomanni (an inferior version of that of Trajan), and, rather unusually, a book of meditations, written in Greek while he was mainly on campaign. These reflections of Stoic philosophy have influenced many writers and men of action, including Sir Thomas Browne, Matthew Arnold and Cecil Rhodes. At his death in AD 180, the empire was once again undergoing a period of general unease. As soon as one revolt was crushed or a barbarian invasion averted, another would break out, or threaten, in a different part of the empire.

THE SEVERANS: THE DISINTEGRATION OF DYNASTY (AD 180–234)

The previous eighty-four years had seen just five emperors; during the next hundred and four there would be no fewer than twenty-nine. The break in the powerful chain of command of the 'five good emperors' is often attributed to Marcus Aurelius, who was alone in nominating his son as his successor. Marcus himself was forty when he assumed the imperial purple gown of an office for which he had been groomed for

FIGURE 4.2 Battle scene from the Marcus Aurelius' column. This massive column, with thirty drums of carved Luna marble, records Marcus Aurelius' German and Sarmatian campaigns. This scene illustrates the miraculous 'divine intervention' of rain (in the form of an old, hairy rain god), which revives the Roman soldiers and destroys the hilly fortifications of the enemy, who end up in a pile of destruction. The Marcomanni soldiers, shown here and at the bottom of the relief above, are depicted with unruly beards and shallow eyes (sometimes shirtless); their bodies are often oddly contorted in death. This image is clearly juxtaposed with the Roman soliders, who have chest armour, helmets and meticulously cropped hair; they also appear spatially above the barbarians. At the side, women huddle with their children and watch the subsequent submission of the barbarians to the emperor. The heads of these figures are deliberately out of proportion, so that the viewer can see their facial expressions clearly. Photo © Barosaurus Lentus/Wikimedia Commons.

more than twenty years. Lucius Aurelius Commodus (AD 161–192) was only nineteen when he became emperor. Given the previous history of young successions (Caligula, twenty-four; and Nero, sixteen), this did not bode well. Like Nero, Commodus initially displayed some grasp of foreign and trade affairs; but then, like Nero, he fell into the hands of favourites and corruptible freedmen; like Nero, his private life was a disgrace and his public extravagances were prodigious; like Nero, he fancied himself in the arena; like Nero, some of his actions bordered on the deranged; and, like Nero, he died ignominiously – a professional athlete was suborned to strangle him in his bath.

Whatever the nature of the final conspiracy, it brought into office, at the behest of the Senate, a better man, Publius Helvius Pertinax, prefect of Rome and a former governor of Britain. But this proved only temporary as an ominous pattern of events unfolded, such as had followed the death of Nero. Pertinax, a disciplinarian, was murdered three months after becoming emperor by the imperial guard, who then offered the empire for sale to the highest bidder in terms of imperial handouts. The winner of this bizarre auction was Didius Salvius Julianus, an elderly senator, but there were three other serious contenders in the field, each an army commander with several legions behind him. Lucius Septimius Severus (AD 146–211), in Pannonia, was nearest to Rome, which he entered on 9 June AD 193, having already been recognized as emperor by the Senate. He promptly stripped Didius of office and sentenced him to death. Having disbanded the imperial guard and replaced it with three of his own legions, Severus embarked on an eastern campaign. In the course of this he killed another rival, Pescennius Niger, at Issus and won victories in Mesopotamia, in recognition of which he dubbed himself 'Parthicus Arabicus' and 'Parthicus Adiabenicus'. To legitimize his claim further, Severus proclaimed himself to be a son of Marcus Aurelius, and renamed his elder son Marcus Aurelius Antoninus (AD 188–217), later nicknamed 'Caracalla', after a Gallic greatcoat.

The third imperial contender, Clodius Albinus, governor of Britain, was put in an impossible position, as he was appointed Caesar, or deputy emperor, by Severus in AD 193 (probably to secure his cooperation). He crossed into Gaul with his army, which proclaimed him emperor, but in AD 197 he was defeated near Lyon by Severus, who purged the Senate and the provinces of Clodius' supporters before departing for a second Parthian war. At the end of the following year, Mesopotamia, annexed by Trajan, then abandoned by Hadrian, was once more a province of the empire. Severus now dubbed himself 'Parthicus Maximus' and promoted Caracalla to Augustus and his younger brother Geta (AD 189–212) to Caesar. He toured the east, including Egypt, with his family in AD 199–202, then set out for a triumphal tour of his native Africa.

Severus was born in Leptis Magna. A professional soldier, he favoured those with military experience when making civil appointments. He campaigned energetically to maintain the empire's frontiers in the east in the face of the marauding Parthians, and spent the last two and a half years of his life in Britain, personally leading a bid to bring Scotland into the empire. It was probably in his time that the prefect of Rome, whose function was primarily military, was invested with jurisdiction in matters of criminal law within 100 miles of the city, and the commander of the imperial guard, a military office, was given similar jurisdiction over the rest of Italy and the provinces. After the execution in AD 205 of Fulvius Plautianus, who had performed the latter duty with rather too much authority, Severus appointed in his place a legal expert, Aemilius Papinianus (d. AD 212), heralding a golden age of the interpretation of Roman law.

Severus was also responsible for a number of monumental restorations in the city of Rome in AD 203 after an earlier fire (including the Porticus Octavia, the Pantheon and the Temple of Divine Vespasian), all of which bear inscriptions with his name. While Cassius Dio (77.16.3) makes this sound as though Severus was rewriting history in his own name, the surviving inscriptions maintain all the original dedications, something which fits far better with his image (he is portrayed on coins as 'Resitutor Urbis'), and clearly set him in the tradition of Rome's greatest dynasties. He furthered dynastic parallels (Figure 4.3) by commemorating the saecular games (also held under Augustus, Claudius and Domitian) with the phrase 'What Happy Times' (perhaps laying on the message of peace and solidarity a bit thick). His relationship with the Senate, which never recovered from the purges of Clodius' supporters in AD 197, remained tense. His relationship with his wife Julia Domna, on the other hand, was remarkably strong, as were the public powers he afforded her (see Chapter 6).

Within the army, the top jobs went to those with the best qualifications, not necessarily those of the highest social rank. Severus improved the lot of the legionaries by increasing their basic rate of pay to match inflation (it had been static for a century), and by recognizing permanent liaisons as legal marriages. It was probably Severus, too, who improved the status of the ordinary soldier by extending the civil practice to allow veterans to style themselves *honestiores* as opposed to *humiliores* (see Chapter 6). Severus' philosophy of rule – which, according to Cassius

FIGURE 4.3 *Aureus* of Septimius Severus. Minted in Rome in AD 206, this small gold coin (7 grams) commemorated the *ludi saeculares* held by Septimius Severus – games which, like his military victories, served to connect Severus, who is labelled 'Pius Augustus', to the emperor Augustus. The reverse of the coin, which reads, 'What happy times!', depicts the lavish splendour of Severus' games, with a ship depicting the *spina* and ornaments of the Circus Maximus as well as four *quadrigae* and various animals, including an ostrich, lions and bison. Photo © Roma Numismatics Ltd. (www.Roma Numismatics.com).

Dio (76.15), he impressed upon his sons before his death in Britain AD 211 – was to pay the army well and to take no notice of anyone else. By 'anyone else' he meant, of course, the Senate. And so the devolution of imperial powers began with an increased dependence on military figures for the stability of the state.

Like Marcus Aurelius, Severus had nominated his sons to rule after him. The 'joint' rule between Caracalla and Geta, unsurprisingly, proved an issue, which Caracalla resolved by having Geta murdered in their mother's arms before instigating a wholesale slaughter of his sympathizers and innocent citizens as well as the *damnatio memoriae* of Geta from all public monuments (and in some cases coinage) (Figure 4.4). This *damnatio* was different to previous examples (see Figure 3.8) for two reasons. First, the young Geta, unlike his predecessors (Caligula, Nero and Domitian) had not had a chance to rule unsuccessfully or to generate unpopularity. Second, fratricide (save for the example of Romulus and Remus) was generally frowned upon, and Geta's close association with Caracalla in so many of Septimius Severus' dynastic monuments made the situation rather awkward. While the removal of a name was a way of condemning an individual, the nasty scar that remained often served to remind the audience – rather than make them forget – about the condemned individual. In the case of Geta, it sometimes seems that Caracalla would rather have forgotten the incident entirely: some inscriptions were reinscribed to remove the name of Geta (as well as the gash on the stone) and one text in Ephesus was entirely recarved to remove any trace of Geta's name.

> There are many who say that Caracalla, after having had his brother killed, ordered Papinianus to play down the crime in the Senate and in public. Papinianus replied that it was easier to commit fratricide than to make excuses for it.
>
> (***Historia Augusta*: Caracalla, 8**)

Unsurprisingly, Papinianus did not retain his post as commander of the imperial guard; he was replaced by Macrinus. However, Caracalla kept faith with his father's advice by increasing the pay of the army by 50 per cent and building a gargantuan public bath complex in Rome (see Figure 7.6), thus initiating a financial crisis. Some sources suggest that it was to solve this crisis (through taxes) that he initiated the final step in the process of universal enfranchisement: granting full citizenship to all free men in the Roman empire in AD 212. A band of discontented officers murdered Caracalla in Mesopotamia in AD 217, while he was attempting to extend the eastern front. The officers wanted Macrinus to take over as emperor, and the Senate agreed, but he never reached Rome: he continued fighting in the east and was killed by Syrian troops who supported the claim of a fourteen-year-old cousin of Caracalla – Elagabalus (AD 203–222). Known for his raucous parties, which made full use of the precursor to the whoopie cushion, this teenager was perhaps exceptionally depraved:

FIGURE 4.4 *Damnatio memoriae* of Geta by Caracalla. This wooden tondo from Egypt (*c.* AD 200), now in the Antikensammlung, Staatliche Museen zu Berlin, is the only surviving painted portrait of an imperial family (though these were quite common in antiquity). It depicts the Severan dynasty: Septimius Severus, wearing a crown; his wife Julia Domna, bedecked with pearls; and their children Caracalla (in the front, below his father, with a smaller gold crown) and Geta (whose head has been erased). This act of *damnatio memoriae* is a clear reminder of the fratricide of which Caracalla was accused. Photo © bpk/Antikensammlung, SMB/Johannes Laurentius.

> The emperor Elagabalus rounded up into a public hall all the prostitutes from the Circus, the Theatre, the Stadium, the baths and everywhere else they frequented. Addressing them like a general would his troops, he called them his fellow soldiers and reviewed with them the various positions and techniques of their profession.
>
> **(*Historia Augusta*: Elagabalus, 26.3)**

Elagabalus lasted less than four years before being lynched by his own guards, having adopted as his successor his first cousin, Alexander Severus (AD 205–235). The latter, far more sensible teenager (he was sixteen when he became emperor) ruled for thirteen years with moderate success, partly because he was a likeable lad who knew his limitations and partly because his mother, Julia Mammaea, gave him plenty of sound advice. His rule thus qualifies as the only imperial matriarchy in the history of the Roman empire. Indeed, having successfully restored order in the east, where the Sasanid dynasty, successors to the Parthians, had threatened to overrun all former Persian territories, Alexander took his mother with him on a campaign against the Alamanni in AD 234. The following year they were both set upon and murdered by mutinous soldiers at the fortress town of Mainz.

This was certainly the work of Maximinus (AD 173–238), a giant Thracian peasant who had risen through the ranks to become commander of the imperial guard. He nominated himself as emperor and promptly doubled the pay of the army. The Senate's choice, Gordian, the eighty-year-old governor of Africa, and his son, Gordian II, had hardly packed their bags for Rome before a supporter of Maximinus attacked and defeated them. Soon afterwards, Maximinus invaded Italy, but he was soon murdered by some of his own troops. The Senate had, in the meantime, deified the Gordians and replaced them with two more candidates. These were then killed by the imperial guard in favour of Gordian III (nephew of Gordian II).

THE THIRD-CENTURY CRISIS? DEVALUATION AND DISORDER (AD 235–284)

The following period is sometimes referred to as 'the third-century crisis' because this was when the Roman empire began to dissolve socially, politically and economically. The captaincy of the imperial guard had become a waypoint on the path to becoming emperor, while the approval of the Senate, which had heralded the era of the 'five good emperors', was no longer a primary concern. In AD 238 no fewer than five emperors died by various means and hands, and while the year of four emperors (AD 69) had ended with a clear successor and the founding of a dynasty, the year of six emperors had no such neat resolution.

Gordian III was only thirteen when he came to power, and though he enjoyed civil and military success for about five years, upon the death of his adviser Furius Timesitheus he was murdered in Mesopotamia in AD 244 while collecting wild animals for his triumphal procession in Rome to celebrate the victories in Persia.

During the ensuing twenty-six years, a total of thirty-four emperors, pretenders and usurpers came and went (usually violently) while the hostile peoples outside the frontiers gathered themselves for the kill. In Germany, the Goths, Franks and Alamanni established the permanent threat to the Roman empire which ultimately led to its annihilation. In AD 259 the Persians even managed to capture the emperor himself, Valerian, who spent the rest of his life very uncomfortably in their hands. He was used as a human mounting-block to assist the Persian king on to his horse; and when he died his skin was stripped off to serve as a permanent symbol of Roman submission. His son Gallienus, who had been joint ruler, carried on alone until he fell in AD 268 – albeit in a more usual way, murdered by his own staff. Some Christian writers suggested that Valerian's fate was punishment for his edicts against Christianity; certainly these were reversed by Gallienus, who appears to have reached an accommodation with the Christians which lasted some years.

The threat of the empire being overrun (from several directions) was temporarily averted by Aurelian (AD 214–275), commander-in-chief of the Roman cavalry, who was proclaimed emperor by his troops while campaigning against the Goths in AD 270. In addition to evacuating the Roman garrisons and abandoning the province of Dacia north of the Danube, he defeated the Alamanni, who had got as far as Ariminium (modern Rimini, on the east coast of Italy). He also dealt with two dangerous outbreaks of separatism.

Numerous petty emperors had surfaced in various parts of the empire. Some were readily disposed of; others were simply murdered by their own troops. In Gaul, however, Gaius Latinius Postumus had established an independent state, with its own senate. In AD 268 the local soldiery murdered him, and then his three successors. The senate of Gaul now appointed Gaius Pius Tetricus as ruler, in which capacity he remained for three years until he surrendered to Aurelian's army. In the meantime, the influential city of Palmyra, under its formidable regent Zenobia, was threatening Roman rule throughout the east. Attacks into Egypt and Asia Minor as far as the Bosporus were repelled, and Aurelian destroyed Palmyra. Zenobia was taken to Rome to walk, with Tetricus, in Aurelian's triumph. Both were allowed to live: Zenobia with a generous pension; and Tetricus with a responsible job in local government in Italy. It was also Aurelian who built the great defensive wall around Rome itself (Map 5, no. 13). Murdered by his own staff, he earned the epitaph 'He was loved by the people of Rome, and feared by the Senate' (*Historia Augusta:* Aurelian, 50). The dreadful game of thrones continued after him, until AD 284, when yet another commander of the imperial guard, Diocles (AD 245–313), a Dalmatian of obscure and humble origin, emerged from the crush of contenders to be proclaimed emperor by the troops.

The role of emperor as a leader in civic, economic and administrative roles was significantly undermined by these constant shifts in power. By the time a coin, a statue or an economic policy was set out in the empire, the man whom it represented was already passé. The image of the emperor as a recognizable figure with singular policies across a vast empire was quickly deteriorating, along with the sense of civic and economic stability and solidarity. Extending universal citizenship had not resulted in a unified empire. Constant campaigns on the borders cost money (especially when every new emperor raised the army's pay) and the devaluation of coinage under Severus (and continued by his successors) resulted in massive inflation, making travel and commerce on the empire's roads (which were increasingly dangerous) ever more risky. Plague struck a number of large cities (including Rome itself) and the formerly open cities of the empire became more insular, erecting walls and fortifications.

RECOVERY: DIOCLETIAN, CONSTANTINE AND CHRISTIAN ROME (AD 284–337)

One aspect of the problem was not so much that the empire was falling apart, but that it had always consisted of two parts. Much of the region which comprised Macedonia and Cyrenaica and the lands to the east was Greek, or had been Hellenized before being occupied by Rome. The western part of the empire had received from Rome its first taste of a common culture and language overlaid on a society that was predominantly Celtic in origin. Diocles, who now called himself Gaius Aurelius Valerius Diocletianus (Diocletian), was an organizer. In AD 286 he split the empire into east and west, and appointed a Dalmatian colleague, Maximian (d. AD 310), to rule the west and Africa. A further division of responsibilities followed in AD 293. Diocletian and Maximian remained senior emperors, with the title Augustus, but Galerius, Diocletian's son-in-law, and Constantius (surnamed Chlorus, the 'Pale') were made deputy emperors with the title Caesar (Figure 4.5). Galerius was given authority over the Danube provinces and Dalmatia, while Constantius took over Britain, Gaul and Spain. Diocletian retained all his eastern provinces and set up his regional headquarters at Nicomedia in Bithynia, where he held court with all the outward show of an eastern potentate, complete with regal trappings and elaborate ceremonial. The establishment of an imperial executive team had less to do with delegation than with the need to exercise closer supervision over all parts of the empire, and thus to lessen the chances of rebellion. There had already been trouble in the north, where in AD 286 the commander of the combined naval and military forces at Boulogne, Aurelius Carausius, to avoid execution for embezzling stolen property, had proclaimed himself emperor, set himself up as ruler of Britain, and issued his own coins. This outbreak of lese-majesty was not quelled until AD 296.

Diocletian ruled for twenty-one years, during which he visited Rome only once, in AD 303, the year of his formal edict against Christianity. On 1 May AD 305, after a health failure, he took the unprecedented step of announcing (from Nicomedia) that he had abdicated, and offered Maximian no choice but to do the same. While his reign had been outwardly peaceful, the years of turmoil had left their mark on the administration of the empire and on its financial situation. Diocletian reorganized the provinces and Italy into 116 smaller units, each governed by a rector or *praeses*, which

FIGURE 4.5 Porphyry sculpture of the tetrarchs, AD 305: (left) Diocletian and Maximian; (behind) Constantius and Galerius (the bearded figure in each pair is older than his clean-shaven counterpart). This depiction of the tetrarchs illustrates the changing attitude towards the empire and imperial rulers. These men are not presented as distinct individuals but as parts of a 'unified' whole – a fitting analogy for Rome's empire. Piazza san Marco, Venice. Photo © Allan T. Kohl/Art Images for College Teaching.

were then grouped into twelve dioceses under a *vicarius* responsible to the appropriate emperor. He strengthened the army (while at the same time purging it of Christians), and introduced new policies for the supply of arms and provisions.

Diocletian's monetary reforms were equally wide-ranging, but though the new tax system he introduced was workable, if not always equitable, his price edict of AD 301 to curb inflation by establishing maximum prices, wages and freight charges fell into disuse, its effect having been that goods simply disappeared from the market. The values of commodity goods and occupational status often bear striking similarities to their modern counterparts (Figure 4.6). Ordinary wine was twice the price of beer, while named vintages were almost four times as much as *vin ordinaire*. Pork mince cost half as much again as beef mince, and about the same as prime sea fish (river fish were cheaper). A pint of fresh, good-quality olive oil was more expensive than the same amount of vintage wine, but there was a cheaper oil as well. A carpenter could expect twice the wages of a farm labourer or a sewer cleaner, with all

FIGURE 4.6 Diocletian's price edict. Issued in AD 301, possibly in Alexandria, it survives in numerous copies (all fragmentary) in Latin and Greek throughout the eastern empire. This one is from Aizanoi, Phrygia (Turkey) and is now housed in the Münzkabinett, Staatliche Museen zu Berlin. Recorded in the text are the prices of men, boys and horses, mules and camels (of different origins and occupations: the best Bactrian camel is worth considerably more than lesser beasts of burden). Like so many laws, despite its ubiquity, it does not appear to have been applied well in practice. It also does not seem to have solved the economic crisis, and may well have resulted in more black-market trading. Photo © bpk / Münzkabinett, SMB.

meals included. A teacher of shorthand or arithmetic might earn half as much again per pupil as a primary-school teacher; grammar-school teachers earned four times as much as primary-school teachers; and teachers of rhetoric five times as much. Costs of education, like the cost of various foodstuffs, reveal a clear hierarchy in social values and commodities that is not, in all respects, vastly different from their modern equivalents.

Confident of his safety, Diocletian had built a retirement palace near Salona, on the coast of his native Dalmatia (the modern town of Split stands around its ruins). Here he lived on until his death in AD 313, gardening and studying philosophy, and refusing to take sides when the system of government he had devised almost immediately foundered. When he retired, Diocletian had promoted Galerius and Constantius to the posts of Augustus and appointed two new Caesars. Trouble broke out when Constantius, while campaigning against the Picts, died at York in AD 306, and his troops proclaimed his son Constantine as their leader. Encouraged by this development, Maxentius, son of Maximian, had himself set up as emperor and took control of Italy and Africa, whereupon his father came out of involuntary retirement and insisted on taking back his imperial command. The situation soon degenerated into chaos. At one point in AD 308 six men were styling themselves Augustus, whereas Diocletian's system allowed for only two. Galerius died in AD 311, having on his deathbed revoked Diocletian's anti-Christian edicts. Matters were not fully resolved until AD 324, when Constantine defeated and executed his last surviving rival. The empire once again had a single ruler, and against all the odds he would continue to rule for some years yet.

Constantine was born in Naissus in Upper Moesia in about AD 272. His father was subsequently forced to divorce his mother (a former barmaid) and marry Maximian's daughter instead. His appellation – the 'Great' – is justified principally because of what he did for the empire's Christians. Under Diocletian especially, Christians had had a terrible time. In AD 313, when the struggle for imperial power was at its height, Constantine initiated the Edict of Milan – this city, not Rome, was now the administrative centre of the government of Italy – which gave Christians (and others) freedom of worship and exemption from any religious ceremonial. It is said that before the Battle of the Milvian Bridge in AD 312, at which he enticed Maxentius to abandon his safe position behind the Aurelian Wall and then drove most of the latter's army into the Tiber, Constantine had dreamed of the sign of Christ. Thereafter, though he was not actually baptized until just before his death in AD 337, he regarded himself as a man of the god of the Christians, and could therefore claim to be the first Christian emperor. Christian influence is often ascribed to the dedication of Constantine's arch in Rome (Map 5, no. 14), where his victory is attributed to '*instinctu divinitatis*'. However, as we have seen throughout Rome's history, citing divine inspiration for victory was a fairly common Roman practice.

In AD 325 he assembled at Nicaea in Bithynia 318 bishops, each elected by his community, to debate and affirm some principles of their faith. The outcome of their deliberations, known as the Nicene Creed, is now part of the Roman Catholic mass and the Anglican service of communion, and is commonly used by many Protestant denominations.

Then, in AD 330, he established the seat of government of the Roman empire at Byzantium (which he renamed Constantinople, 'City of Constantine'), thus ensuring that a Roman (but Hellenized and predominantly Christian) empire would survive the inevitable loss of its western part. Its capital stood, until the middle of the fifteenth century, as a barrier between the forces of the east and the as yet ill-organized tribes and peoples of Europe, while each struggled to find a permanent identity and culture.

Although the Edict of Milan meant the empire now officially 'tolerated' Christians, Christianity – a faith, like Judaism, that excluded worship of any other gods – was not universally accepted. This was especially true in Rome itself, where pagans and paganism (as well as the use of the catacombs for clandestine Christian burials) would continue throughout the fourth and fifth centuries. While some estimates suggest that a third of the population in Rome was Christian at the time of Constantine, these people were generally not from the wealthy classes, nor were they necessarily literate (the spelling on their funerary monuments is often poor). However, the fervour and faith of these individuals are attested through the inscriptions on their monuments. Often carved on reused marble (sometimes clearly taken from the previous owner of a sarcophagus), Christian inscriptions reveal high mortality rates, especially for children and women, as well as the prevalence of strangely humble names, such as 'Liar' (Calumniosus) and 'Filth/Dung' (Stercus).

While many early Christian funerary monuments include elements that are found on pagan monuments, such as terms like *bene merenti* ('well deserving'; in the dative case) and an indication of the person's age, there are also distinctions: if a person had converted, their life as a Christian might be recorded separately; and images, especially fish (the Greek word *ICHTHYS* was used as an acronym for 'Jesus Christ Son of God our Saviour'), are often key features. The stele of Licina Amias (Figure 4.7) is an excellent example of the combination of pagan and Christian styles: the stone begins with the pagan D. M. (the Roman formula for a monument 'to the gods of the departed') but goes on to depict the Christian symbols of the fish and the anchor (often associated with hope). The Greek text reads, 'the living fish' while the Latin below follows the common pagan epithet *benemerenti* and presumably ended with the deceased's lifespan (*vixit* . . . – 'she lived'). Many of the images that define Christianity today – the ship, the good shepherd, 'Mary Orans' (a woman with a covered head, praying) – have their origins in these humble early Christian monuments.

Constantine was ambivalent about the Jews: while the Edict of Milan is also known as the Edict of Toleration, Judaism was seen as a rival to Christianity, and among other measures he forbade the conversion of pagans to its practices. In time he became even more uncompromising towards the pagans themselves, enacting a law against divination. He also destroyed temples and confiscated temple lands and treasures, which gave him much-needed funds for his personal extravagances. His reign comprised a series of field days for architects, whom he encouraged to celebrate the religious revolution by reinventing the basilica as a dramatic ecclesiastical edifice. The head, arm and a foot of his colossal statue, found in the Basilica Nova (a large basilica off the Forum Romanum), are now displayed in the Capitoline museum (Figure 4.8).

Constantine was also a dynamic military commander. He had a great victory in AD 332 over the Goths, 40,000 of whom subsequently enlisted in the Roman army as

FIGURE 4.7 Christian stele to Licina Amias from the third century AD, found in a necropolis near the Vatican (now housed in the Museo Epigrafico, Rome). Considered by some to be one of earliest Christian tombstones in Rome, the text reveals the hidden language of early Christianity as well as the need to consider both Christian and pagan audiences. Indeed, the crown between the 'D' and the 'M' (which was fairly unusual in pagan epitaphs) could give the abbreviation 'DOM', which would become the abbreviation for *dominus* ('lord') in later Christian monuments. Photo by author.

FIGURE 4.8 Head from a colossal statue of Constantine, *c.* AD 313–315, on display in the courtyard of the Capitoline Museum, Rome (inv. MC 757/S). This portrait, which was originally labelled not as Constantine but as part of a colossal statue from Greece, survived for years as part of the Capitoline collection before it was correctly identified as the head of the first Christian emperor (based on the image itself and its context in the Basilica Nova – a complex Constantine renovated after defeating Maxentius). A contrasting misattribution occurred in the case of the Vatican's famous bronze equestrian statue of Marcus Aurelius, which survived the Renaissance only because it was believed to be a statue of Constantine. The object on the plinth just below the head is an iPhone, to give a sense of scale. Photo by author. Courtesy of Roma, Musei Capitolini.

allies. Two years later he defeated the Sarmatians, 300,000 of whom then settled within the empire. He also developed Diocletian's reforms, and completed the division of the military into two arms: frontier forces; and permanent reserves, who could be sent anywhere at short notice. He changed the system of command so that normally the posts of civil governor and military commander were separate. He disbanded the imperial guard and established a chief of staff to control all military operations and army discipline. The praetorian prefects (commanders of the imperial guard), who had hitherto held military ranks while also being involved in civil affairs, became supreme appeal judges and chief ministers of finance.

While Constantine's reign marks the beginning of Christian Rome, it was also the end of an era, particularly in terms of the city of Rome and its centrality. After Diocletian's transfer of the imperial seat to Milan (AD 284), Rome was no longer the administrative centre of the empire: the Senate remained but it had little authority or influence. Constantine then went much further and moved the capital of the empire to Constantinople. He returned to Rome only briefly, in AD 312–313, 315 and 326. The empire had been a divided for some time but the imperial departure from Rome, like the large fortifications that arose around the city, monumentalized a fundamental change in the city's role – from the beating heart of an inviolate empire to an increasingly tacit mausoleum of history. While we continue to describe the citizens of the empire as 'Romans', from this point onwards their links to Rome itself – in terms of their powers, policies and identities – grew ever more tenuous.

FURTHER READING

Bennett, J., *Trajan: Optimus Princeps*, Routledge, 1997.

Birley, A.R., *Septimius Severus: The African Emperor*, Routledge, 1999.

Birley, A.R., *Hadrian: The Restless Emperor*, Routledge, 2000 (new edition).

Birley, A.R., *Marcus Aurelius: A Biography*, Routledge, 2000 (new edition).

Bjorn, C. and Norena, C., *The Emperor and Rome*, Yale Classical Studies, 2010.

Elsner, J., *Imperial Rome and Christian Triumph: The Art of the Roman Empire AD 100–450*, Oxford University Press, 1998.

Gibbon, E., *The History of the Decline and Fall of the Roman Empire*, ed. J.B. Bury, Methuen, 1909 (2nd edition).

Heckster, O., *Rome and Its Empire: AD 193–284*, Edinburgh University Press, 2008.

Ick, M., *The Crimes of Elagabalus: The Life and Legacy of a Decadent Boy Emperor*, I.B. Tauris, 2013.

Jenkyns, R. (ed.), *The Legacy of Rome: A New Appraisal*, Oxford University Press, 1992.

Meijer, F., *Emperors Don't Die in Bed*, Routledge, 2004.

Pohlsander, H.A., *Emperor Constantine*, Routledge, 2004.

Potter, D.S., *Constantine the Emperor*, Oxford, 2013.

Southern, P., *The Roman Empire from Severus to Constantine*, Routledge, 2001 (2nd edition).

5   ROMAN RELIGIONS AND MYTHOLOGY

The Romans had a pragmatic attitude to religion, as to most things. Insofar as they had a religion of their own, or an indigenous mythology, it was not based on any central belief, but on a mixture of fragmented rituals, taboos, superstitions and traditions which they had collected over the years from a number of sources, including their own Indo-European roots. To the Romans, religious faith was effectively a contractual relationship between mankind and the forces that they believed controlled people's existence and wellbeing. The result was essentially twofold: a state cult whose significant influence on political and military events outlasted the republic; and a private concern, in which the head of the family supervised the domestic rituals and prayers in the same way as the elected representatives of the people performed the public ceremonials. As circumstances and people's view of the world changed, individuals whose personal religious needs remained unsatisfied turned increasingly to the cults of the east – to Christianity and to the tenets of the Greek philosophers.

ROMAN DIVINITIES

Many of the gods and goddesses worshipped by the Romans had their equivalents in Greek mythology. Some came by way of the Etruscans or the tribes of Latium. The Diana to whom Servius Tullius built a temple on the Aventine hill was identified with the Greek Artemis (Figure 5.1): she is depicted as a virgin huntress with hunting dogs. But some of the rites attached to her at Aricia, the centre from which he transferred her worship, went back to an even mistier past. The priest of Diana at Aricia, who was always a runaway slave, held the title of king. He took office by killing his predecessor, and held it for as long as he was able to defeat other runaway slaves in

FIGURE 5.1 Statue of Diana. This statue, now in the Louvre, is thought to be a Roman first–second-century AD copy of a bronze Greek original (c. 325 BC). Found in Italy, Pope Paul IV gave it to King Henry II in the sixteenth century allegedly because it reminded the king of his mistress (also named Diana). Scholars have speculated that it was originally from either Nemi, the site of a famous shrine to Diana, or Hadrian's villa at Tivoli (from where Cardinal Ippolito D'Este collected a number of Roman copies of Greek statues in the sixteenth century). Photo © Musée du Louvre, Dist. RMN-Grand Palais / Thierry Ollivier.

single combat. Any fugitive slave could challenge him by breaking off a branch from a particular tree in the sacred grove; so, naturally, the resident priest kept a close watch. Aricia is modern Ariccia, near Lake Nemi, the ancient lake into which a stream flowed from a sacred grotto beside the temple. The lake was known as 'Diana's Mirror' because at one time the reflection of the moon upon it could be seen clearly from the temple. Nemus means 'grove', and the priest of Diana had the title Rex Nemorensis. Some vestiges of earlier magic accompanied Diana to her new site in Rome:

> In the country of the Sabines there was bred on the property of a certain head of family a heifer of astonishing size and perfection of form; to which its horns testified, for they hung in the entrance court of the temple of Diana for many years. The beast was held to be the subject of an omen: seers prophesied that the state whose citizens sacrificed it to Diana should be the leading power in the land. This prediction came to the notice of the priest of the temple in Rome. On the first day which seemed appropriate for the sacrifice, the Sabine brought the heifer to Rome, drove it to the temple of Diana, and stood with it before the altar. The Roman priest, much impressed by the size of the victim, which was famous, and knowing the prophecy, said to the Sabine: 'What are you doing, stranger? Would you sacrifice to Diana in a state of uncleanliness? You must purify yourself in running water. The Tiber is at the bottom of the valley.' The Sabine, conscious of correct procedure and wanting to do everything by the book so that the prophecy might be fulfilled, immediately went down to the river. While he was away the priest sacrificed the heifer to Diana, for which the king and his subjects were exceptionally grateful.
>
> **(Livy, 1.45)**

Many goddesses (and their cult statues) were cordially invited to Rome. Livy records the ritual of *evocatio* (literally a 'calling out') after the famous Roman general Camillus captured Veii in 396 BC. The statue of Veian Juno was asked (either in jest or earnest entreaty), 'Juno, would you like to come to Rome?' and she consented (some said by a nod of her head, others by speaking) (Livy, 5.23). Occasionally tradition threw up a deity whose antecedents had been forgotten. The festival of the goddess Furrina, who gave her name to the grove in which Gaius Gracchus met his death, was regularly observed on 25 July; but by the middle of the first century BC no one could remember who she was or why she was being celebrated.

The Romans inherited their preoccupation with examining every natural phenomenon for what it might foretell from the Etruscans, who had developed the practice if not into a science then at least into an art. The Etruscans employed three main kinds of divination, which were said to have been communicated to them by a mysterious lad called Tages, who appeared to them after literally being ploughed up from the earth while it was being tilled:

1   Divining the future from examining the entrails of victims sacrificed at the altar – the liver was of particular significance (Figure 5.2).
2   Observing and explaining the meaning of lightning and advising on how sinister predictions might be averted.
3   Interpreting any unusual phenomena and taking necessary action.

Many early societies practised animism – the belief that natural and physical objects are endowed with mystical properties. Alongside an appreciation of the divinity that resided in gods and goddesses with human attributes and human personalities, the Romans invested trees, springs, caves, lakes, animals and even household furniture with *numina* (singular: *numen*), meaning the 'divine will' or 'divine powers' of a deity. Significant gods and goddesses had multiple functions; minor administrative roles were often undertaken by attendant spirits, known as *indigitamenta*, into whom the deity projected the *numen* of that particular activity. Ceres, for instance, in her capacity as goddess of the grain harvest, employed no fewer than twelve individual spirits, to whom reference should be made in all prayers appropriate to the occasion. These

FIGURE 5.2 Bronze sheep liver for divination. This Etruscan object is a life divination tool, used by a Harupsex in the second century BC. It is inscribed with the names of sixteen Etruscan deities, including Selva (Silvanus), Uni (Juno), Mar (Mars) and Herc (Hercules), some of which are disputed on account of the abbreviations used. Museo Civico, Piacenza, Italy. © 2014. Photo Scala, Florence.

included Vervactor (first plougher of the season), Reparator (second plougher of the season), Occator (harrower), Sarritor (hoer) and Surruncinator (raker).

From Rome's foundation as a city, boundary markers between one person's property and the next had a special significance (a lesson Remus learned the hard way when he trespassed on Romulus' wall on the Palatine). The word for a boundary stone was *terminus* and there was even a great god Terminus, a massive piece of masonry which stood permanently in the Temple of Jupiter on the Capitoline hill, because, according to the poet Ovid (43 BC–AD 18) in his Fasti, a calendar of rites and traditions, it refused to budge, even for Jupiter.

PRAYER AND SACRIFICE: BLESSINGS AND CURSES

The contractual relationship between mankind and the gods involved each party in giving, and in return receiving, services. The Romans believed that powers residing in natural and physical objects had the ability to control the processes of nature, and that man could influence these processes by symbolic action. The first is a primitive form of religious creed; the second is a type of magic.

The 'services' by which Romans hoped to influence the forces that guided their lives were firmly established in ritual – the ritual of prayer and the ritual of offering. In either case, the exact performance of the rite was essential. One slip, and you had to go back to the beginning and start again. The very multiplicity of deities caused problems. 'Whether you be god or goddess' is a common formula in Roman prayers, introduced to offset a lack of knowledge of a particular deity of a certain location or situation, or to avoid giving offence to a deity of foreign origin. The poet Horace (65–8 BC) dedicated to Augustus an ode calling for divine assistance to restore the fortunes of Rome, but is clearly unsure to whom his appeal should be addressed: 'Upon which of the gods should the people call to revive the failing empire?' (*Odes* 1.2). He plays safe by starting at the top of the hierarchy: 'To whom will Jupiter assign the task of receiving atonement for our crimes?' He then cites four candidates in turn: Apollo, Venus, Mars and Mercury.

Many Roman deities went by a variety of names, and might not respond if wrongly addressed. So Catullus (*c.* 84–54 BC), in a hymn to Diana (Poem 34), is careful also to invoke her as 'Latona's daughter, splendid child of Jove . . . called Juno Lucina by those in childbirth's pangs, and also queenly Trivia, and Luna, she who shines with borrowed light.' The poem ends on a note of respectful exasperation, and with a ritual escape clause: 'Accept our prayer under any name by which it pleases you to be addressed.' These lines throw up another identity problem in that Juno Lucina (Lucina here means 'bringing into the light') is not Diana, but Juno, consort of Jupiter, appearing here in her guise as goddess of childbirth. Juno had at least ten other names or surnames for use on special days or in particular circumstances, including Juno Moneta (Juno the 'Mint'), because her temple on the Capitoline hill housed the state mint, where money was coined and stored.

Some prayers were realistic and modest, for example Horace's 'Poet's Prayer', which ends: 'I pray, Apollo, let me be content with what I have, enjoy good health and clarity of mind, and in a dignified old age retain the power of verse' (*Odes* 1.31). This is, however, about the nearest any Roman usually got to praying for anything but material blessings. On some occasions prayer was offered not for a blessing but for a curse. There was a prayer for the return of stolen property and another for the diversion of some unspecified piece of ill-fortune to someone. The vengeful cursing of a thief (whether they have stolen a cloak or a heart) is a practice that can be found across Rome's empire from the Greek east and Egypt to the baths of Roman Britian. While the ritual and medium (papyrus, stone or metal) varied, a curse was inscribed, an act which itself may have been a ritual to invoke 'magic' (sometimes the text is written backwards). These **curse tablets**, not meant to be read by mortals, are often poorly carved and written in vernacular language with creative spelling, implying that the people who made them were not fluent writers.

Curses can be quite formulaic: invoking a deity, often a Chythonic (earth/elemental deity, like those invoked by Dido after Aeneas' defection in Book 6 of the *Aeneid*), and recording the crime (e.g. the theft of one's cloak from a bath house: one can see how this might be humiliating). Then a 'blanket statement' was made to cover all possible perpetrators in the curse (male, female, slave, freedman) in the punishment, which often took the form of elements: payments in water or blood. Curses reveal not only religious practice but aspects of local language and culture, as well as the fact that many Romans felt the need to 'take the law into their own hands'.

Prayer was almost invariably accompanied by some form of offering, or sacrifice. This did not necessarily involve the ritual slaughter of an animal. The offering often merely had to represent life in some form: it could be cakes made from corn, fruit, cheese, bowls of wine, or pails of milk. Each deity had his or her own preferred sacrificial animal – a ram for Janus, a steer for Jupiter. For Mars, it was usually a combination of ox, pig and sheep, but on 15 October it had to be a winning horse from a chariot race. This was slaughtered at the altar, its tail was cut off, and the blood that dripped from it was preserved as a charm. The sex of a chosen animal was also significant: male for gods, female for goddesses. So was its colour: white beasts were offered to deities of the upper world; black to those of the underworld; and a red dog was sacrificed to Robigus, symbolizing the destruction of red mildew.

The sacrificial routine was elaborate and messy (Figure 5.3). The head of the victim was sprinkled with wine and bits of sacred cake made from flour and salt. The *victimarius* then stunned the animal with a mallet before cutting its throat and disembowelling it to ensure there was nothing untoward about its entrails. If there was, this was a bad omen

FIGURE 5.3 First-century AD altar relief from the Sanctuary of the Genius of Augustus in the forum at Pompeii. It depicts a bull led to a tripod altar in front of a temple hung with bunting. The *victimarius* holds an axe with which to stun the victim before its throat is cut, while the presiding officer, his head veiled, holds out a *patera*, the dish used for offerings. Photo © VRoma: Barbara McManus. Courtesy of del Ministero dei Beni e delle Attività Culturali e del Turismo – Soprintendenza Speciale per i Beni Archeologici di Pompei, Ercolano e Stabia.

and the whole process had to be repeated with a fresh animal until it came out right. The vital organs were burned upon the altar and the carcass cut into pieces and eaten. Then the priest (or presiding sacrifant), with his toga drawn up over his head, would say prayers under his breath while a flute was played. Any unintentional deviation from the prescribed ritual meant not only a new sacrifice, but an additional one in expiation of the error. Before high occasions, on which a replay of the entire ceremony might be an embarrassment, an expiatory sacrifice was performed as a matter of course on the previous day, in the hope of 'covering the bases' for the next day's ritual.

Human sacrifice was unusual in Roman religion. Acts of sacrilege were regarded as symptoms of impending doom and then the Sibylline Books, the national store-house of prophetic utterances (see below), were consulted for remedies against further disasters: 'Among other sacrifices, a Gaulish couple and a Greek couple were walled up alive in the cattle market, in an underground tomb which had once before [in 228 BC] been stained with human victims, an un-Roman practice' (Livy, 22.57). However, Livy does record the act of *self*-sacrifice, known as *devotio*. During the Latin War of 340 BC, one of the consuls, Decius Mus, decided that a sacrifice was needed to redress Rome's dire situation. Instructed by a priest, he went through the ritual of dedicating himself and the enemy to the gods of the underworld. Then he leapt on his horse and rode deep into the enemy lines, causing much consternation, until he was buried beneath a hail of missiles. The Roman formations rallied and won the day.

OMENS

A sibyl was a Greek prophetess. The story goes that one of her kind offered to Tarquinius Superbus at a high price a collection of prophecies and warnings in the form of nine books. When he refused, she threw three of the books into a fire and offered him the remaining six for the original price. He refused again, so she burned three more and offered him the final three, still at the same price. This time, he bought them. The Sibylline Books were consulted on the orders of the Senate at times of crisis and calamity, in order to learn how the wrath of the gods might be allayed. However, they were accidentally burned in 83 BC, and envoys were sent all round the known world to collect a set of similar utterances. Augustus had the new collection put in the Temple of Apollo on the Palatine hill, where it remained until it was finally destroyed in the fifth century AD.

Disasters were seen by the Romans as manifestations of divine disapproval, and unusual phenomena as portents of catastrophe. In the winter of 218–217 BC, just before the Battle of Trasimene, but with Hannibal already ensconced in Italy, the following portents were said to have been observed:

> In Rome a six-month-old freeborn infant shouted 'Victory' in the vegetable market; in the cattle market an ox climbed up three flights of stairs on its own and then jumped out of a window in fright when the inhabitants screamed; phantom ships glowed in the sky; the Temple of Hope, in the vegetable market, was struck by lightning. In Lanuvium a sacrificial corpse moved and a crow flew down into the Temple of Juno and alighted on her sacred couch. In the district of Amiternum, ghostly men in shining garb materialized in many places but did not approach anyone. In Picenum it rained stones. At Caere oracular tablets shrank. In Gaul a wolf stole a sentry's sword from its sheath and ran off with it.
>
> **(Livy, 21.62)**

Reports of these phenomena could cause panic among a people for whom superstition was a way of life, especially at times of national uncertainty. The Sibylline

Books were duly consulted and various methods of appeasement emerged, including the ceremonial purging of the city of Rome, sacrifices, gifts to temples of Juno of gold ingots (each weighing forty pounds) and bronze statues, and a series of symbolic feasts at which statues of the gods reclined on couches round a banqueting table. At the end of it all, Livy reports, the Roman people felt considerably relieved. The awe in which the Sibylline Books were held and the reverence with which their revelations were treated illustrate their significance in the Romans' relationship with their gods.

The taking of auspices (literally 'signs from birds') was a standard procedure before any state activity. This is illustrated in the story of the legendary founding of Rome itself and in the plan of a Roman temple (Figure 5.4), which often had a larger front porch from which to observe the birds (see Chapter 7). An official augur, who acted as a consultant, prepared the statutory square space and then handed over to the state official who was to perform the ritual. He observed the flights of any birds he could see, noting their species, height, position, speed and direction of flight. If there was any doubt about the interpretation of what the official saw, the augur would advise. Later, armies took with them a portable auspice kit, consisting of a cage of sacred chickens, in front of which bits of cake were placed to see what would happen. It was

FIGURE 5.4 Maison Carrée, Nîmes, probably finished in 16 BC, is the most complete surviving temple of the Augustan era. Dedicated to Gaius and Lucius, sons of Agrippa and Augustus' daughter Julia, it reflects the loyalty of the local provincial community to the imperial family. The slender columns, each just over nine metres high, are surmounted with capitals in the Corinthian style. Photo © Allan T. Kohl/Art Images for College Teaching.

a bad sign if the birds refused to eat; good if they ate the cake and let bits of grain fall from their beaks. In 249 BC the consul Claudius Pulcher 'began a sea-battle though the sacred chickens had refused to eat when he took the auspices. In contempt of religious practice, he threw the chickens into the sea, remarking that if they would not eat, they could drink' (Suetonius, *Tiberius* 2). He was very lucky to escape from the ensuing debacle, during which ninety-three Roman ships and their crews were captured by the Carthaginians. How much the Romans believed in the results of auguries (they would seem to be easy to manipulate with enough birdseed) is unknown.

Public business was frequently interrupted so that the omens (*omina*; singular: *omen*) could be consulted. A law passed by an assembly or an election could be declared invalid if the correct procedure had not been followed. There was no need to resort to the tactic of filibustering in political assemblies to obstruct proceedings: religious grounds could suffice. In 59 BC Julius Caesar's consular colleague Marcus Calpurnius Bibulus proposed to offer religious justification for the rejection of Caesar's legislation in the assemblies. Fearful, in the prevailing unrest, of venturing out of his house, he sent messages that he was watching the sky for omens. As bad omens had to be announced in person before the start of business, this raised an awkward precedent. Caesar overruled Bibulus' tactics, but for some time his laws were regarded with suspicion.

There was a distinction between signs that were solicited and those that appeared without invitation. The more startling or unexpected the sign – for instance, a sudden flash of lightning or a member of an assembly suffering an epileptic fit – the more seriously it was taken. It was not unknown for an interested party to feign a fit in order to obstruct proceedings. Lightning which appeared while auspices were being taken was good news; not so when it came unbidden.

WORSHIP IN THE HOME

Two national deities had their place in private worship, too: Vesta, goddess of the fire and the hearth; and Janus, god of doorways. The latter, who gave his name to the month of January, is often depicted as having two faces, one looking in each direction. There are several interpretations of this: that it represents opening and closing a door, going in and coming out, or viewing (and thus guarding) both the inside and the outside of a house. The door itself was so highly regarded that it required the attention of two more deities: Cardea, goddess of hinges, and Limentinus, god of the threshold. To trip as one went through a door was regarded as a thoroughly bad omen, so it was customary for brides to be carried over the threshold. Vesta was particularly important to the women of the household, for the open hearth was where the food was prepared and cooked, and the meal was eaten beside it. Prayers were said to

Vesta every day, and during a meal a portion of food might be thrown into the fire as an offering, and also to seek omens from the way in which it burned.

The particular gods of the household were its *lares* and *penates*. The *lares* (one of them was designated *lar familiaris* ('family spirit') and was specific to that household) were supposed to be the spirits of dead ancestors and they had their own shrine, which they inhabited in the form of tiny statuettes (Figure 5.5; see also Figure 7.2). Daily prayers and offerings were made to them, with more elaborate ones on the sacred days of each month and notable occasions, such as a birth, wedding, birthday, departure or return, or when a son of the house spoke his first word. The *penates* looked after the larder, its contents and their replenishment, and also had their own cupboard. The statuettes of the *penates* were taken out and put on the table at mealtimes, and were sometimes given the names of particular state gods. When a family moved, their *lares* and *penates* went with them.

Each household had in addition its *genius*, whose image was a house-snake. *Genius* might be described as a 'spirit of manhood', since it was supposed to give a man the power of generation, and its particular sphere of influence was the marriage bed. The household *genius* was especially honoured on the head of the family's birthday.

FIGURE 5.5 Wall painting in the *lararium* (shrine of the *lares*) of the House of the Vettii, Pompeii. The *genius* of the household is flanked by two *lares*. Photo © Allan T. Kohl/Art Images for College Teaching. Courtesy of del Ministero dei Beni e delle Attività Culturali e del Turismo – Soprintendenza Speciale per i Beni Archeologici di Pompei, Ercolano e Stabia.

Births and deaths had their special rituals. Juno Lucina was the main deity of childbirth, but there were other spirits who watched over the unborn child and its mother from the moment of conception to birth. A series of child-development deities watched over the baby's breastfeeding, bones, posture, drinking, eating and talking, including its accent: Levana helped it get up from the ground; Statanus taught it to stand; Abeona supported its first steps.

On the ninth day after the birth of a boy (the eighth in the case of a girl), the ceremony of purification and naming was enacted, presided over by the goddess Nundina. Free-born children received an amulet – gold for a child of the rich, bronze or merely leather for poorer families – which a girl would wear until her marriage, and a boy until he exchanged his *toga praetexta*, the robe of a child (which was also worn by girls), for the *toga virilis*, the garb of a man, between the ages of fourteen and seventeen.

While a spirit of some kind watched over a person at most times and on most occasions, from conception to death, at the actual moment of death there was none. The religious element in the funeral rites was directed towards a symbolic purification of the survivors. After the burial or cremation, a sow was sacrificed to Ceres to cleanse the house, and any refuse in it was solemnly swept out, while the family was sprinkled with water, and then invited to step over a ceremonial fire. After that, everyone sat down to a feast. Once the corpse was buried – and even in the case of cremation one bone was preserved and put in the ground – its own spirit joined all those other spirits of the dead, which were known collectively as *manes* and required regular worship and appeasement.

WORSHIP IN THE FIELDS

To the countryman, the natural world teemed with religious significance. The fields, orchards, vineyards, springs and woods all had their attendant deities or spirits – every oak tree, for instance, was sacred to Jupiter. Silvanus, god of the woods and fields, guarded the boundary between farmland and forest, and the estate had to be regularly protected from natural and supernatural hazards by lustration – the ritual of purification involving sacrifice and a solemn procession round its perimeter. The country year was crowded with festivals of appeasement, prayer and rejoicing.

The farmer's annual round began in the spring, which the original Roman calendar reflected by the year beginning on 15 March. The establishment of what is now New Year's Day in Christian countries on 1 January was for sheer administrative convenience. In 153 BC, in order to enable the arrival in Spain of the incoming consul to coincide with the start of the campaigning season, the beginning of his term of office, and thus of the year, was advanced to 1 January, and there it remained. The first celebration of the country year was the Liberalia on 17 March, in honour of Liber, god of fertility in the fields and vineyards. This was also the traditional date on which a teenage boy abandoned his *toga praetexta* for the *toga virilis*.

The latter part of April was a riot of festivals, each with its own special significance. At the Fordicia on 15 April, pregnant cows were sacrificed to the earth-goddess Tellus, and in Rome itself foetuses were burned and the ashes kept for use at the festival of the Parilia the following week, during which the sheep were purified by being driven through bales of blazing straw. Ceres, goddess of agriculture and especially of corn, had her festival on 19 April, as Virgil records in his verse handbook on farming, the *Georgics* (1.338–350):

> First thing of all is to revere the gods, especially Ceres: to her greatness dedicate the yearly rites. Perform them on the grass which burgeons at the very end of winter, in the bright days of spring. The lambs are fat, the wine is at its softest, sleep is sweet, and all the shadows thicken on the hills. This is the time when all your country folk should worship Ceres. Mix the mellow wine with milk and honey, lead the sacrifice three times the circle of your new-grown crops, while all your fellow workers follow on behind, chanting and calling Ceres to their homes.

Here again we have the lustration ritual as an act of purification and bringing of luck. After the Vinalia Rustica, probably a drunken revel to celebrate the end of winter, and the sacrifice of the red dog to Robigus, god of mildew, the month closed with the Floralia, a festival ostensibly to petition for the healthy blossoming of the season's flowers, which lasted from 28 April to 3 May.

When the corn was cut in August, there were celebrations to Consus, god of the granary, and Ops, god of harvest wealth, and a further Vinalia Rustica; the real festival of thanksgiving for the wine crop, the Meditrinalia, was observed on 11 October. Sowing took place in December, during which there were repeats of the festivals of Consus and Ops. The Saturnalia was on 17 December. This festival was observed in the country as a genuine celebration of seed-time. In towns it was a longer celebration which embodied some of the secular traditions later associated with Christmas, including holidays from school, candles, exchanges of gifts, the mingling of household staff with the family, and even the wearing of party hats.

THE RELIGION OF THE STATE: OFFICES AND THE FESTIVAL CALENDAR

The religion of the Roman state reflected the ways of private worship, while retaining traditions from the period of the kings. Under the nominal direction of the *pontifex maximus*, administrative and ritualistic matters were the responsibility of four colleges, whose members, with one or two exceptions, were appointed or elected from the ranks of politicians and held office for life. The members of the Pontifical College, the senior body, were the *rex sacrorum*, *pontifices*, *flamines* and the Vestal Virgins. *Rex sacrorum* ('king of religious rites') was an office created under the early republic to maintain the tradition of royal authority over religious matters. Though in later times he still took precedence at religious ceremonies over all other dignitaries, including the *pontifex maximus*, by then it had become largely an honorary position. The sixteen *pontifices* (priests) were the chief administrators and organizers of the religious affairs of the state, and authorities on procedure and matters of the calendar and festivals, and on the designation of particular days on which certain public business could not be conducted. The *flamines* were priests of particular gods: three for the major gods, Jupiter, Mars and Quirinus, and twelve for the lesser ones. These specialists had the technical knowledge of the worship of the particular deity to whom, and to whose temple, they were attached, and performed the daily sacrifice to that deity. The *flamen dialis* ('priest of Jupiter') was the most important of them, and on certain occasions he ranked alongside the *pontifex maximus* and *rex sacrorum*. His life was hedged around with taboos and hazards. In the second century AD, Aulus Gellius recorded 'those I can remember':

> He may not ride a horse . . . If a person is brought into the house of the *flamen dialis* in fetters, he must be untied and the bonds pulled up through the open skylight on to the roof and then let down into the street . . . Only a free man may cut his hair. It is the custom that the *flamen dialis* may not touch or even mention a nanny-goat, uncooked meat, ivy, or beans . . . He may not go out without his cap of office; it has only recently been decided by the priests that he can take it off indoors . . . If he loses his wife, he must resign his office. His marriage cannot be ended except by death.
>
> **(Attic Nights 1.15)**

The six Vestal Virgins were chosen from patrician families at an early age to serve at the Temple of Vesta. By tradition, they normally served ten years as novices, the next ten performing the duties, and a further ten teaching the novices, though staying on for the full thirty years seems to have been an option. They had their own convent near the Forum, and their duties included guarding the sacred fire in the temple, performing the rituals of worship, and baking the salt cake that was used at various festivals throughout the year. Punishment for any lapse in ritual or conduct was rigorous: whipping for letting the sacred fire go out; whipping and being walled up underground, with a few provisions, for a breach of the vow of chastity. The last known case of this punishment occurred during the rule of the emperor Domitian (AD 81–96):

> [Cornelia, the chief Vestal Virgin,] continued to protest right up to the place of punishment; whether she was guilty or innocent, I don't know, but she certainly

had the demeanour of innocence. And here's another thing! As she was being conducted into the underground vault, her gown caught on something. She turned to pull it free. When the executioner offered to give her a hand, she recoiled in horror from his touch, an unspeakable violation of her purity and chastity.

(Pliny the Younger, *Letters* 4.11)

The fifteen members of the College of Augurs exercised great learning, and presumably diplomacy, in the interpretation of omens in public and private life, and acted as consultants in cases of doubt. Each carried a crooked staff, without any knot in it, with which he marked out the square space of ground from which official auspices were observed.

The members of the College of Quindecimviri Sacris Faciundis ('Fifteen for Special Religious Duties') were the keepers of the Sibylline Books, which they consulted and interpreted when requested to do so, and ensured that any actions prescribed were properly carried out. Their functions were originally performed by just two officials, but by the time of Sulla the number had mushroomed to fifteen; Julius Caesar added another, but the name remained the same. This college also had responsibility for supervising the worship of any foreign deity which was introduced into the religion of the state, usually on the recommendation of the Sibylline Books. One such was Cybele, the Phrygian goddess of nature – the 'Great Mother' – whose presence in Rome in the form of a sacred slab of black meteoric rock was recommended in 204 BC after, as Livy records, it had rained stones more often than usual. Cybele's cult, symbolized by noisy processions of attendant eunuch priests and flagellants, was exotic and extreme, in direct contrast to the stately, methodical practices of state religion. Roman citizens were discouraged from participating in its rites until the time of Claudius. The annual public games in honour of Cybele, however, were held in considerable style from 4 to 10 April, and were preceded by a ceremonial washing and polishing of her stone by members of the college.

The seven office-holders of the College of Epulones ('Banqueting Managers') belonged to the smallest and most junior of the four colleges. It was founded in 196 BC, presumably as a result of the amount of organization required to put on the official feasts that had become integral parts of the major festivals and games by then.

The earliest state religious festivals were celebrated with games, such as the first to be recorded in Rome – the festival to Consus at which the Sabine women were kidnapped (see Chapter 1). The Consualia, traditionally celebrated in Rome on 21 August, was also the local 'Derby Day', the main event of the chariot-racing calendar. Whether it was a case of cause or effect, the underground granary, which housed the sacred shrine of Consus where the opening sacrifice was conducted, was conveniently situated in the middle of the Circus Maximus (Map 5, no. 3), where the racing took place.

Religious festivals could be grave as well as joyful. February saw both kinds. During the nine days of the Parentalia, during which the family dead were worshipped, state officials did no business, temples were closed and marriages were forbidden. In contrast, the ancient rites of the **Lupercalia**, which took place on 15 February, were a more raunchy and raucous version of Valentine's Day. The deity honoured was probably Faunus, god of fertility, but the proceedings reflected the origins of Rome itself. They started in the cave where Romulus and Remus were supposedly suckled by the wolf. Several goats and a dog were sacrificed, and their blood was smeared over two noble youths. Then, according to Plutarch's account in the *Life of Caesar*, the two youngsters ran through the city in loin cloths, smacking eager young ladies who lined the streets with their hands out, hoping for a whip of fertility. Rome continued to celebrate this highly popular festival until the fifth century AD. In 2007, claims were made that a cave near the remains of the palace of Augustus was the site where the opening proceedings took place, but the identification remains controversial.

The marathon festivities for Mars – from 1 to 19 March – were even more exhausting for the participants. Two teams, each consisting of twelve celebrants known as *salii* ('jumpers'), donned the helmets, uniforms and armour of Bronze Age warriors and leapt through the streets, chanting and beating their shields. Each night they rested, and feasted, at a prearranged hostelry or private house. Once a member of the *salii*, always a member! It was a rule of the order that if you were out of Rome while the celebrations were taking place, you had to stay where you were for the duration. In 190 BC, this held up a military campaign when a Roman army waited at the Hellespont while its commander was immobilized by the festival en route to join his troops.

There was not a month in the Roman calendar which did not have its religious festivals. August, the sixth month of the old calendar, hosted, in addition to the Consualia, festivals to Portunus (god of harbours), Vulcan (god of fire), Volturnus (god of the river Tiber) and Hercules (god not just of victory but of enterprise in business). In the course of his life on earth, Hercules pulled off some celebrated, but decidedly shady, commercial deals. He was thus popular with the business community, who were in the habit of offering him a proportion of their profits as a thank-you for services and in the hope of further assistance. August was also the month when the ancient festival of Diana was remembered on the Aventine.

That January should find itself the first month in the revised calendar was entirely appropriate. Janus, who gave his name to it, was a god unique to the Romans and he has no equivalent in any other mythology. He was the god of beginnings as well as of the door, which you meet when you first enter a house. He not only began the year and received the first state sacrifice annually at the Agonia on 9 January, but the first hour of the day was sacred to him, and his name took precedence over all others in prayers. Gaius Duilius (see Chapter 2) set up a victory temple in his honour to commemorate his naval victory at Mylae and may also be associated with the minting of his bearded, double-headed face on early (*Aes grave*) bronze coins in the mid-third century BC. The gates of his temple in the north-east corner of the Forum were (it is said on the orders of Numa) kept wide open in times of war. According to Livy, this meant that they were closed only twice in the succeeding seven centuries.

CHURCH AND STATE: EMPERORS AND RELIGION

Augustus, as part of his national morale-boosting campaign, reaffirmed the traditional forms of worship. According to his own account (*Res Gestae Divi Augusti*) and a bronze inscription placed outside his mausoleum, he restored eighty-two temples in and around Rome. In 12 BC, after the death of Lepidus, who had held the post since 44 BC in succession to Julius Caesar, Augustus had himself appointed *pontifex maximus*, an office which thereafter was restricted to emperors. Thus the head of state was once again the head of religious affairs. Augustus promoted the god Apollo, with whom his own family was said to have special affinities, to the status of a major deity, and dedicated a magnificent new temple to him on a site on the Palatine hill, which was his personal property. He did not take the connection between religion and rule so far as to allow himself officially to be regarded as a god in his own lifetime, but he prepared the way to being deified after his death by confirming the divinity of Julius Caesar and dedicating a temple to him.

Augustus, however, was happy to accept the worship of non-Romans, provided that his name was coupled with that of Rome (or Roma, the goddess who personified the city). His deification enabled the proliferation throughout the empire of Rome's most potent export: the **imperial cult**, or emperor worship. In this way, the loyalty of inhabitants of the provinces of Rome could be focused on an individual rather than on a concept of government. People could more easily relate to an individual (even if that person was subsequently damned by the Senate). The imperial family also provided a model of conduct and benefaction that could be followed on a local scale by provincial aristocrats. Even one of the most pragmatic of Augustus' successors, Vespasian, dedicated a new temple to the divine Claudius; he also encouraged the establishment of emperor worship in the provinces of Baetica (south-east Spain), Gallia Narbonensis and Africa, to strengthen the ties between their inhabitants and his family.

Emperor worship bound together the largely Hellenized eastern empire and the predominantly Celtic and Germanic provinces of the west (see Figure 5.4). While many cultures, east and west, accepted the imperial cult, this did not necessarily come at the expense of local gods. In the Greek east the emperor and his cult did not overrun local deities. For example, in the city of Ephesus (and many other cities in the Greek east) the majority of buildings are dedicated to the predominant local deity (in this case Ephesian Artemis), the emperor and the Ephesian people (in that order). In the Roman west, though the names of Roman deities are often adopted, the process of cultural transmission moves both ways, as evidenced in dedications to the Celtic goddess Sulis in Bath by a Roman centurion. However, Roman interference occurred only in cases of obnoxious practices, such as human sacrifice, or for political reasons. Except in army camps and Roman colonies, the Roman religion and attendant culture had little impact on the Hellenized east, where responsibility for the temples and their priesthoods was largely left to the local authorities.

RELIGION IN THE PROVINCES: EAST MEETS WEST

One issue with religion and culture is that its transmission is seldom a one-way street. Indeed, the success of the Roman empire was inextricably linked to its ability to accept and interact with foreign nations. When McDonald's travels across the globe, some elements remain but some are altered: hence, the McDijonaise (France), the McFalafel (Israel) and the McChicken Tikka Burger (London). Our ability to observe and understand these cultural adaptations, however, is dependent on our knowledge of both cultures. While Rome's eastern provinces are often well documented from previous historical (Greek, Egyptian, Persian) accounts, sources from indigenous cultures of the west are limited. The result of this disparity is scholars' tendency to focus on elements of 'Romanization' in the west. As studies of the Roman west proliferate, this 'transformation' becomes less clear. Both eastern and western areas of the empire present gods with traditional Roman (or Greek in the east) names (e.g. Minerva Sulis in Roman Britain or Zeus Megistos in Dura Europos). In both cases, these epithets probably refer to a local god (Celtic Sulis and Near Eastern Bel). Just because the names have been 'Romanized' (by a Roman source), that does not mean the cult was completely 'Romanized' in practice. For some eastern cults, such as those of Mithras and Isis, we know (from earlier sources) that the Roman version of the cult deviated from its Persian and Egyptian origins. Certainly, Rome influenced the religions of its provinces, but equally Rome was influenced by the cults of these provinces. The religions that emerged from this exchange, like the global range of McDonald's menus, were likely cultural hybrids.

The survival of a religious faith depends on a continual renewal and affirmation of its beliefs, and sometimes on adapting its ritual to changes in social conditions and attitudes: expansion is possible only through active and organized proselytizing, and by the relevance of its teachings to those to whose attention it is brought. To the Romans, the observance of religious rites on occasions of state was a public duty. Their beliefs were founded on ancient rituals and on a variety of mythological traditions, many of them derived from Greek rather than Italian models. Without any basic creed to counter, foreign religions made inroads into a society whose class structure was being blurred and whose constitution was being changed by the increased presence of freed slaves and incomers from abroad. The brilliance of some of the major foreign cults had considerable attraction for those brought up on homespun deities of the hearth and fields. The first to reach Rome was that of Cybele in 204 BC, according to Livy. The worship of **Mithras** (Figure 5.6), the emissary of light who symbolized the

FIGURE 5.6 Statue of Mithras from the Baths of Mithras at Ostia (now in the Museo Ostiense). As places of worship, Mithrea were fundamentally different from Roman temples: often underground (sometimes connected to a spring or other water source), the cave-like structure had little natural light and usually contained a central nave or path with an image of Mithras at the centre. The origins of Mithras' cult are debated, although they were possibly Persian. He is depicted here – with flowing locks, a Phrygian cap and the short toga that was popular in Anatolia – just before he slices the bull's neck in sacrifice. © 2014. Photo Scala, Florence, courtesy of the Ministero Beni e Att. Culturali.

fight to disseminate life-giving forces in the face of the powers of darkness and disorder, was practised from the first century AD and had particular appeal among the army. Shrines to Mithras, originally a Persian god, can be found across the Roman empire, such as in a British temple (excavated in London in 2012), in residential areas of Ostia and in army camps in Syria (Dura Europos). Tacitus (*Histories* 3.24) dramatically illustrates the preliminaries to the second Battle of Cremona during the civil war in AD 69. After Antonius Primus, leader of Vespasian's faction, had harangued his troops, 'There was a shout from the whole army, and the men of the Third Legion turned to the east and saluted the rising sun, in accordance with the custom in Syria.'

The worship of Isis, an Egyptian goddess who brought her husband Osiris back from the dead, arrived in Rome in the early years of the first century BC. Initially scorned in the city, it became a popular cult with branches all over Italy, including Pompeii, where a temple to Isis survives. Its significance is powerfully reflected in the fictional prose narrative *Metamorphoses* (also known as *The Golden Ass*) by Lucius Apuleius (fl. *c.* AD 160), who became a priest of Isis and her consort Osiris. The protagonist, also called Lucius, is accidentally turned into an ass while experimenting with an ointment supplied by the maid of the house. After several adventures and misadventures he appeals to Isis for help, having realized the omnipotence of the 'supreme goddess'. She duly appears to him:

> I come in answer to your prayers, Lucius: I, mother nature, ruler of all the elements, original child of time, most powerful of divine spirits, queen of the dead, supreme in the heavens, the single face of all gods and goddesses. With a nod I arrange the glowing arch of the sky, the healthy sea breezes, the bitter silence of the underworld. I am one god, worshipped throughout the world in many forms, with different rites, and under a variety of names . . . The Egyptians, who are skilled in ancient lore, celebrate my being with forms of worship which are unique to me and address me by my real name, Queen Isis.
>
> **(Lucius Apuleius, *Metamorphoses* 11.5)**

This is not just a description of a powerful deity, or even of a chief divine: it is an expression of monotheism. The worship of Isis in the Roman empire was just one of the cults known as 'mysteries', which presented exotic and erotic imagery and secret rituals. The mysteries based on those practised at Eleusis, to whose ancient annual festival initiates flocked from the Greek-speaking world, and those of Cybele and Bacchus, were also significant. They all have in common a ceremony of purification of the initiate, a sense of personal relationship with the deity, and the notion of a life beyond death.

The rituals of the mysteries were supposed to be known only to initiates. True to their names, these cults remain shrouded in mystery. However, in addition to literary allusions, we have fascinating glimpses of the cults of Isis and Bacchus in the form of temples and wall paintings excavated at Pompeii (Figure 5.7). These scenes, which have been subject to numerous scholarstic debates, represent a series of symbols and acts that could have been parts of an actual ritual or simple allegories for life, death and/or marriage.

FIGURE 5.7 The Villa of the Mysteries at Pompeii was built in the middle of the second century BC and remodelled and redecorated around 60 BC. One hall carries round its walls a continuous series of paintings in bright tones. These have been taken to symbolize a bride's preparations for marriage, while also reflecting elements associated with the mysteries of Dionysus (Bacchus). In this section, which goes round a corner, a kneeling woman (far left) begins to uncover an object that some have suggested is an enormous phallus. Next, a winged female figure raises a whip to strike a half-naked girl whose back is bared by the woman in whose lap she buries her face. On the right a clothed woman holds the *thyrsus*, the wand carried by Bacchus and his adherents, while a naked companion, clashing cymbals above her head, dances in ecstasy. Photo © C.M. Dixon. Courtesy of del Ministero dei Beni e delle Attività Culturali e del Turismo – Soprintendenza Speciale per i Beni Archeologici di Pompei, Ercolano e Stabia.

JEWS AND CHRISTIANS

Traditional beliefs were also affected by the Jewish diaspora. By the time of Augustus' death in AD 14, there were considerable areas of Jewish settlement throughout the eastern empire, in the provinces of Africa and Mauretania, in southern Spain and Gaul, and in Italy, Corsica, Sicily and Sardinia, with major communities in Rome, Alexandria, Ephesus, Antioch and Damascus. A Jewish force enabled Julius Caesar to extricate himself from an embarrassing military situation in Egypt in 47 BC, and in return he granted Jews in communities outside Judaea privileges which included freedom of worship, the ability to remit contributions to the Temple in Jerusalem, permission to answer to their own laws, and exemption from military conscription. A significant part of the Jewish community in Rome was founded by the prisoners brought back by Pompey from Jerusalem in 63 BC as spoils of war taken in the course of sorting out Roman problems in the east (see Chapter 2). Freed by their owners, they, and their descendants, were allowed by Augustus to observe their traditions and worship while still holding Roman citizenship. If the handout of the monthly grain ration fell on the Jewish Sabbath, his agents had instructions to hold back the supplies due to the Jewish population until the following day.

Roman policy was that other cultures within the empire should be allowed to maintain their own traditions provided that they were willing to accept the trappings of imperial rule and religion, and that there were no breaches of the peace. Opposition to Jews occurred mainly in Hellenized cities, though conflicts of culture also emerged when Romans began worshipping their emperors. The most significant charge that could be brought against the Jews in Roman times was that they were different. To them, religion had such a bearing on daily life that it was impossible to eat with their fellow citizens or participate in their festivals. Though they were at times exempted from emperor worship as long as they offered sacrifices and prayers for his health and wellbeing, this could still be interpreted as disloyalty to the state. Slaves in Roman households worked all day, every day, including festivals. Servants in Jewish households did not work on the Sabbath. The injunction that agricultural land should lie fallow every seventh year gave Jews an undeserved reputation for idleness.

Many Romans, however, responded to a creed much of whose tradition was based on written law and sound medical practice. A form of semi-Judaism became fashionable, especially among women: one did not have to be a full convert to attend services in synagogues. These people were known as 'god-fearers'; among them, according to Josephus, the Jewish historian who accompanied Titus back to Rome after the fall of Jerusalem in AD 70, was Nero's empress Poppaea Sabina.

During the rule of Tiberius, a devout young Jewish thinker and teacher, the son of a Nazarene carpenter, had been executed in Jerusalem under Roman law. His name was Jesus, and his followers claimed he was the Messiah. His death was hardly noticed by Roman historians, but if he had not died, he might have been completely forgotten, for it is central to the Christian faith that he came back to life. His original adherents were the Jewish Christians. That this sect of Judaism became a separate and vibrant movement was due to another Jew, Saul, from Tarsus. His name in Greek was Paul, and the Roman citizenship acquired by his father extended to him. Though he was in Jerusalem towards the end of Jesus' life, they never met, but Paul was violently opposed to the Jewish Christians, and in AD 36 he supported the death by stoning of the deacon Stephen, accused of preaching 'against the Temple and the Law'. Sent by the Temple authorities to assist in rounding up Jewish Christians in Damascus, Paul had a searing vision on the road and experienced the voice of Jesus. He was subsequently baptized in Damascus by Ananias, a member of the local Jewish Christian community.

Paul's mission became to establish across the Roman empire a faith based on the life, death, resurrection and divinity of Jesus, instead of on Jewish law. Pagans were allowed to be Christians without first becoming Jews. Christianity appealed especially to the lower orders, to whom this new and personalized religion seemed to offer a bond of unity with one another, and a means of worshipping a single spiritual god by giving honour to a being with whom they could identify. In the course of his lengthy, tireless and often dangerous missionary travels, described in the Acts of the Apostles, Paul was arrested by the Roman authorities in Jerusalem for being the cause of a riot against himself. The commander of the guard ordered him to be interrogated under flogging. As he was being tied up, Paul demanded to know whether it was legal to flog a Roman citizen who had not yet been found guilty of any crime. This was reported to the commander, who asked him, 'Are you a Roman citizen?' Paul said that he was. The commander observed, 'It cost me a large sum to become a Roman citizen.' Paul replied, 'I am a citizen by birth.' The charges were hastily dropped.

In AD 61 Paul arrived in Rome, and from then on he used the city as a base for his mission. He was arrested, and probably executed, in about AD 67, during one of Nero's anti-Christian periods. The monotheistic practices of Jews and Christians made them subject to ridicule and persecution for centuries in the Roman empire (see Chapter 4). Christian worship was practised in caves and cellars far outside the city, and many of their number were buried in catacombs, sometimes provided by a wealthy Christian patron, such as Domitilla, for the benefit of all her brothers and sisters in faith. The catacombs of San Sebastiano, built in the early fourth century AD along the *Via Appia*, illustrate that Christians buried their dead in the same areas of the city as pagans, and also adopted established styles for their funeral monuments, for instance by using terms such as 'well deserving' (*bene merenti*) and giving the age of the deceased. Hence, although the lines that divided Christian and pagan practice were certainly significant, the commonalities which the two groups shared should not be neglected.

San Sebastiano's catacombs were the only ones to remain in use throughout antiquity. The bones of Paul and Peter were once kept there, and many inscribed *ostraka* (pieces of broken pottery) bearing their names attest to the shrine. The dark and dank multi-levelled labyrinth of tombs, which stretches for miles underground, later became an object of Gothic fascination, with the journey into the dark shadows and then back into the light seen as mirroring the rise of the soul from a hard and brutal existence into a newer and brighter life.

FURTHER READING

* indicates sourcebook

Adkins, R. and Adkins, L., *Dictionary of Roman Religion*, Oxford University Press, 2001.

Beard, M., North, J. and Price, S., *Religions of Rome*, vol. 1: *A History*, *vol. 2: *A Sourcebook*, Cambridge University Press, 1998.

Cameron, A., *The Last Pagans of Rome*, Oxford University Press, 2011.

Clark, G., *Christianity and Roman Society*, Cambridge University Press, 2004.

Clauss, M., *The Roman Cult of Mithras: The God and his Mysteries*, trans. R. Gordon, Routledge, 2001.

Ferguson, J., *The Religions of the Roman Empire*, Thames & Hudson, 1985 (new edition); Cornell University Press, 1993 (new edition).

Grant, M. and Hazel, J., *Who's Who in Classical Mythology*, Routledge, 2001 (reissue).

Lane Fox, R., *Pagans and Christians in the Mediterranean World from the Second Century AD to the Conversion of Constantine*, Penguin, 2006 (new edition).

North, J., *Roman Religion*, Oxford University Press, 2000.

Price, S. and Kearns, E., *The Oxford Dictionary of Classical Myth and Religion*, Oxford University Press, 2004.

Rüpke, J. (ed.), *A Companion to Roman Religion*, Blackwell, 2011 (2nd edition).

Scheid, J., *An Introduction to Roman Religion*, Edinburgh University Press, 2003.

Turcan, R., *The Gods of Ancient Rome*, Routledge, 2001.

6 SOCIETY AND DAILY LIFE

Roman society, under both the republic and the empire, was rigidly and recognizably structured, while inherent social and economic factors ensured that inequality was maintained. The top ranks in society had the wealth and status to control and exploit property, and to manipulate the legal system. The lower ranks depended for their position on how far they were able to influence the means of production. Land meant wealth, and remained in the family as long as there were natural or adopted heirs. When a family ceased to exist, it was often favoured freedmen or even slaves who reaped the benefit.

In assessing the daily life of an ancient Roman, we enter a world that is seldom documented by its participants (particularly in literary evidence), so this chapter will focus more on material evidence, with a collection of case studies from the port town of Ostia (*c.* twenty miles from Rome). Here we have an unusual combination of imperial intervention (as well as projects undertaken by members of the Roman elite, including Cicero and Clodius) together with facets of everyday life (and death): *collegia* (guilds) of tradesmen, launderers, granaries, bars, brothels, fire brigades and apart-ment blocks. (For further images and information about the site of Roman Ostia, please visit the excellent archaeological website http://www.ostia-antica.org.)

The old patrician aristocracy, decimated by numerous wars, for the most part died out as republicanism took hold, to be replaced in time by a new nobility, comprising the families of patricians and wealthy plebeians who had successfully stood for office and then entered the Senate. Through their strings of hereditary hangers-on, their clients (*cliens* (plural *clientes*) means 'listener', and thus 'follower'), the nobility became the ruling class (see Chapter 1). With senators barred from participating in state contracts and restricted in trading overseas, a new equestrian class emerged, to whom Gaius Gracchus (see Chapter 2) effectively granted the status of an order of society by giving non-senators who possessed 400,000 sesterces (the same qualification as for senators) the right to bid for tax collection in the provinces, and to have control over the jury courts.

Augustus created a senatorial order (see Chapter 3), membership of which was at his discretion. Senators, and their sons, were entitled to wear a toga with a broad stripe (*latus clavus*) of purple (more accurately, a reddish pink). To promote the dynastic principle, senatorial status was also conferred on senators' wives, and on three generations of their descendants. To maintain an aristocratic strain, senators were now barred from marrying freedwomen. To avoid bad publicity, senators and their families (as well as equestrians) were forbidden to participate in public spectacles. However, the number of subsequent laws 'reaffirming' (if not increasing) penalties for elites who voluntarily transgressed into public performance (e.g. the *Senatus Consultum of Larinum* of AD 19) suggests that, then as now, 'bad publicity' was better than no publicity.

Augustus also raised the qualification portal for senators from 400,000 sesterces to one million sesterces. A decree in the time of Tiberius stipulated that a prospective equestrian and his two previous generations must be free born. Otherwise, it is not generally known whether membership was automatic or conferred by the emperor. Certainly, the equestrian ranks provided the state with a host of army officers and provincial officials (including provincial governors), and latterly with palace dignitaries.

As the rich grew richer and the poor poorer, the *plebs urbana* (city plebs), originally composed mainly of artisans and shopkeepers, became less of a respectable class of society and more of an uncontrolled (and uncontrollable) rabble, comprising also ruined peasants from the countryside vainly seeking work and those attracted by the grain dole. They had voting power, for they were always on the spot to exercise it. In AD 14, responsibility for the election of state officials was transferred to the Senate. A new division of society emerged in Rome: plebs who were professional people (teachers, architects, physicians, tradesmen) and *plebs quae frumentum accipiebat* (plebs who received the grain dole). Especially because the latter could still cause trouble on the streets, Augustus had also interested himself in the supply of housing and water, had provided them with public games, and had distributed cash benefits.

There was a distinction between society in the capital and society in the towns (*municipia*) of Italy. Each despised the other. When, in the time of Augustus, the powers of the city officials diminished, and the towns themselves received attention from the centre of government, politically minded local citizens began to look for recognition in their own towns, rather than in Rome, laying a basis for local government which has been one of Rome's most significant legacies. The value of the charity is monumentalized on Trajan's arch at Benevento (Figure 6.1), which depicts the *alimenta Italiae*, a scheme devised by Trajan to help feed the poor children of Italy (the opposite of Augustus' legislation, which encouraged procreation among the aristocracy). The image of Trajan giving handouts to young children and infants is a rare portrayal of an emperor interacting directly not just with the common men of

FIGURE 6.1 Scene from Trajan's arch at Benevento. This scene, from the interior central panels of the arch, shows the emperor with personifications of various cities (the ladies with crenellated crowns) and children of all ages, babes in arms and a toddler on his father's shoulders (the father wears the short toga of the lower classes). It is an unusually poignant scene, though one wonders if those who received the benefits would have regarded it with the same feeling. Alinari Archives, Florence. Photo © Alinari, Fratelli.

Italy but with their offspring. The only known precedent from a state relief is a panel of the *Ara Pacis* (see Figure 6.7), and even here the children come from wealthy families. The aim of this programme, according to Pliny the Younger (*Panegyricus* 26), was to increase the number of potential military recruits. Trajan's arch, which commemorates his Dacian victory alongside his social reforms, suggests that he did not necessarily distinguish between the two agendas.

As the status of non-citizens in the provinces became more of a concern, a new division of society emerged which did not discriminate between citizens and non-citizens when it came to the administration of the law (see Chapter 4). From the early second century AD, citizens and non-citizens alike were either *honestiores* (men of privilege) or *humiliores* (men of humble rank), with separate punishments for the same crime. Whereas *humiliores* could be sentenced to hard labour in the mines, *honestiores* were merely banished for a short term. The most common form of punishment for a minor offence was flogging, from which *honestiores* were immune.

TRADITIONAL VALUES AND CUSTOMS

The Romans were sticklers for tradition as well as for order – Julius Caesar stressed in public that he was, through his mother, descended from the fourth historical king of Rome and through his father from the goddess Venus, and it was not unknown, under the empire, for successful entrants to the new nobility to invent fictional genealogies for themselves. To support an obsession with the passing of laws, in which everyone was able to participate, and the creation, in the form of the Twelve Tables in 451–450 BC (see Chapter 2), of a digest of current legal practice, the Romans claimed a system of *mos maiorum* –the 'way [or custom] of our ancestors'. The application of tradition and precedent often had more potency than the law itself, and in addition methods for resolving legal situations covered all aspects of public and daily life, including the conduct of the family and the inviolability of the home. It was this ideology and the role of the *paterfamilias* that Augustus, later elected the title '*pater patriae*', would claim to restore to the Roman people.

The Latin term *familia* is usually translated as 'family' or 'household', while *domus* stands for 'house' or 'home'. In Roman times, however, each had a variety of connotations, depending on the circumstances. Thus, *familia*, according to the legal writer Ulpian (d. AD 223), could refer to all those subject to the father's authority (*patria potestas*), including his wife (if married under rites which gave him this authority, known as *manus*), children, adopted children and sons' children; all those related through the male line (*agnates*) to the household, such as brothers and their children, unmarried sisters, but not the sisters' children; all those related through the male line to a common ancestor (also known as *gens*); or all the slaves belonging to a house or farm. In practice, *domus* also came to be used to refer to relatives outside the particular household, but often including those descended through the female line. This broader definition of family applied not only in life but in death, with funerary monuments often mentioning not only the wives and children of the patron but his freedmen and their children. For example, a family tomb monument on the Isola Sacra in Ostia records that 'Tiberius Claudius Eutychus made [this monument] for his well-deserving wife Claudia [offspring of] Memnon, himself, his children, his ex-slaves, male and female, as well as their descendants'.

The term *virtus* described the male quality of steadfastness. Meanwhile, women, as well as men, were expected to possess to a considerable degree that essentially Roman quality of *pietas*, which is untranslatable except as a combination of duty, devotion and loyalty, especially to the gods, but also to one's country, parents and other relatives.

ECONOMY AND MONEY

Much of the hard and menial work was done by slaves. Leisure hours for citizens of Rome were comparatively long and leisure pursuits were subsidized. Public holidays were plentiful (as we observed in the trial of Verres; see Chapter 2) and public entertainment was free. In the times of Julius Caesar and Augustus, 150,000 of the inhabitants of Rome received free grain. Nero was in the habit of handing out gifts of astonishing value and variety during the games which he inaugurated:

> Every day all manner of free gifts were thrown to the people: on a single day 1000 birds of different kinds, a variety of food parcels, and tokens for corn, clothing, gold, silver, jewellery, pearls, paintings, slaves, farm beasts, even wild animals, as well as ships, tenement blocks and agricultural land.
>
> **(Suetonius, *Nero* 9)**

The economy of ancient Rome was an issue of the greatest complexity, and Roman numerals were not in any case designed for easy computation. Imports into Italy, especially of grain, olive oil and wine, were astronomical, as were those of luxury goods from other parts of the Roman world (see Diocletian's price edict; Chapter 4). Consumer spending was restricted by the fact that so many of the population were slaves, while others, especially in Rome itself, were on the bread line. Meanwhile, the army, whose presence anywhere had the effect of boosting the local economy, was spread around the provinces. The provinces themselves were meant to be self-supporting and indeed to provide the fiscal treasury with taxes, while also supplying Rome with staple goods. Some of them were more successful at this than others. There was mass production of pottery, especially the distinctive and often decorated red-coated bowls, plates, serving dishes, cups and lamps that have been found even on sites of dwellings of the rural poor. Archaeological evidence has further revealed that branches of Italian potteries began to operate in Germany and Gaul, which then became major manufacturing centres in their own right, exporting their wares to other provinces, and even back to Italy. A testament to this level of trade is Monte Testaccio in Rome, an artificial mountain (or ancient landfill) composed of shattered pottery shards, mostly amphora, from across the empire (Gaul, Spain and North Africa; see Map 5, no. 15).

Vast sums were expended on public works and entertainments, and on the armed forces. At the end of the day, though, the emperor was usually blamed for shortages, shortfalls and anything else to do with the economy.

> [In AD 32] the exorbitant price of corn almost led to rioting; as it was, there were frantic demands made in the theatre for several days, even more outspoken

against the emperor [Tiberius] than was customary. Stung by these, he reprimanded the state officials and the Senate for failing to use their authority to control the people, listing the provinces from which he had obtained corn and emphasizing that he had imported greater quantities than Augustus. In response the Senate drafted a statement censuring the people in old-fashioned terms of severity, and the consuls issued one which was equally tough. Tiberius' public silence on the matter was not, as he thought, regarded as a constitutionally tactful move, but as arrogance.

(Tacitus, Annals 6.13)

However, the emperor always had considerable resources of his own on which to draw, particularly from estates which were bequeathed to him or acquired by other means. According to Pliny the Elder, Nero confiscated the entire properties of six men who between them owned almost all the grain land in North Africa, and these were still being cultivated as imperial possessions under the rule of Hadrian, sixty years later. The whole of Egypt, too, had from the time of Augustus constituted an imperial perquisite, in that he had (in his estimation) acquired it by right, and he passed on to his successors the tradition that the ruler owned the land and those who worked it were his tenants. Nerva and his immediate successors, Trajan, Hadrian, Antoninus and Marcus Aurelius, inherited from Domitian and his father the habit of moderation in personal expenditure. During their rules, however, there was considerable improvement in the provision of roads and harbours, central government money was granted for new buildings in the provinces, and new public assistance programmes were introduced, particularly for the children of poor families in the municipalities; similarly, increased allowances of wine and olive oil, as well as of grain, were made to the public in Rome.

The successful conclusion of Trajan's invasion of Dacia, begun in AD 101, and especially the output of the Dacian gold and silver mines, boosted the imperial exchequer, but it needed a period of comparative peace, and the careful and dedicated attention of Antoninus and Marcus Aurelius to the levying and collecting of taxes, before comparative liquidity was finally, albeit only temporarily, achieved. Indeed, as Rome and her empire grew, so her needs for supplying the capital increased. Roads offered one means of doing this, but travel by water (sea or river) was not only faster but often more secure for large and/or heavy shipments. Moreover, while it was vital to maintain a good supply of grain for Rome, it was dangerous to have large amounts of grain in a city where riots over foodstuffs were commonplace. As a result, Rome developed a substantial commercial urban centre in the port of Ostia (Cicero is recorded in the restoration of its city walls). The town expanded under Claudius and Nero and even more so during the reigns of the 'five good emperors' (Figure 6.2).

FIGURE 6.2 Depiction of the port at Ostia on a bronze sestertius from the reign of Nero (*c.* 29 grams). Struck in Rome *c.* 64 AD, on the obverse of this coin is the laureate Nero (not shown). On the reverse is the port of Ostia with six ships within, framed on either side by a portico and an arcade; at the bottom is a reclining figure (signifying the river Tiber, which connected to the port); and at the top is a *pharus* (lighthouse) with a statue of Neptune. Photo © CNG Coins.

WORK

Romans rose early and usually worked a six-hour day. A woman's place was firmly in the home: even queuing for the little wooden token entitling a family to the monthly grain dole appears to have been a male prerogative. Free men and freedmen who had work were out and about on their business for the whole morning, contributing to the noise and bustle of urban activity, of which the poet Martial (*c.* AD 40–*c.* AD 104) wrote: 'There's no place in Rome for a poor man to think or rest. Schoolmasters disturb life in the morning, bakers at night, while the coppersmiths hammer all day long' (*Epigrams* 12.57).

The import business was centred on Ostia, where goods from overseas were unloaded, checked and stored in warehouses before being transferred to barges for the journey upstream. The building industry accounted for a continual supply of skilled labour in the form of architects, surveyors, supervisors, foremen, sculptors, stonemasons, carpenters and brickworks' managers. These workers often founded *collegia* or **guilds in Ostia**, which featured not only a place for work but a hall for dining and a means of defining themselves socially. The significance of this identity is evident not only in the colleges and market stalls of the Piazzale delle Corporazioni, a large portico behind the theatre at Ostia (Figure 6.3), but also in honorary inscriptions and funerary monuments, where these roles and collegial associations are recorded.

In the cities and towns, wholesale and retail markets operated, craftsmen plied their trades, and little shops, taverns and inns did their business. They, in their turn, were supplied with raw materials and foodstuffs by the agricultural estates. In accordance with the *mos maiorum*, sons tended to follow the trades of their fathers.

FIGURE 6.3 Mosaic from Ostia. This floor mosaic is from a market stall (stall 18) at the Piazzale delle Corporazioni (a covered market behind the theatre). One can see the entrance, the brick columns and the interior space in this photograph. The scene depicts two single-masted Roman merchant ships, steered by an oar at the stern. The inscription reads 'Navicul. Karthag. de suo' ('belonging to the *navicularii* [private ship owners] from Carthage'). If it had no other cargo, such a ship might carry 6000 amphorae, each weighing 50 kilos. Photo by author.

Apart from the army, the only respectable occupations for the upper classes were the law and politics, since so many professional posts in such fields as architecture, medicine, surgery, dentistry, teaching and agricultural management were held by freedmen. This left a sizeable group of educated, if not always aristocratic, unemployed, many of whom pursued the calling of client. Queues of them formed at dawn at the houses of the rich, waiting patiently in their best clothes for some pathetic gift of money or food, which the patron solemnly dispensed to each in order of social seniority. Called the '*salutatio*', this alms-giving often took place in the atrium (receiving room) of the Roman house (see Chapter 7).

> Now the meagre handout is sitting on the doorstep for the toga-wearing rabble to grab. The master scrutinizes your face first – he's afraid that you are an impostor and have come to claim the handout under a false name. You'll get it if he recognizes you. He orders a slave to summon the nobles – they claim descent from the Trojans – who are irritating the doorstep as much as we are. 'Give a handout to the praetor first, then to the tribune.' But a freedman is in front. 'I was here first,'

he says. 'Why should I be afraid or hesitate to keep my place? The tribunes will wait, let money talk. The man who has just come into the city with feet whitened with the chalk-dust of slavery shouldn't give precedence to the sacred rank of a tribune.'

(Juvenal, *Satires* 1.95–111; trans. Clive Letchford)

The more humble or poorer clients would do the rounds of patrons to collect as many donations as possible. That done, the client would return to his writing, if he was a poet like Martial, or mingle with the crowds in the Forum or the market, which were as much meeting-places as centres of public or private business, or read the daily newspaper which was posted up in various public spots, or take an early bath. For, after work, for women as well as men, a visit to the public baths was usually the order of the day (see Chapter 7). For the better-off poet, or one such as Horace, who boasted a generous patron, the day was less active:

I lie in until eight o'clock, then take a walk or, after reading or writing something which will satisfy me during times of contemplation, rub myself down with oil . . . But when the noonday sun tells my exhausted frame that it is time for the baths, I avoid the Campus and the game of ball. After a light lunch, enough to prevent my having to last out the day on an empty stomach, I loaf around at home.

(*Satires* 1.6.122–128)

THE ROLE OF WOMEN

'Our ancestors, in their wisdom, considered that all women, because of their innate weakness, should be under the control of guardians' (Cicero, *Pro Murena* 12). The guardian might be father, husband or male relative, or someone appointed by the will of the father or husband, or by an official of the state. The only exceptions up to the time of Augustus were the six Vestal Virgins; after Augustus, the rule was relaxed in cases of free-born women who had had three children and freedwomen who had had four, provided that there was no father or husband to exercise control. Of fundamental importance when engaging in a study of women in Rome is to remember that nearly all the voices of Roman women, from literature to tombstones, are recorded by men. Nothing, it seems, was a woman's own:

Your maidenhead is not entirely yours: a third belongs to your father, and a third to your mother. You own the rest. Don't resist your parents: they have handed over their rights of guardianship to their son-in-law, together with your dowry.

(Catullus, Poem 62.63–66)

It was customary for marriages to be arranged, and the size of the dowry was expected to match the social standing of the prospective bridegroom:

> To Quintilian
>
> Though you yourself have few needs and have brought up your daughter as befits a child of yours and a grandchild of Tutilius, she is, however, to be married to a man of great distinction, Nonius Geler, whose status in the community demands a certain ostentation by way of gowns and attendants (not that these enhance a bride's value, only show it off to its best advantage). Now I know that you are not blessed with as much wealth as you are with intellect. So I am taking upon myself part of your responsibility and, in the capacity of an additional father, propose to settle on our girl fifty thousand sesterces. It would be more, but I reckon only an insignificant sum could prevail over your modesty and, that being so, you will not refuse it.
>
> **(Pliny the Younger, *Letters* 6.32)**

In the history of letter-writing, few men do a better job of recording their tact and generosity than Pliny the Younger (see Chapter 8).

There were several ways of celebrating a **Roman marriage**, of which the simplest involved the consent of both parties, without rites or ceremony. The three others each gave the husband legal power over his wife (*manus*):

1 By cohabiting for a year without the woman being absent for more than a total of three nights (*usus*).
2 By a symbolic form of purchase, in the presence of a holder of a pair of scales and five witnesses (*coemptio*).
3 By full ritual (*confarraetio*), in the presence of the *pontifex maximus*. This was obligatory for patrician families, and comprised a form of religious service with prayer, a bloodless sacrifice, the offering and eating of sacred bread, and the taking of auspices. The bride and bridegroom sat on two chairs, bound together and covered with lambskin.

The first two – 'making use of' (*usus*) and being 'bought' (*coemptio*) in a notional sale – fail to escape the implication that women are treated as property, though the final ritual (*confarraetio*), reserved for the upper classes, implied some level sharing in the ritual bread-breaking (from the Latin *farraeus*, a spelt cake).

After the second century AD a different kind of ritual emerged, which began with a formal betrothal, at which the prospective bride slipped a gold ring on to the finger now known as the 'wedding finger' in the presence of guests. For the marriage ceremony itself, she wore a veil of flaming orange-red, surmounted by a simple wreath of blossom. There was animal sacrifice and the inevitable examination of the entrails for happy omens, after which the couple exchanged vows and the guests shouted their congratulations. In one of his poems (number 62) Catullus describes a raucous exchange between the boys and girls at a wedding that would not be out of place in a modern Bollywood movie.

Funerary inscriptions provide further insights into what married life was like in the Roman world. It is worth noting that these monuments, like literature, were often of the work of a grieving husband; as such, they probably represent more of an 'ideal' image of a wife than the reality. For example, husbands sometimes claim that they lived *sine querella* ('without a quarrel') for a number of years. The images they invoke, often in the form of superlatives – *carissima* ('most dear'), *castissima* ('most chaste'), *piissimia* ('most pius') – tend to refer to the aspect of a wife most valued by her husband: namely, fidelity. A first-century BC monument to Aurelia Philematio and her husband Aurelius Hermia (two slaves who had been freed during their lives – as indicated by 'L. L: *Lucii libertus/a*') (see Appendix 2) depicts the couple in the centre of the relief and Aurelia's head is covered. She looks down (in a gesture of modesty), but her hand is joined with Hermia's (*dextrarum iunctio*), as it may have been when they were ritually bound during the marriage ceremony. At first Aurelia is described in a typical manner: chaste, modest, unknown to the crowds and faithful to her man. However, the nature of their relationship appears mixed, as Hermia records that he was 'more than parent', taking her 'on to his lap when she was only seven years old' (Figure 6.4). There are clearly different ways of interpreting this passage, but (regardless of one's interpretation of *gremio* as 'lap' or 'bosom') this monument illustrates that the role of husband (especially with a marriageable age of twelve or thirteen) was, in some cases, more akin to that of a father. This could also explain the disparity often observed between husbands and wives; as not only a legal superiority but a simple age distinction. When assessing the role of Roman women, therefore, it is vital to consider context and to compare laws and recorded rituals with practice in the form of material culture and historical events.

In Roman times, women, though discriminated against and subjected to abuse by such poets as Horace and Juvenal (*c.* AD 55–*c.* 140), were still capable of standing up for themselves. One of the most contentious pieces of Roman legislation was the Oppian Law, introduced after Hannibal's victory at Cannae in 216 BC with the object of reducing spending on luxury goods: for example, no woman could possess more than an ounce of gold, wear a dress dyed in a number of colours, or ride about the city in horse-drawn carriage. Livy (34.1) describes the events of the year 195 BC, when a proposal to repeal the law was submitted to the Tribal Assembly:

> Neither modesty nor the persuasion or authority of their husbands could keep the women indoors. They blocked all the streets and entrances to the Forum,

FIGURE 6.4 Funerary monument to Aurelia Philematio and her husband Aurelius Hermia from the first century BC. Originally from Rome, now in the British Museum (reg. no. 1867,0508.55). Photo © The Trustees of the British Museum.

> vociferously arguing that at a time of prosperity, when men's personal fortunes were increasing daily, women too should be restored to their former splendours. The press of women increased day by day, as they came in from the towns and outlying districts. They even grew so bold as to waylay and interrogate the consuls, praetors and other officials.

There was a prolonged and impassioned debate, in which Cato the Elder, ever for austerity, argued to keep the bill (see Chapter 2).

> The next day an even greater crowd of women poured out of their houses into the streets, and mass-picketed all the entrances to the homes of the two Brutuses, who had announced that they were vetoing their colleagues' proposal. Nor would they let up until the tribunes agreed to withdraw the veto. There was now no doubt that all the tribes would vote for the motion: the law was duly rescinded, twenty years after it had first been passed.

> **(Livy, 34.8)**

While laws, literature and depictions of the 'ideal' woman in literature create one image of a caged woman, other accounts of women in politics can provide an interesting contrast.

In such a restricted environment, it is not surprising that there seems to have been a comparatively small number of women in professional jobs. There are, however, records of a few female doctors, clerks and secretaries, hairdressers (for whom training was obligatory), teachers, and the occasional fishmonger, vegetable-seller, dressmaker and wool or silk merchant. There were certainly female gladiators, too. Martial makes a point of mentioning them in his book celebrating the shows put on by Titus in AD 80 in the recently completed Colosseum:

> You demand more, Caesar, than to be served under unconquerable arms by warlike Mars: Venus herself is also at your command . . . Noble tradition tells how Hercules slew the lion in the wastes of the Nemean valley. Let the ancient tale be reduced to silence: after your shows, Caesar, we can say that we have seen such deeds performed by a woman's hand.
>
> **(Spectacles 7, 8)**

It would seem, from a relief now in the British Museum, that when women fought each other in the arena, they did not wear helmets.

There were also prostitutes, who were required to register with the aedile (Figure 6.5). A law of Augustus declared adultery by women a public offence. A subsequent court ruling forbade men from having sex with an unmarried or widowed woman of the upper class, and banned upper-class women from having any sexual relationship outside marriage. This led some upper-class women to register as prostitutes, even though this barred them from receiving legacies. In AD 19, under Tiberius, the Senate eliminated this loophole by making daughters, granddaughters and wives of senators or equestrians ineligible to register as prostitutes. Caligula was the first to tax prostitutes, probably on a monthly basis, with the levy set at the sum they normally charged for a single sexual encounter (Suetonius, *Caligula* 11); and Alexander Severus used a tax on pimps and prostitutes to fund restoration of the public buildings where they plied their trades (*Historia Augusta* 24.3). Alongside these laws is the portrayal of figures such as Julia the Elder, Augustus' daughter (from a previous marriage), who was married (for the first time at the tender age of fourteen) to a series of Augustus' candidates for succession (Marcellus, Agrippa, then Tiberius). Utterly under her father's control, she flouted his marriage legislation with a number of affairs and debaucheries. When asked how all her children looked like their fathers, she allegedly replied, 'I only take on passengers when the boat is full' (Macrobius, *Saturnalia*, 2.5.9–10).

Another side to the legislation against women's adultery is reflected in the story of Lucretia (see Chapter 1), as told by Livy. She is technically – and, under laws passed in Livy's lifetime, legally – guilty and feels she must pay the penalty. Lucretia's nobility and constancy in legend are matched historically by Cornelia, mother of the brothers

FIGURE 6.5 Erotic floor mosaic (sometimes captioned 'prostitute with client') from the second half of the fourth century AD in a bedroom of the Villa del Casale, Piazza Armerina, Sicily. Photograph © Allan T. Kohl/Art Images for College Teaching, courtesy of the Museo Regionale della Villa Romana del Casale, Piazza Armerina.

Gracchus (see Chapter 2). With her husband, Tiberius Sempronius Gracchus, censor, twice consul and twice awarded a triumph for his victories, she had twelve children, only three of whom lived to adulthood. He died in 154 BC. Though she was still nubile, to judge from the fact that she had a proposal of marriage from King Ptolemy VIII, she preferred to remain a widow and dedicate herself to the upbringing and education of her children. That both her surviving sons were inspired by civic, rather than mere political, duty to bring about changes in the system suggests some maternal influence. Whether she actively motivated them, or tried to control their excesses of enthusiasm for their causes, is a subject of debate. Certainly, according to Plutarch, she prevailed upon Gaius to withdraw a law aimed at banning from public office anyone who had once been voted from office by the people, as had the tribune who tried to get his elder brother's land bill referred to the Senate.

After the death of her son Tiberius, Cornelia retired to a villa near Misenum, where twelve years later she was brought the news that Gaius had also been killed because of his beliefs. It was said that she bore their loss with the greatest nobility of spirit, and for the rest of her life devoted herself to literary and other cultural pursuits, and to entertaining learned men, particularly Greeks, who flocked to see her. Only a single whiff of scandal was ever attached to her name – that she was implicated in the death of her daughter's husband, Cornelius Scipio Aemilianus Africanus, conqueror of Carthage, who had nullified the operations of the Gracchi's agrarian commission by initiating a senatorial decree passing its powers to the consuls. After her death, the citizens of Rome erected a bronze statue of her, with the inscription 'Cornelia, mother of the Gracchi'.

As attested on their tombstones, Roman women were expected to possess considerable *pietas*, particularly to their husbands. The most patient wife, in this respect, seems to have been Octavia (*c.* 70–11 BC), sister of Octavian. She had only recently been married to Gaius Claudius Marcellus when, in 54 BC, Caesar proposed that she should marry Pompey (while Caesar himself married Pompey's daughter Pompeia). However, Pompey declined all offers, and Octavia remained married to Marcellus, with whom she subsequently had a son and two daughters. When Marcellus died in 40 BC, she was immediately married off to Marc Antony, as his third wife, to cement the agreement between him and Octavian to divide responsibility for the empire. That same year, Antony and Cleopatra's twins were born.

Antony and Octavia's daughter Antonia (grandmother of Nero) was born in 39 BC. Octavia spent that winter and the following year in Athens with her husband, after which, pregnant with their second child, she was sent back to Italy, while Antony dallied with Cleopatra in Antioch. In 35 BC, she returned (on behalf of Octavian) to Athens with troops, money and supplies for Antony, who accepted them but sent Octavia home without even bothering to see her. With Octavian and Antony at loggerheads in the Senate, Octavian begged her to leave her husband. Octavia refused. Her reward was to be divorced by Antony in 32 BC, while her brother went to war against her ex-husband and his mistress. After the death of the two lovers, Octavia brought up her three children with Marcellus and her two daughters with Antony, as well as Antony's three children with Cleopatra and his surviving children with his previous wife.

Certainly some women were able to attain a degree of education and to absorb and reflect the culture of the times. We are on shakier ground when trying to assess the characters of **imperial women**, especially the talented and politically adept models of two early imperial wives, Livia (58 BC–AD 29), wife of Augustus and mother of Tiberius, and Agrippina the Younger (AD 15–59), wife of Claudius and mother of Nero (see Chapter 3). Tacitus implies that both poisoned their husbands. Irrespective of whether suggestions of strings of other murders and, in the case of Agrippina, of lovers too (including her brother and her son) are justified, each woman undoubtedly manipulated the system to ensure that her son by an earlier marriage became emperor, and each of those sons eventually demonstrated considerable distaste for his mother.

Livia had a distinguished aristocratic pedigree, besides having been married to Tiberius Claudius Nero (d. 32 BC), who had, however, had a chequered political career. One of Caesar's right-hand men, he had advocated a reward for the dictator's assassins. He then supported Marc Antony's brother against Octavian at Perusia (see Chapter 3), joined Sextus Pompey in Sicily, and finally switched allegiance to Marc Antony in Greece. He and his family were allowed to return to Rome under the terms of the Treaty of Misenum (39 BC) between Octavian, Antony and Sextus Pompey. Soon afterwards, nineteen-year-old Livia – who was six months pregnant – and Tiberius divorced in order that she could marry Octavian, who had conveniently divorced his own wife. After they had faced down the public outcry over the circumstances of their marriage, the union, during which she received unprecedented honours, lasted for fifty-three years.

Though they had no children, she was in other respects a traditional and suc-cessful Roman upper-class wife who even spun and wove material for her husband's clothes. And, as a traditional Roman wife, she organized the household and much else besides: she received imperial clients and provincial embassies, commissioned public buildings and dedicated them in her name, established charities, presided at banquets. As a good wife should, she helped her husband with his correspondence, and altogether eased his imperial burden, while undoubtedly increasing her own influence. This unprecedented crossing of the boundary between private and public spheres made ancient historians such as Tacitus and Cassius Dio uneasy, and may be the reason for their hostility towards her. But there had never been a Roman empress before, and someone had to lay down the ground rules.

Livia filled the position very well, as is suggested by Augustus' public recognition of her role. Statues were erected to her. She sat with the Vestal Virgins at public shows, she had the right to manage her own affairs, and she was even granted the same tribunician privileges as her husband. In his will, Augustus formally adopted her into his line – with the name Julia Augusta – and subsequent empresses came to adopt the title of Augusta, too. Livia's prestige was such that she was awarded the services of a lictor to walk before her, but there is some confusion as to whether he ever materialized. When she died, the Senate voted that a triumphal arch should be erected in her memory. Her son Tiberius accepted it on her behalf, agreed to meet the cost, then forgot about it. She was finally deified in AD 42, at the instigation of her grandson Claudius.

The fifty-nine-year-old Claudius may have had Livia's role in public affairs in mind when he married his thirty-four-year-old niece Agrippina. As with Livia, much of what we know about Agrippina comes from historians to whom the notion of a woman wielding political clout was anathema. The eldest daughter of Claudius' brother and Vipsania Agrippina, granddaughter of Augustus, she was no stranger to public controversy. During the rule of Caligula, she and her two sisters were officially cited in prayers, but in AD 39 she was implicated in a plot to assassinate Caligula and banished. When recalled to marry Claudius, she established herself and her son by her first marriage in virtually unassailable positions.

She was granted the title of Augusta, which even Livia had not received until after her death. Her portrait, and details of her honours, appeared on the reverse of Claudius' coins, an unprecedented privilege for a ruler's wife during her lifetime. She rode in a ceremonial carriage such as was usually reserved for priests and holy statues, and extended her geographical influence by founding a settlement for army veterans at her birthplace in Germany. She also ensured that her nominee, Burrus, became sole commander of the imperial guard, and persuaded Claudius to betroth his daughter Octavia to him. The following year, AD 50, her son was formally adopted by Claudius and took the name Nero. Being three years older than Claudius' own son Britannicus, he took precedence over his stepbrother (and now his brother by adoption). If Agrippina was responsible for Claudius' death in AD 54, then it may have been because her husband's unpredictable nature made her position precarious, and because she wanted to exercise full control while Nero was still too young to take charge of his own affairs.

Not only was she now the widow of a god, but in the east she was herself hailed as divine. Even in Italy, she made her position clear: gold and silver coins of AD 54 carry portraits of her and Nero facing each other, but it is her inscription that surrounds them – 'Agrippina Augusta, wife of the divine Claudius, mother of Nero Caesar'; Nero's inscription is relegated to the reverse of the coin (Figure 6.6). She was, in effect, regent for her teenage son, but he was still influenced by Burrus and Seneca. When the situation began to unwind for Agrippina, the situation was reversed. Both heads still appear on the coin's obverse, but facing in the same direction, with Nero slightly obscuring his mother: the inscriptions have also changed places. Several factors, or a combination of them, have been suggested for Nero's decision to get rid of his mother. Agrippina wished to be seen to be in control. In the time of Claudius, she had attended meetings with foreign diplomats, but sat apart from the emperor. Now, on one occasion, it was clear that she intended to sit beside Nero on the platform. Seneca managed, by quick thinking, to circumvent a major lapse in protocol by whispering to Nero to rise and go to meet her. Agrippina interfered, too, in the emperor's emotional entanglements. Nero, who was psychotic about his personal safety, was probably also motivated by fear to take the actions he did. So, after several botched attempts, he successfully orchestrated the murder of a woman with a most remarkable curriculum vitae: to successive Roman emperors, she had been great-granddaughter, granddaughter (by adoption), sister, wife (and niece) and mother.

Although the reigns of Livia and Agrippina were long over by the third century AD, their legacies would be recalled by a number aspiring women in the later years

FIGURE 6.6 Gold *Aureus* issued in AD 54, the first year of Nero's reign, showing the new emperor and his mother face to face on the obverse (twice actual size). The inscription is hers; his is relegated to the reverse. The design was changed the following year to make both figures face in the same direction, with Nero partially obscuring Agrippina. Photo © The Hunterian, University of Glasgow, 2014.

of the Roman empire, including Julia Domna, mother of the emperor Caracalla (see Figure 7.1), Julia Maesa and Julia Mammaea, grandmother and mother, respectively, of the emperors Elagabalus and Alexander Severus (see Chapter 4).

SLAVES AND SLAVERY

By using slave labour, the Romans perpetuated an institution that had existed in Egypt since at least 2600 BC and was commonplace in the empires of China, India and Babylon as well as Greece. After the gradual decline of peasant farming in Italy from about 200 BC, Romans based much of the social and economic fabric of their empire on slavery. One of the functions of official provincial tax-collectors, especially in Asia Minor, was to kidnap potential slaves and ship them to the specialist slave markets, one of the biggest of which, at Delos, could process 10,000 men, women and children in a single day. Acquisition of slaves by conquest was standard practice. Julius Caesar records that during one of his campaigns of aggression, 'The next day the gates were broken down, there being no one to defend them, and the troops marched in. Caesar sold off the whole town lock, stock and barrel. The dealers gave him a receipt for 53,000 head of people' (*Gallic War* 2.33). This was not excessive by the standards of the time, especially as the warriors inside the town had gone back on their word. He was, however, more uncompromising on another occasion:

> Caesar, aware that his compassion was widely recognized, was not at all concerned that harsher treatment of the inhabitants of the town might be regarded as innate brutality, but at the same time he could not see any satisfactory outcome of his plans if more of the population in other parts of the country took the same action. He therefore decided to make an example of them to deter the rest. He spared the lives of those who had taken up arms against him, but cut off their hands, a punishment intended clearly to demonstrate the evil of their ways.
>
> **(*Gallic War* 8.44)**

Until the empire, marriage between slaves was not recognized, and their children automatically assumed the status of slave themselves. A slave could keep what he could save towards buying his freedom, but if he ran away and was caught, the punishment was either branding or death. There was hardly any aspect of daily life, or work, or the leisure industry, in which slaves were not involved, and their treatment, which was entirely the responsibility of their owners, varied according to their skills and the labour that was demanded of them. They were trained to fight each other, and wild animals, to the death in the arenas of the empire. It was from a training establishment for gladiators that Spartacus the Thracian led out a band of slaves and in 73 BC began his two-year campaign of revolt. During the later republic, gangs of slaves worked in fetters on the agricultural estates and were chained up in semi-underground barracks at night. Others did not suffer so much. Great numbers of herdsmen were required, and in 8 BC Gaius Caecilius Isodorus, himself a former slave, left a staff of 4116, most of whom would have been employed in this capacity. Cato the Elder, who acquired young slaves as an investment and sold them for a healthy profit after training, laid down that a staff of twelve (a manager and eleven hands) was the right number to work a farm of 150 acres devoted to olive-growing and sheep-rearing.

Slaves worked in the mines, and in the potteries. They constituted the state's labour force for building and maintaining public works, and in other government services, such as the mint and the grain supply; they were also its 'white-collar' workers, who kept the machinery of bureaucracy and administration ticking over. They served as clerks and accountants in private businesses, and as secretaries, teachers, librarians, doctors, scribes, artists and entertainers. And they were the private staff of villas, townhouses and palaces. Household slaves had perquisites. Even in the house of the bombastic and vulgar freedman Trimalchio, a character in Gaius Petronius' novel *Satyricon*, they got what was left over after the dinner parties, though this often came at the price of dramatic humiliation for the entertainment of his guests. In addition, Trimalchio names his carver 'Cut', so that he can wittily call and order him in a single phrase: 'Cut, Cut!' (*Satyricon* 31). In the course of a single evening, he strips and berates a slave, then rewards him with a silver cup, orders a clumsy slave to kill himself, then graciously pardons him, and finally announces his intention to free all his slaves upon his death.

> As he says this, a boy drops a wine glass. Trimalchio looks at him and says, 'Kill yourself, and be quick about it. You're such an idiot.' The boy immediately pleads with him, lip quivering. 'Why do you ask me?' Trimalchio replies. 'It's as if *I* were being a nuisance to *you*. I suggest you tell yourself to stop being an idiot.' We beg him and he finally lets the boy off.
>
> **(Petronius, *Satryicon* 52; trans. Clive Letchford)**

The poet Martial (*Epigrams* 8.23), by his own account, laid into his cook if a meal was not up to scratch:

> You think me barbaric, Rusticus, and too fond of my food, because I beat my cook when my dinner is below standard. If that seems to you a trivial reason for the lash, what other excuse is there to flog a cook?

Pliny the Younger would invite the better-educated members of his staff to join him after dinner for conversation, and remarked of his villa at Laurentum that most of the rooms in the wing which housed his slaves were also perfectly suitable for putting up guests. This kind of sentiment is echoed by Seneca, when he expresses one of the principles of Stoicism (see Chapter 4):

> Remember that he whom you call your slave came into life by the same route as you, basks in the same sky, and breathes, lives and dies in the same way as you do. You can observe the free man in him just as he can see the slave in you. In the proscriptions of Marius many high-born men, on the military ladder to a seat in the Senate, were reduced by fate to being shepherds or janitors. You look down at your peril on someone in whose place you could come to be even while you look down on him. I don't want to get too involved in the broader issues of the treatment of slaves, to whom in general we are extremely arrogant, cruel and abusive. This, however, is the sum of my advice: treat your inferiors as you would want to be treated by your masters.
>
> **(Epistles 47)**

Nevertheless, slaves could still suffer some unusually harsh punishment, as two accounts from the early imperial era testify:

> Vedius Pollio, Roman knight and a friend of the divine Augustus, practised his barbarity with the assistance of moray eels, into whose tanks he threw condemned slaves: not that wild animals would not do, but because with no other creature could he watch a man being torn to pieces utterly and instantaneously.
>
> **(Pliny the Elder, *Natural History* 9.39)**

> [In AD 61] the city prefect, Pedanius Secundus, was killed by one of his own slaves; the murderer had either been refused his freedom after the price had been agreed, or had fallen in love with a youth and could not bear to have his master as a rival. Whatever the reason, when the time came to take out to execution all the slaves of the household, as was the time-honoured tradition, there was almost a revolution as the people, bent on sparing innocent lives, got together and

besieged the Senate. In the Senate house itself there were those who protested that the punishment was unfair, though the majority saw no reason why the law should not be observed.

(Tacitus, *Annals* 14.42)

While the experience of Roman slaves who worked on the vast estates of Italy was probably not much different from that of African slaves on the American and West Indian plantations in the eighteenth century (and while household slaves were probably no worse off than domestic staff in Europe at a later date), attempting to compare the systems of slavery in ancient and modern contexts can be problematic. However, it is worth noting a few fundamental differences in the Roman system. Roman slaves came from all over the known world, from a number of cultures, races and religions. In some cases, such as the historian Polybius (see Chapter 2), taken as a war hostage from Achaea, they were highly educated. The range of roles they could occupy was, therefore, diverse (as witnessed above). Perhaps more importantly, slavery was not a lifelong sentence in the Roman empire. Emancipation, such as that promised by Trimalchio, was a viable prospect. A slave could purchase his freedom or achieve it by a process of manumission, which was at the discretion of the owner but became so popular at the beginning of the empire that Augustus introduced laws to restrict it. Freedmen had full rights of citizenship except that of holding public office, and some became even richer than the masters they had once served. Others also influenced affairs of state, as did Claudius' personal advisers. Only from about AD 100 did equestrians start to replace freedmen as senior civil servants.

Cicero's slave, Tiro, who is credited with the creation of a form of shorthand, remained with his master even after he was freed in 53 BC, and he is mentioned repeatedly in Cicero's letters to his friends. While slaves in the countryside, the gladiatorial barracks and the quarries (who are most often associated with inciting rebellion) had very difficult lives, urban slaves were surrounded by freedmen who had earned their freedom, set up successful businesses and retained positive working relationships with their former employers (often by offering 'mates' rates'). These slaves were brought into a comfortable Roman household, where they learned the language and a trade. They sometimes even received an honourable mention on the family burial monument (see above). The social mobility of freedman clearly had its limits. However, the fact that wealthy, aspirant freedmen such as Trimalchio became objects of ridicule for imperial court poets such as Petronius, Martial and Juvenal suggests that they could achieve sufficient levels of success to provoke resentment and bitterness among impoverished members of the elite.

EDUCATION

At the beginning of the republic, education was a case of *mos maiorum*, being left entirely to the parents, and consisting of a mixture of martial and practical arts. Boys were expected to emulate their fathers, and girls their mothers. From about 250 BC, largely as a result of the influx of educated Greek slaves, tutors were employed in richer homes or were set up as teachers of informal schools. Towards the end of the republic, a two-tier educational system evolved, leading to higher education in oratory and philosophy.

At about the age of seven, children of the privileged classes were sent to a primary school (often presided over by a single teacher), where from dawn to the middle of the afternoon, with a break for lunch at home, they learned reading, writing and arithmetic. Girls as well as boys could benefit from this basic schooling, which seems often to have been in premises designed as shops, with an open front on the street. Pupils sat on wooden benches and wrote out their exercises on tablets which they rested on their knees. While the lack of identifiable school buildings has been used to cast aspersions on the amount of general schooling that took place in the ancient world, it is equally possible that a number of public venues (temple steps, theatres or arenas) were used for schooling, as is implied in Martial's description of urban cacophony (see above) and could be attested by the alphabet graffiti and game boards found on the steps and seats of public buildings throughout the empire. Formal education ceased for girls at the age of twelve, but boys who showed academic promise were sent on, if their parents could afford the fees, to 'grammar' school, where they remained until they assumed the *toga virilis*, pursuing a curriculum which emphasized Greek as well as Latin literature.

Much has been made, from allusions in literature and from an often-reproduced fresco uncovered at Herculaneum, of the brutality of schoolmasters. There seems, however, to be no evidence that corporal punishment in Roman times was any more frequent or severe than it was in many twentieth-century British schools. And though Horace writes of remembering verses 'dictated to me as a boy by flogger Orbilius' (Epistles 2.1.70–71), Suetonius describes a man who was less of a disciplinarian:

> Marcus Verrius Flaccus, a freedman, was renowned for his teaching methods. He stimulated his pupils' efforts by competition: setting those at the same level of attainment a subject on which to write and offering a prize for the best essay. This would be a book of antiquarian interest for its beauty or rarity. As a result of his success he was chosen by Augustus to teach his grandsons, and moved into the palace with his whole school on the understanding that he would not take on any more pupils.

> **(On Teachers 17)**

According to Suetonius, rhetoric was taught in schools 'in the early days'. By the time of Quintilian (towards the end of the first century AD), it had become accepted that rhetoric should be taught in special schools at a higher level, though a pupil might be expected to have had an introduction to the subject before embarking on higher education.

Rhetoric, as a subject as well as an art, originated in Sicily in the fifth century BC, and was developed in Athens and Asia Minor, before becoming an accepted subject for study in Rome. There were basically three branches of oratory: the display of one's art, often in the form of a panegyric or invective (the latter had its counterpart in the medieval Scottish 'flyting'); the persuasion of an audience to a particular point of view; and the defence or prosecution of a defendant in a court of law. Each of these involved five separate skills: selection of content; arrangement; language; memory; and delivery.

While the schools taught traditional religious observances and supplemented the training children received at home in conduct and morality, older boys, as they grew up, were also exposed to the influence of the various branches of Greek philosophy, in which the upper classes at least came to find a more acceptable guide to life than they did in the religion of the state. Leading citizens employed resident philosophers. When Cicero was about eighteen, he attended lectures in Rome given by Phaedrus the Epicurean; shortly afterwards, he listened to Philo of Larissa, head of the Academic school of philosophy, to whose doctrines he remained generally faithful for the rest of his life. When Horace was 18, he studied philosophy in Athens, where, in addition to the Academics and the Epicureans, he would have come under the influence of the Stoics and the Peripatetics (see Chapter 8).

Beyond the elitist oratorical education, many Romans, especially the freedmen of Petronius' *Satyricon*, admired the practical skills of numeracy, basic reading and/or a trade over elaborate but somewhat less useful talents:

> I didn't learn further maths, literary criticism or any rubbish like that. But I do know my letters and I can do any calculation when it comes to cash. Look, how would you like it if we had a little bet? Come on, I'm putting this on the table. You'll soon understand that your father has wasted his money on school fees, however well you understand literary criticism.
>
> **(Petronius, *Satyricon* 58; trans. Clive Letchford)**

DRESS

The Romans applied their ingenuity and use of basic materials and principles not only to solving complicated architectural and engineering problems, but also to their clothes. These had to be simple. Only wool and, to a lesser extent, linen were available, and because needles were of bronze or bone, and thread only of the coarsest quality, stitching or sewing was neither elegant nor particularly effective. Buttons and buttonholes were therefore rarities, and clothes were fastened or held together mainly with enormous safety-pins, belts, knots or not at all.

To say that the Romans slept in their underwear is not to suggest, as would be true of many later civilizations, that they did not wash, for bathing was a feature of daily life. It was simply that the time for taking one's bath was in the afternoon. A woman might have a brassiere in the form of a band, the purpose of which was to keep her breasts up rather than in. Otherwise, both men and women wore a loin cloth knotted round the waist, with a belted tunic or shift with short or long sleeves. The male tunic reached to the knees, while women and girls wore one that was longer, sometimes down to the ground. In winter a Roman might wear two tunics, one on top of the other; those particularly susceptible to cold, such as Augustus himself, might wear as many as four. For the poorer classes, slaves and small children, that was the limit of their attire, though Pliny the Elder allowed his shorthand writer to wear gloves in cold weather, which enabled the latter to continue to record his master's thoughts effectively.

The outer garment, the classic toga for men and the *palla* for women, was the standard, and statutory, formal dress for a Roman citizen (Figure 6.7). It was simply a vast blanket of undyed light wool, draped round and over the body, leaving one arm free, and probably held together only by its own weight and its folds, or by faith alone. The *palla* was rectangular in shape. Archaeologists and scholars have concluded, from practical experiments, that the toga was in the form of a segment of a circle, along the straight edge of which ran the purple stripe of the *toga praetexta* (worn by children and certain officials, and latterly by men of senatorial rank), and that it was about five metres long by two metres wide (at its widest point). Putting it on, getting the folds to fall correctly and keeping it adjusted while performing daily tasks appear to have been almost as problematic for the Romans as they have proved to be for modern scholars: Suetonius clearly admires Vespasian's unusual talent for conducting conversations with callers while getting dressed. Those who were standing for public office were in the habit of whitening their togas with chalk, and were thus known as *candidati* ('clothed in glittering white'). For dinner parties, at which the toga could have been an intolerable burden, it was often replaced by the *synthesis*, a kind of dressing-gown. Martial is particularly biting about a rich acquaintance who changed his *synthesis* eleven times during a single meal. The emperor Elagabalus insisted on wearing only brand-new togas, and this was considered a great extravagance (although, to be fair, 'cleaning' a toga often involved soaking it in vats of urine mixed with a clay detergent).

Cloaks were worn out of doors in bad weather. There was little difference between the footwear of men and women; both usually wore sandals tied round the

FIGURE 6.7 Relief from the *Ara Pacis* (now in the Ara Pacis Museum, Rome). The *Ara Pacis Augustae* (Altar of Augsustan Peace) was commissioned by the Senate in 13 BC to mark Augustus' safe retrun from Gaul and Spain. It was dedicated on the Campus Martius in 9 BC. Depicting various members of the imperial family, including women and children, it illustrates the standard toga (on the men) and the equally complex *palla* on the women. One wonders how Romans, and especially young children, managed in this complicated attire; indeed, the youngest boy, holding his mother's hand, grips his toga with his left hand and appears to be almost stepping on it with his right foot. Similarly, both men and women seem to have at least one hand affixed to their clothing at all times in a gesture of modesty, necessity, or perhaps both. Photo by author.

ankle with thongs, and on more formal occasions the *calceus*, a soft leather shoe. For men, shaving was the rule between about 100 BC and AD 100, performed with iron razors by a slave or at one of the innumerable barber's shops that were a feature of urban life. Women wore their hair up in a variety of styles, varying between the simple, often with a knot or lock at the back falling to the nape, and the intricately curled and over-ornate.

FOOD AND DRINK

The ordinary Roman diet was fundamentally more vegetarian based; the word *frumentum* (grain) also means military food supplies or rations. The army diet, which was carefully supervised, was a balanced one of grain (which the soldiers themselves ground and made into porridge, bread or biscuits), some meat (usually bacon), fish, poultry, cheese, vegetables, fruit, salt, olive oil and raw wine. When there was a delay in getting the grain ration through and meat had to be substituted, the soldiers complained. Officers fared rather better, even in what has been traditionally regarded as the most uncomfortable posting of all – northern Britain. Entries in documents (in the form of thin wooden tablets) relating to the accounts of the commanding officer's household in about AD 100, found since the 1970s at the fort of Vindolanda on Hadrian's Wall, record fresh produce such as pork crackling, pork cutlets, pig's trotters, piglets, ham, chicken, venison, anchovies (or other small fish), oysters, eggs, radishes, apples, lentils, beans, pork fat, lard and butter. At home, porridge and bread were the staple foods of most Romans, with many city-dwellers forced to rely on the grain dole for their needs (see the extract from Juvenal's *Satires* below).

In well-to-do homes the regimen was different. *Jentaculum* (breakfast), for those who wanted it, might be bread dipped in wine, or eaten with cheese, dried fruits or honey. The equivalent of lunch was *prandium*, again a light meal, often consisting of left-overs from the previous day. The main meal of the day, *cena*, was eaten in the middle of the afternoon, after work and the daily bath, and could – and often did – go on for hours. Dinner parties were elaborate, and could be dignified or disgusting affairs, depending on the discrimination of the host and his choice of guests. Cicero wrote to his friend Atticus that when Julius Caesar stopped overnight at his country villa in Pozzuoli (Puteoli) in 45 BC with his retinue (who had to be entertained in three dining rooms), Caesar 'had a bath at about one . . . oiled his body, and came into dinner. He took an emetic, and so was able to eat and drink to excess, with obvious enjoyment' (*Ad Atticus* 13.52). Dinner guests reclined on their left elbow at an angle of about forty-five degrees to the table, on couches set against three sides of it, and ate with their fingers.

The meal consisted of three parts, within each of which there could be any number of courses, served individually or together. Hors d'œuvre might be eggs presented in a variety of ways, salads, cooked vegetables, shellfish, snails and occasionally stuffed dormice (Figure 6.8). The main courses could include anything from beef, lamb, pork, venison, hare, bream, hake, mackerel, mullet, oysters, sole, chicken, duck, goose and partridge to veal, sucking pig, boar, wild goat, porpoise, crane, flamingo, ostrich and turtle-dove. In the dinner at Trimalchio's house, form was clearly valued over substance:

> So we took our places at last. Some boys from Alexandria poured snow-cooled water over our hands and others took their place and gave attention to our feet and removed our hangnails with great skill. They were not silent even in this tedious task but they kept on singing as they went. Anyone who was asked to bring anything did the same – you would think you were in the middle of the chorus of a pantomime, not the dining room of a leading man. The starter was brought in – very luxurious . . . On the platter there was a donkey made of Corinthian bronze which had two saddle-bags. There were black olives in one and green olives in the

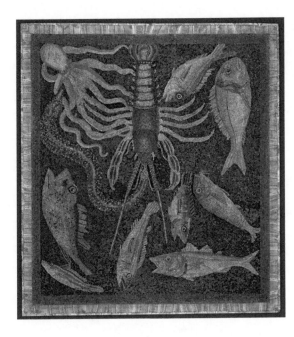

FIGURE 6.8 A panel from a mosaic floor, c. AD 100, depicting fish from the Mediterranean: (clockwise from top left) octopus, spiny lobster, dentex, gilt-headed bream, red mullet, comber (*serranus*), common bass (bottom right), green wrasse, rainbow wrasse, scorpion fish, moray eel. Now in the British Museum (reg. no. 1989,0322.1). Photo © Trustees of the British Museum.

other. Two dishes accompanied the donkey and Trimalchio's name and their weight in silver was inscribed on the edges. Metal stands held dormice sprinkled with honey and poppy seeds. There were sizzling sausages arranged on a silver griddle and, beneath the griddle, Syrian plums and pomegranate seeds.

(Petronius, *Satryicon* 31; trans. Clive Letchford)

We know how some of the dishes were cooked from the only surviving Roman cookery book. It is attributed to a noted gourmet of the time of Tiberius called Apicius, who, it is said, having spent nine-tenths of his considerable fortune on good living (which still left him with ten million sesterces), killed himself. The book is a later compilation, and many of the recipes have been made to work under modern conditions. They reveal that the ambitious host was usually more concerned with exotic ingredients than with exotic tastes – for instance, peacock features, but only as rissoles. Most main dishes were served in sauce, the basic ingredient of which was a factory-made fish stock called *liquamen* or *garum*, concocted from the entrails of mackerel. The meal would finish with dessert: fruit, cakes and puddings.

In marked contrast to Trimalchio's exotic buffet, at a seven-person dinner party in the country Martial offered his guests:

Mallow leaves [good for the digestion] . . . lettuce, chopped leeks, mint [for burping], rocket leaves . . . mackerel garnished with rue and sliced egg, and a sow's udder marinated in tuna-fish brine . . . that's the hors d'œuvre. For the main course, all served together, tender cuts of lamb, with beans and spring greens, and a chicken and a ham left over from three previous dinners. When you are full, fresh fruit and vintage wine from Nomentum with no dregs.

(Epigrams **10.48.7–19)**

Wine was the national, and natural, drink, usually diluted with water; beer was for Britons and Gauls. Wine was also mixed with honey to make *mulsum*, a cooling aperitif which accompanied the first course at dinner. This was usually made from must, the first treading of the grapes, but Pliny the Elder recommended that dry white wine should be used instead. For those modern readers inclined to try, about two tablespoonfuls of honey to a bottle of wine has been suggested. The best wine-producing region in Italy was on the border between Latium and Campania, from which came the excellent Caecuban, Setian, Falernian and Massic vintages.

HOLIDAYS AND THE GAMES

So what about the Roman rabble? They follow success – as always – and hate those who have been found guilty. If fortune had smiled on Sejanus and Tiberius had been struck down while off-guard, the same people would have proclaimed Sejanus emperor within the hour. Since none of us sells our votes any more, the rabble has cast off any worries. The rabble used to grant power, consulships, legions – everything. But now it keeps to itself and only has two things it really wants – bread and circuses.

(Juvenal, *Satires* 10.77–81; trans. Clive Letchford)

While Juvenal associates the public's love of 'bread and circuses' with their loss of voting privileges under the empire, it is worth noting that games had existed (and were popular) throughout the republican period. However, the games, and indeed the venues where they were staged, were taken to a whole new level under imperial munificence.

Not only was the official Roman working day a short one by modern standards; there were comparatively few working days in the year, except for slaves, who in any case were not allowed to attend public entertainments as spectators. In the reign of Claudius, 159 days of the year were designated public holidays, on 93 of which shows were offered at public expense. By the middle of the fifth century AD, there were 200 holidays a year, on 175 of which public games were held. Originally these games had religious significance, but under the republic ever more secular games were introduced into the calendar, ostensibly to celebrate notable events, some of which lasted as long as a fortnight. There were two kinds of games: *ludi scaenici* (theatrical events) and *ludi circenses*.

That the *ludi scaenici* suffered overwhelming competition from the other forms of spectacle is attested by the much smaller audiences that the stage theatres seated (see Chapter 7), by the fewer days allocated to them, and by the evidence of the playwright Terence (*c.* 185–159 BC). A revival of his comedy *The Mother-in-Law* was staged as a part of the funeral games in 160 BC for Lucius Aemilius Paullus, who had been twice consul, and censor, while mixing cultural sensitivity with considerable brutality. All was going well during the first act, Terence says in a prologue to a further performance that year, when someone announced that the gladiatorial show was about to begin. The audience did not so much melt away as surge out.

Ludi circenses took place in the custom-built circuses, or race-tracks, and amphitheatres. In these days of live, and televised, sporting mass entertainments – motor-racing, horse-racing, physical team sports such as soccer and rugby, football played under American and Australian rules, and even cricket played between teams wearing coloured tracksuits – it should not be difficult to appreciate the Romans' passion for chariot-racing. One can understand, too, their devotion to the particular team they supported – and its colours of white, green, red or blue – while not necessarily condoning the violence that often ensued between gangs of rival supporters. The public acclaimed the most successful drivers, and there was heavy on-course and off-course betting. The drivers were slaves, but they were also professional sportsmen who could earn vast sums.

The chariots themselves were deliberately constructed to be as light as possible, and were drawn by two, four or sometimes even more horses; the higher the number, the greater was the skill required of the driver, and the more sensational were the crashes and pile-ups. A race was usually seven laps of the track – a total of about 4000 metres in the Circus Maximus in Rome – with a hair-raising 180-degree turn at each end of the *spina*, the narrow wall that divided the arena. Though the start was staggered, there were no lanes and apparently no rules, yet during the first and second centuries AD several star charioteers notched up over 1000 wins each, and there are records of individual horses being in a winning team several hundred times. Gaius Appuleius Diodes, who died at the age of forty-two after driving four-horse chariots for twenty-four years, earned 1462 wins from 4257 starts (and he was placed 1437 times). In the reign of Augustus there might be ten or twelve races in a day; during and after the time of Caligula, twenty-four a day was commonplace.

Of course, the *ludi circenses* of the amphitheatres have given the Romans a deserved reputation for blood lust, though there is some evidence that the Etruscans also attached religious significance to the gladiatorial combat. The single rule of such bouts was that similarly armed contestants or teams of contestants did not normally fight each other. The most usual contest was between a moderately protected and

FIGURE 6.9 Floor mosaic from the Villa Borghese, Rome, c. AD 320. The scene depicts a gladiator, Astacius, twice: first in a victory stance (top middle) and defeating Astivus. The Greek letter theta (circle with a line through it) refers to the death (*thanatos*) of the gladiators at the bottom of the mosaic. © 2014. Photo Scala, Florence, courtesy of the Ministero Beni e Att. Culturali.

helmeted swordsman and a *retiarius*, armed only with a net and a trident (Figure 6.9), or between teams of these. It was each man for himself, and any who appeared less than enthusiastic were prodded into activity with red-hot irons, while other attendants stood by to drag off the corpses. It was sometimes left to the crowd to signify whether a wounded and downed gladiator should be finished off by his opponent. They did so by waving their handkerchiefs for mercy, or giving the 'thumbs down' signal for death. Gladiators were slaves, or condemned criminals, or prisoners of war, all of whom were regarded as expendable.

The same was true of wild animals, which were rounded up in their natural habitats and transported in their thousands to be hunted down and slaughtered in the confines of the arenas of the Roman empire, as a morning's overture to the gladiatorial contests in the afternoon. To celebrate the opening of the Colosseum in AD 80, 5000 wild beasts and 4000 tame animals were killed in one day. For variety, animals would be goaded to fight each other: elephants versus bulls was a feature of a games in 79 BC. Nero introduced a novel turn, the marine contest: 'Fights between wild animals of the forests are less interesting, now that we have seen seals against bears' (Calpurnius, *Eclogues* 7.64–65). Alternatively, or as an additional attraction, the animals might tear apart contingents of condemned and unarmed criminals. Martial (*On Spectacles* 7) records the epic death of a criminal called Laureolus, who was mauled by a bear for his gruesome crimes:

> As Prometheus was trussed up on a Scythian rock . . . so Laureolus dangling on a
> cross, defenceless, relinquished his guts to a Caledonian bear. His mauled limbs
> survived though the parts dripped with gore, and his whole body had lost the

appearance of a human form. The punishment was deserved: we are told he had either murdered a parent, robbed a temple, or set fire to the city.

The more gruesome the crime, the more violent the death. Even in capital punishment, the Romans showed both creativity and flair. Different types of combat (and their musical accompaniment), such as hunts and gladiatorial fights, are depicted on the Zliten Mosaic (now in the Jamahiriya Museum in Tripoli, Libya).

The third and most spectacular form of combat, which involved flooding the arena or transferring the whole show to a suitable stretch of water, was the *naumachia*, or sea-fight. The idea seems to have originated with Julius Caesar, an impresario of great ingenuity and ambition. He had an artificial lake dug, on which he pitted against each other two fleets of 10,000 oarsmen, with 1000 soldiers dressed up to represent men of Tyre and Egypt. Particularly popular in later years was a reconstruction of the Battle of Salamis (480 BC), which was replayed several times during the first century AD. Claudius staged the biggest *naumachia* of all in AD 52:

> The tunnel dug through the mountain between the Fucine lake and the river Liris had now been completed. [Brick-lined, and 5600 metres long, it had taken 30,000 workmen eleven years to construct.] In order that as many people as possible might admire the impressiveness of the achievement, a naval battle was arranged on the lake itself . . . Claudius put 9000 armed combatants into two fleets of ships with both three and four banks of oars. He positioned rafts round the edge of the lake to block off any escape routes, leaving enough space in the middle for the display of the power of the oarsmen, the skill of the coxes, the speed of the ships, and all the other arts of such a contest. Platoons and companies of the praetorian cohorts were stationed on the rafts, protected by ramparts, from behind which they fired catapults and missile-throwers. Covered ships manned by marines occupied the rest of the lake . . . The battle, though contested by criminals, was fought as bravely and spiritedly as if the combatants were men of free will, and after considerable bloodshed they were excused death.
>
> **(Tacitus, *Annals* 12.56)**

Hazards were not always confined to the arena itself. When the Circus Maximus was still used for gladiatorial contests, Pompey put up iron barriers to protect the audience during a fight between twenty crazed elephants and bands of armed hunters. The barriers buckled and some of them broke. In AD 27, a jerry-built amphitheatre at Fidenae collapsed, throwing 50,000 spectators (according to Tacitus; a mere 20,000, according to Suetonius) to the ground and burying them in debris. A redeeming feature of this disaster was the way in which emergency services were provided by the rich, who drafted in medical supplies and doctors from their own households. The government's response was to issue guidelines for such entertainments: 'No one with a capital of less than 400,000 sesterces may present a gladiatorial show, and an amphitheatre may only be built on solid ground' (Tacitus, *Annals* 4.63).

FURTHER READING

* indicates sourcebook

Adkins, L. and Adkins, R.A., *Handbook to Life in Ancient Rome*, Oxford University Press, 1998 (new edition).

Barrow, R., *Greek and Roman Education*, Bristol Classical Press, 1998.

Bauman, R.A., *Women and Politics in Ancient Rome*, Routledge, 1994.

Bradley, K., *Discovering the Roman Family*, Studies in Roman Social History, Oxford University Press, 1991.

Bradley, K., *Slavery and Society at Rome*, Cambridge University Press, 1994.

*Cooley, A.E. and Cooley, M.G.L., *Pompeii: A Sourcebook*, Routledge, 2004.

Crook, J.A., *Law and Life of Rome*, Thames & Hudson, 1984 (new edition); Cornell University Press, 1984.

Croom, A.T., *Roman Clothing and Fashion*, Tempus, 2002.

Dalby, A., *Food in the Ancient World from A to Z*, Routledge, 2003.

Davies, J. and Wilkes, J. (eds), *Epigraphy and the Historical Sciences*, Oxford University Press, 2012.

Fantham, E. *et al.*, *Women in the Classical World*, Oxford University Press, 1994.

*Futrell, A., *The Roman Games: Historical Sources in Translation*, Blackwell, 2006.

Gardner, J., *Women in Roman Law and Society*, Routledge, 1987 (new edition).

*Gardner, J. and Wiedemann, T., *The Roman Household: A Sourcebook*, Routledge, 1991.

Habinek, T., *Ancient Rhetoric and Oratory*, Blackwell, 2004.

Harris, W.V., *Rome's Imperial Economy*, Oxford University Press, 2011.

Kleiner, D.E.E. and Matheson, S.B. (eds), *I Claudia II: Women in Roman Art and Society*, Yale University Art Gallery, 2000.

*Lefkowitz, M.R. and Fant, M.B., *Women's Life in Greece and Rome: A Sourcebook in Translation*, Duckworth, 2005 (3rd revised edition); Johns Hopkins University Press, 2005.

*Lomas, K., *Roman Italy, 338 BC–AD 200: A Sourcebook*, Routledge, 1996.

Mouritsen, H. *The Freedman in the Roman World*, Cambridge University Press, 2011

Robinson, O.F., *Ancient Rome: City Planning and Administration*, Routledge, 1992.

*Shelton, J.-A., *As the Romans Did: A Sourcebook in Roman Social History*, Oxford University Press, 1997 (2nd edition).

Stambaugh, J.E., *The Ancient Roman City*, Johns Hopkins University Press, 1988.

Treggiari, S., *Roman Social History*, Routledge, 2002.

Wiedemann, T., *Emperors and Gladiators*, Routledge, 1995.

*Wiedemann, T., *Greek and Roman Slavery: A Sourcebook*, Routledge, 1980.

*Pompeii and Herculaneum database: http://ancientgraffiti.wlu.edu/.

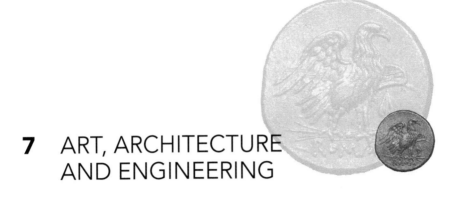

7 ART, ARCHITECTURE AND ENGINEERING

Rome's art and architecture found inspiration in a number of different cultures (Greek, Roman, Near Eastern), which were incorporated into different types and styles of buildings. The remains of Roman arches, columns, roads, aqueducts and statues, found in so many different locations across the globe, tend to imply the continuity of Roman architecture. This perspective, however, overlooks the most dynamic features of Roman building: how it adapted, like culture and religion, to varying locations, climates and people through a vast empire. For example, in Near Eastern cities such as Palmyra and Apamea, we find few (if any) examples of a 'forum' (an open square for a market); instead, there are long colonnaded streets with a covered portico. This not only represents local traditions but simple practicality: in a hot environment, an open market place is suboptimal. Equally, in drier climates, such as those of North Africa, large cisterns for collecting rainwater were more common than they were in the houses of Roman Britain (for obvious reasons). Although Romans could build free-standing theatres and amphitheatres, they continued to use natural features such as hills (e.g. the theatre at Orange) or to dig into the ground (e.g. the theatres at Palmyra and Pompeii). Hence, the adaptability and dynamic nature of Roman buildings and art played a crucial role in its acceptance and transmission across the empire.

The overriding impression the material arts of Rome offer is one of opulence, solid permanence and the application of practical skills that were largely inherited but also adapted to the economic and expansionist tendencies that resulted in the growth of the empire. Roman sculpture, learned from the Greeks and Etruscans, reached a peak in the first and second centuries AD which has hardly been matched since. It was, however, the development of the arch, the vault and the dome, and the use of concrete, which gave distinction, serviceability and grandeur to Roman domestic and public architecture and civil engineering. The ability to control light, water, temperature and physical space was, especially in an urban environment, both a boon and an ideological statement about the divine authority, security and superiority of Roman culture.

SCULPTURE

Two influences in particular drove the Romans to explore and develop the art of sculpture: the worship and reverence of images, not only of gods and goddesses but also of dead ancestors; and the recording of ritualistic and triumphant events in bas-relief on pillars, arches and tombs. Whereas the faces of Greek 'classical' portrait sculptures (e.g. the Parthenon sculptures or those at the Temple of Zeus, Olympos) tend to display an image of perfection rather than expression or emotion, the development of Roman sculpture represents a fascinating range of styles from Etruscan art (similar in some ways to Greek archaic art), such as the Louvre Vase (Figure 1.1), to Veristic styles in the late republic and Flavian periods (e.g portraits of Pompey (Figure 2.6) and Vespasian (Figure 3.6)). The drilling of the eyes in Roman portraits from the second century AD onwards, to indicate the ring of the iris and the reflection of light on the pupil, added further expression to such statues (Figure 7.1), and in the third and fourth centuries AD dramatic facial expressions were used to convey emotion (e.g. the portraits of the tetrarchs (Figure 4.5) and Constantine (Figure 4.8)). With the exception of Augustus' perpetual 'classical' youth and quadragenarian six-pack, Romans often favoured reality over flattery in their portraits, both on statues and on coins (see Figures 2.6, 3.2, 3.3, 3.6 and 4.3).

Similar transitions can be seen on public monuments, where the sculptural skills acquired during the later republic were breathtakingly employed to embellish the north and south friezes of the great marble edifice which is the *Ara Pacis Augustae* (see Figure 6.7; Map 5, no. 7). The life-size figures of Augustus and his extended family, officers of state, senators and priests, some with their wives and children, are caught in a moment of pause as they progress towards the entrance. The composition of this scene is beautiful, with the eye of the viewer led from character to character: children, on the lower part, tug on the adults' robes and look up towards them. Each individual plays a specific role, and it is not only their poses but their faces that make them real and relatable.

The *Ara Pacis Augustae* scene contrasts with reliefs from Trajan's column, set up in his imperial forum (*c.* AD 113; see Figures 9.1 and 9.2; Map 5, no. 10), which depict both his military victories and everyday life in the Roman army. While there are a number of portraits of Trajan himself, the art on this column is more narrative in style: telling stories through the scenes depicted rather than the figures themselves (more than 2500 in total were contained therein). The column is 30 metres high and the reliefs formed a spiral band about a metre deep and 200 metres long that wound 23

FIGURE 7.1 Portrait of Julia Domna from Gabii, c. AD 193–194, now in the Louvre (inv. no. MA1103). Compared with idealized and expressionless portraits of Livia and Agrippina, Julia Domna's inscribed eyes are penetrating, her raised brows (almost a unibrow) express concern and the dimples at the side of her mouth are almost a smile. Her real hair is hinted at by the soft locks at the side of her face beneath her heavy 'helmet-hair' wig. The Roman tradition that women took no official part in public life was conclusively broken by Julia Domna, who came from a royal priestly family in Syria and travelled with her husband Septimius Severus on his campaigns across the empire. Photo © RMN-Grand Palais (musée du Louvre)/Jean Schormans.

times round the column in 155 continuous scenes. The idea that anyone might have walked around the column twenty-three times in the small space afforded (the column was set between two libraries) is ridiculous (one starts to suffer from vertigo by about the fifth circuit). However, the seemingly endless catalogue of events (from sailing out of Italy, to setting up camp, to building a bridge) serves to illustrate the discipline and order that lay behind Rome's victories. It is a monument as much to the army as to Trajan himself. While Augustus depicts safety and security in Rome in an idealized civic scene, Trajan's image of Rome is much more martial.

Similarly, the column of Marcus Aurelius (see Figure 4.2) begun in AD 180 and completed in AD 192, which records his victories against the German tribes along the Danube, depicts increasing violence and suffering. The heads of decapitated barbarians are contorted and out of proportion, made abnormally large so the Roman audience is left in no doubt about their torment. This is conveyed with more dramatic drillwork which increases contrast but also has the effect of making the art look less natural (togas, for example, appear more thick and chunky). The brutal imagery reflects an empire at its height, in which the expression of dominance and might has superseded the desire to create a sense of security and peace; or, perhaps more honestly, it merely acknowledges the true cost of internal peace and prosperity.

Finally, as we advance into the tetrarchy, we lose the image of the individual almost completely, even when there are only a handful of people in a particular work of art (Figure 4.5). The portrait of the tetrarchs shows two pairs of individuals, almost indistinguishable from one another, clinging to each other in a desperate gesture of unity with one hand, while gripping their swords firmly with the other. Only a beard sets the older of the two men in each pair apart, and both look out determinedly with beady eyes and deep furrows between their brows. The natural, idealized youth of the Augustan age has been replaced with a more sombre, abstract and emotional image of a ruler, one that is more of an icon of a leader than a portrait of an individual, carved on shiny, dark purple porphyry stone from Egypt.

In the past, some scholars postulated that Rome's best artisans died of the plague in the fourth and fifth centuries, which caused her art to move towards abstraction (a bit like suggesting that all of the Impressionists had cataracts). However, when one considers the social, political and economic climate of the late empire, a more complex and deliberate development of artistic styles seems more likely.

PAINTING AND MOSAIC

Roman painting and mosaic, found both in private homes and in public buildings, such as baths, show similar developments over time. During the republic there was a vogue for collecting and exhibiting narrative paintings of battles and mythological scenes, mainly by artists from the Hellenistic world. Pliny the Elder is the source of information for some of these. An imaginative war artist depicted in 201 BC the victories of Cornelius Scipio Africanus over Hannibal in Africa. Lucius Hostilius Mancinus – who claimed, as a naval commander in the Third Punic War, to have been the first to break into Carthage – displayed paintings of his exploits in the Forum and provided a personal commentary. (One wonders if Trajan did the same for his column.) This stunt, according to Pliny, gained him a consulship in 145 BC. Julius Caesar dedicated the Temple of Venus Genetrix (his divine ancestor) in Rome and decorated it with two Greek mythological paintings and, according to Appian, a statue of his current mistress, Cleopatra.

In imperial times, as far as we know, paintings ceased to be portable and were used almost exclusively to cover walls inside houses. These frescoes, many of which are splendidly preserved at Herculaneum and Pompeii, are brightly coloured and often depict scenes from Greek mythology (see Figures 8.2 and 8.3). The art on display reflected the home-owner's taste: for instance, we are told that Trimalchio had two scenes from the *Iliad* and the *Odyssey* alongside a picture from a recent games of Laenas (rather like having Rubens and Renoir prints and a Manchester United poster on the same wall) (Petronius, *Satyricon* 28). Landscapes were employed to give the impression of picture windows – Nero's *Domus Aurea* even has some enclosed in window frames, which are also painted on the wall – while the effect of a garden was often extended and enhanced by landscape frescoes along its boundary walls. Still-life paintings and mosaics were also made of game birds, fish (see Figure 6.8) and vegetables. These may have represented the gifts that guests would take away from a party. Overall, these literary allusions, landscapes, depictions of exotic scenes and animals were designed to impress the viewer with the wealth and education of their patron, though some were clearly more successful than others.

The art of mosaic seems to have originated in Babylon, and it was widely practised in Egypt under the Ptolemies in the third century BC. Because a mosaic is comparatively indestructible and the medium spread throughout the Roman empire to its very outposts, it has come to represent Roman pictorial art to many who have never seen the sculptures and paintings which Italy has to offer. Museums, which often mount floor mosaics on walls, take the art both out of its original context (in a specific room) and out of the perspective from which it was meant to be seen (from above). There were three main kinds of mosaics. *Opus sectile* consists of small pieces of different-coloured marble cut into various shapes and fitted together in a geometrical pattern. In *opus tessellatum*, the dice are square and all of the same size. In *opus vermiculatum*, the dice are of varied shapes and sizes, sometimes of minute proportions, and are often set in wavy lines (*vermiculatus* means 'resembling the tracks of worms'). Sometimes more complicated works were made in a studio before being transferred to the site and embedded in concrete, either as wall decorations or as pavements. These might be scenes from legend or daily life, or even portraits. A fourth mosaic style, *opus incertum*, was much employed during the second century BC to decorate the walls of concrete buildings: it consisted of pieces of rubble fitted together to make rough patterns.

Mosaics follow similar themes to paintings, representing mythological and historical events (e.g the Alexander Mosaic from the House of Menander in Pompeii) or scenes from literature (see Figures 8.2 and 8.3) as well as exotic fauna (see Figure 6.8) and gladiatorial games or hunts (see Figure 6.9) in domestic contexts, such as houses. Like paintings, however, they were also used in commercial contexts: on the floors of taverns in Ostia, where they encouraged patrons to drink, labelling the stalls at the Piazzale delle Corporazioni (see Figure 6.3), and on the floors of public and private baths.

DOMESTIC ARCHITECTURE

Scholars like to distinguish between 'public' and 'private' space, while also often treating **'domestic' space** as a separate element. Although this approach can provide helpful distinctions, it is worth noting that domestic space was not necessarily private. Indeed, the process of *salutatio* (see Chapter 6) meant that a patron would receive many people in the atrium of his home, making this the most visible 'showroom' of a house where family relics were kept. The Roman tradition of hierarchy applied even inside the house, where certain parts of the building (often the peristyle gardens and dining rooms) were more 'private' than others, reserved only for distinguished guests and acquaintances.

The early Roman townhouse was little more than a single room, known as the atrium. The roof sloped inwards and downwards to a rectangular opening, beneath which was a basin, the *impluvium*, set into the floor to catch rainwater. The water in the *impluvium* was used for drinking (it was probably disinfected with a liberal amount of wine first), but it also had a decorative function (reflecting the sunlight in the room) and helped to regulate the temperature (water absorbs heat in the day and retains it longer at night). As time went on, small extra rooms were built inside the atrium, against its walls or separated off by partitions. By the second century BC, Greek influence had brought a further extension in the form of a *peristylum*, a garden court (sometimes with a fountain in the middle) surrounded by a colonnaded passage off which were further rooms (often dining rooms). Between the atrium and the *peristylum*, and opening into both, was the *tablinum*, which had various uses: dining room (especially in summer, when it would be the coolest part of the house), reception room, or office for the head of the household. A dining room is sometimes called *triclinium* in reference to the three couches that were often placed strategically below a wall painting (usually a mythological scene).

The house in Figure 7.2 is known as the House of the Vettii. It is located in Region VI of Pompeii, off the northern end of main north–south road in the city (the *cardo decumanus*) on a back street, across from a bar. The house (actually two houses that have been combined) was owned by a family of freedmen (their signet rings were found inside) who had only just redecorated after the earthquake of AD 62. The main entrance into the house was set back from the street and approached through a small *vestibulum*. Here, entrants to the house were greeted by a large painting of Priapus,

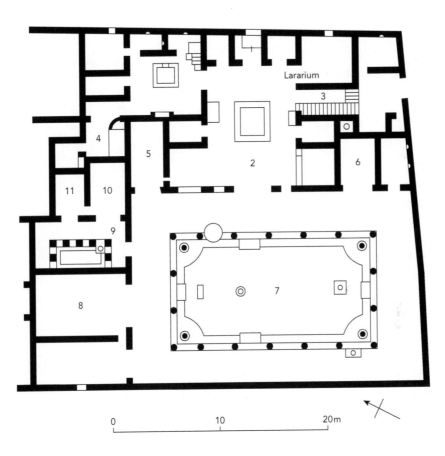

1. Vestibule
2. Atrium
3. Staircase to upper storey
4. Kitchen
5. Dining room (triclinium)
6. Dining room (triclinium 'Pentheus room')
7. Peristyum
8. Oecus
9. Small peristylum
10. Dining room/sitting room
11. Bedroom

FIGURE 7.2 Plan of the House of the Vettii, Pompeii.

the god of male potency, whose massive erection is weighed against piles of gold: welcome indeed! The larger and relatively brighter atrium, where light shone down and was reflected by the waters in the *impluvium*, housed a *lararium* (near the steps to the second storey), which is well preserved (see Figure 5.5). The atrium was dwarfed by the larger but more exclusive garden court (*peristylum*), which was surrounded by dining rooms. This garden was teeming with an array of bronze and marble statues as well as benches, pillars with herms and marble basins.

While one can easily imagine Trimalchio hosting a dinner party in something similar to the House of the Vettii, many Romans could not afford such extravagance, especially in an urban environment. For these individuals, there were apartments above shops (a feature of small towns) and apartment blocks called *insulae* in cities such as Rome (e.g. the Casa D'Aracoeli at the base of the Capitoline hill) and Ostia. Like modern apartment blocks, these offered various levels of amenities.

Urban congestion was a problem in Rome from early times. It has been estimated from statistics compiled at the time that in the second century AD there were only 1782 houses in the city, providing accommodation for 50,000 people, many of whom would have been household slaves. The other 1.5 million lived, as the majority do in Rome today, in tenement blocks, six or even seven storeys high. Augustus limited their height to twenty metres; Trajan lowered this to eighteen. Many of them were cheaply built on unsound foundations, so collapsed blocks were commonplace, rent irregularities were rife, and sanitation was superficial. Unlike modern blocks, where the penthouse is the height of luxury, comparatively well-to-do flat dwellers lived on the ground floor, which was cooler and had access to public sewers and/or a water source. Even in the purpose-built new-town apartment blocks of Ostia, such as the Insula of Diana (see Figure 7.3), ground-floor apartments were more spacious, with higher ceilings and more light. They were also closer to local amenities. Upper-floor tenants in Rome had to make their own arrangements, though there were public lavatories for those who could afford them and sometimes baths were even included in the apartment block. The rest had chamber-pots, the contents of which they emptied into a well at the foot of the stairs, or simply threw out of the window into the street below (a practice that continued in the overpopulated cities of Europe into the eighteenth century).

For the rich, there were two kinds of villa or country house. The *villa rustica* was a glorified farmhouse which contained living quarters for the owner of the estate when he happened to be in residence. The *villa urbana* was where one luxuriated or retreated for a holiday from the bustle of Rome, or stopped off for a night on a journey, or from which one commuted to the city. Cicero, who was by no means one of the richest men of his time, owned seven houses in the country, each of which he used from time to time. The poet Catullus praises his villa in Sirmio (Sirmione, on Lake Garda): 'Is there any greater blessing than to toss one's cares away, when the mind

FIGURE 7.3 The western façade of the Insula of Diana at Ostia. Photo © Houston, George (1968) 'Ostia house of Diana (II)' Ancient World Image Bank (New York: Institute for the Study of the Ancient World, 2009).

casts off its burden and exhausted by the rigours of travel, we come home and fall upon a longed for bed?' (Poem 31.7–10). Pliny the Younger had at least four villas, one of which, on the seashore at Laurentum (near enough to Rome for him to ride home after a full day's business in the city), was especially opulent.

In a typical villa the principal parts of the townhouse were usually reversed: the entrance opened into the *peristylum*, behind which was the atrium. Plans of villas that have been excavated reveal their shape, size and the probable uses to which the various rooms were put. In a letter to his friend Gallus, Pliny the Younger describes in detail what many of the rooms in his winter villa looked like, and for what they were used. Apart from the usual features, it had two towers, with bedrooms commanding magnificent views, a series of sitting rooms, several studies (one of which had built-in bookcases and received the sun all day through a bay window), a centrally heated bedroom, an outdoor gymnasium for the staff, a tennis court and a swimming-pool. Some, if not all, of the windows were glazed. The only drawback, according to Pliny, was that there was no running water, but he adds that there were three public baths in the nearby village if, for any reason, it was inconvenient to heat up the water at home. Central heating was invented by Sergius Oresta in about 100 BC and was achieved by circulating hot air from a furnace through cavities under the floor and inside the walls. Unsurprisingly, it seems to have been a common feature in British villas.

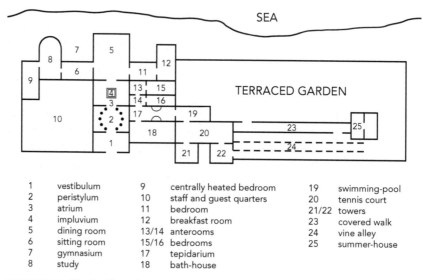

FIGURE 7.4   Pliny's villa at Laurentum.

1	vestibulum	9	centrally heated bedroom	19	swimming-pool
2	peristylum	10	staff and guest quarters	20	tennis court
3	atrium	11	bedroom	21/22	towers
4	impluvium	12	breakfast room	23	covered walk
5	dining room	13/14	anterooms	24	vine alley
6	sitting room	15/16	bedrooms	25	summer-house
7	gymnasium	17	tepidarium		
8	study	18	bath-house		

THE ARCHITECTURE OF PUBLIC BUILDINGS

At least three different types of buildings fall under the category of public buildings: temples, entertainment centres (theatres, circuses, amphitheatres and baths) and urban armatures (aqueducts, roads and monumental arches or fountains). While these structures had different functions, they all existed within the same urban space and thus were spatially, if not physically, associated with one another. These relationships are clearly evident in the most fundamental illustration of public buildings: Roman urban plans. While Romans are well known for their square grid pattern with a main north–south (*cardo decumanus*) and a main east–west (*cardo maximus*) road, often with a forum structure in the middle (e.g. the urban plan of Timgad, Algeria, an early second-century AD Roman settlement), the true nature of urban growth, as seen in the city of Rome (see Map 5), was often much more organic and disorganized.

Vitruvius' *De Architectura* (*On Architecture*), our foremost authority on the principles of **Roman architecture** during the reign of Augustus, records dimensions, proportions and canonical models for many of Rome's buildings. However, his 'ideal' Roman theatre has not yet been found, and he appears to have spent more time studying architecture than practising it. In fact, his descriptions of architectural ideals for all public buildings often do not match the surviving remains, in which adaptability to local climates, resources and traditions emerges as the principal defining feature of Roman architecture. This chapter will offer cases studies from Rome, from the western provinces of Gallia Narbonensis (modern Provence), such as Nemausus

(Nîmes) and Arausio (Orange), and from Roman Britain, such as Aquae Sulis (Bath) and Verulamium (St Albans), together with examples from eastern provinces, such as the city of Palmyra (Syria). This should lead to a better understanding of the Romans' dynamic approach to architecture, in terms of style, function and building materials.

The Romans clearly drew upon existing Etruscan and Greek traditions, including the three orders of architecture – Doric, Ionic and Corinthian, based on different forms of column and the capital that surmounted it – and added to them a hybrid of their own, known as Composite. However, these decorative similarities do not necessarily represent similarities in ideology or function. For example, while Greek temples tend to reflect symmetry (having a front and back porch with a low platform), Roman temples were planned axially (probably on an Etruscan model), with a frontal approach and a large podium that raised them higher off the ground. The Maison Carree in Nîmes (see Figure 5.4), a temple dedicated around 16 BC by Agrippa to his sons Gaius and Lucius, has a high podium and a large frontal porch (but no back porch), and the columns are engaged (carved into the *cella* building) rather than freestanding. As this building is contemporary with Agrippa's construction of the Pantheon, it could provide a model for the original form of that building (Map 5, no. 11).

Of course, as Roman engineering (particularly concrete) developed, so did her architectural pretensions. The emperor Hadrian could not resist employing a giant hemispherical dome (43.28 metres in diameter), which required a special 'super-light' concrete, in his restoration of the Pantheon (*c.* AD 120–124). This fundamentally changed the structure so that light fell only through a circular hole, eight metres wide, at the apex of the dome (Figure 7.5). Similarly, provincial temples show both tradition and innovation. The temple dedicated to Minerva Sulis at Bath (late first century AD) has a classic Roman-style plan – high podium, large front porch, frontal approach – but an unusual pediment decoration with a male face (perhaps a Gorgon). The Temple of Bel in Palmyra (first century AD) resembles a Greek-style temple with a *temenos* (a large outer area), a low podium and freestanding columns running along the outside, but its decoration, side entrance and two inner sanctuaries are clearly neither Greek nor Roman in origin.

Rome's entertainment buildings were defined by arches and barrel vaults that allowed the architects to build massive freestanding structures regardless of location or proximity to natural resources. The arch enables wide spaces to be crossed with the minimum of materials, thus relieving weight that would otherwise place an intolerable burden on the structure. *Pozzolana* (pumice), a chocolate-coloured volcanic earth, found first in Puteoli but also quarried in Rome, was mixed with lime to form a powerful, waterproof cement and/or mortar. In turn, this was mixed with aggregate (e.g chips of rock and broken brick) to make concrete. These inventions made possible the construction of the barrel vaults and aqueducts that carried water

FIGURE 7.5 The Pantheon. To construct the dome, Hadrian's architects had to apply special 'light concrete' (made by adding pumice stone to the mixture) in successive layers. They also carved intricate coffers to decrease the weight of the dome further. Photo © Jon Arnold Images Ltd./Alamy.

to urban baths and facilitated the re-enactment of massive sea-battles (*naumachia*; see Chapter 6).

Among the most massive Roman structures are the Baths of Caracalla (Figure 7.6; Map 5, no. 12), just outside the Appian gate to the south-east of the city. Measuring 412 by 393 metres, they could accommodate 1600 bathers at a time and used 17.5 million brick pieces for the facing alone. Such large bathing complexes, built

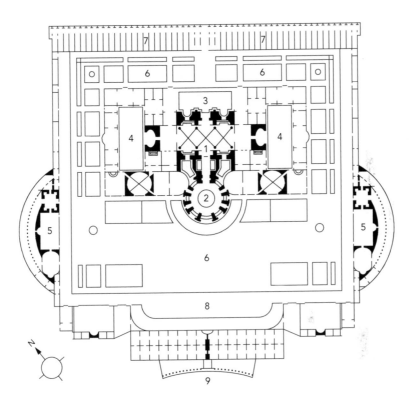

1. Central hall (tepidarium)
2. Calidarium
3. Natatio (frigidarium)
4. Palaestra
5. Lecture halls and libraries
6. Gardens
7. Shops
8. Stadium (?)
9. Aqueduct and reservoirs

0   100   320   FEET

0   50   100   METRES

FIGURE 7.6 Plan of the Baths of Caracalla. This complex, complete with a stadium, a park, lecture rooms, libraries and shops and lounges, as well as baths, toilets and lockers, was a feast for the senses and a perfect place (off the *Via Appia*) to freshen up on one's way into Rome.

during the empire, are known as *thermae*. Neither remains nor reconstructions can reliably reflect their sheer height or the inspiration which governed their design. In their construction of public baths as luxury-cum-cultural leisure and sports centres, the Romans combined their passion for opulence with their flair for hydraulics. The water was heated by furnaces and circulated by means of a network of cisterns and pipes. The essential rooms, separate for men and women, were the centrally heated *tepidarium*, where bathers were encouraged to sweat after removing their clothes; the *calidarium*, where they bathed in tubs of hot water; and the *frigidarium*, where they took a cold plunge.

These baths were the epitome of opulence, with larger-than-life marble sculptures, an Olympic-size swimming pool, elaborate mosaics, brightly coloured pink and grey granite, yellow, red and green marbles from across the empire, giant glass windows, toilets carved in the shape of chariots and private lockers with erotic scenes (to make it easier to remember where one had left one's toga). Baths also included shops, libraries and gymnasiums: something for everyone. Seneca (*Moral Epistles* 56), who had lodgings over a bathing complex, describes a veritable cacophony of noise, including the grunts of weightlifters, the slaps of masseurs' hands on skin, exuberant singing in the showers, pickpockets fleeing the scene of the crime, young men cannonballing into the pool, and vendors selling food or depilation services, all echoing across the vast open spaces and wide pools of water.

Provincial baths illustrate a number of variations upon this theme. The bathing complex at Bath in Roman Britain was gigantic, given the relatively modest population of the town, and was clearly a place for religious pilgrimage as well as a sort of health spa, as it was built around a natural hot spring that had long been a sacred site for the local Celts. The Hunting Baths in Lepcis Magna, North Africa, built by a guild of men who collected and sold exotic beasts (possibly for the games in Rome), is another very well-preserved bathing complex. It features concrete barrel vaults and a segmented 'pumpkin' dome.

Roman theatres employed some elements of the traditional Greek theatre plan, with tiers of seats in a semicircle facing on to a stage building (Figure 7.7). However, from the start (see Polybius' account of Greek theatre in Rome in the first century BC: Chapter 2), Romans made substantial adaptations in both theory and practice. Here, too, the values of axiality and hierarchy reigned supreme: the two side entrances (*paradoi*) of Greek theatres were replaced with a complicated series of entrances that allowed the social strata to be distinguished, even within a unified space. Augustus' *Lex Julia Theatralis* set these distinctions in stone, prescribing certain seats for senators, *equites*, Vestal Virgins, women and slaves.

Theatres in Rome during the republic were temporary structures, made of wood. The ability to house a large gathering without a riot was a statement of order and security that was not monumentalized until the end of the republic. The Theatre of

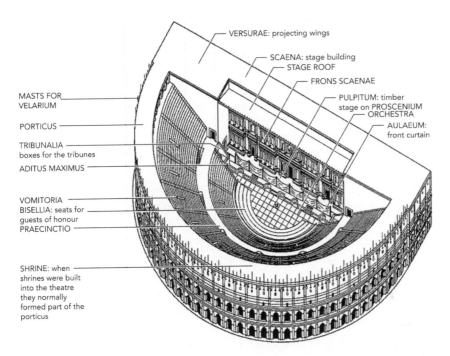

VERSURAE: projecting wings
SCAENA: stage building
STAGE ROOF
FRONS SCAENAE
PULPITUM: timber
stage on PROSCENIUM
ORCHESTRA
AULAEUM:
front curtain

MASTS FOR
VELARIUM

PORTICUS

TRIBUNALIA
boxes for the tribunes
ADITUS MAXIMUS

VOMITORIA
BISELLIA: seats for
guests of honour
PRAECINCTIO

SHRINE: when
shrines were built
into the theatre
they normally
formed part of the
porticus

FIGURE 7.7 A typical Roman theatre. The whole theatre could be covered by the *velarium*, a great canvas roof hung on masts to protect the audience from the sun. The audience entered and left the auditorium through openings known as *vomitoria*. Drawing by Richard Leacroft.

Pompey (55 BC; Map 5, no. 6), Rome's first stone theatre, was (in theory) a victory temple to Venus Victrix, but it happened to include a large monumental complex with a theatre, a portico and a curia (meeting room). In practice, the victory temple was an ornament at the top of the seating *cavea* that allowed Venus to overlook the performances and be seen from the top of Rome's numerous hills. Pliny the Elder tells us that the portico employed sculpture, paintings and exotic marbles from across the empire (*Natural History* 35.59), while Valerius Maximus (2.4.6) records other amenities, such as air conditioning (running water in the aisles and saffron-scented air spray). The size and scope of this statement of wealth would have appalled a republican censor such as Cato the Elder, who had torn down at least one theatre in his day. Pompey's theatre was a monument to the consolidation of power and wealth that characterized the late republic, and it served as a model for his imperial successors. That such a building was permitted and used by the Senate as a meeting-place illustrates just how far Rome had come from its humble agrarian beginnings and traditional republican values of austerity.

A typical Roman theatre

Pompey's theatre became famous for two very different reasons: first, as a universally popular meeting-place for lovers in the shaded portico by the gardens (according to Catullus, Poem 55; Martial, *Epigrams* 11.47; Ovid, *Ars Amatoria* 1.67; Propertius, *Elegies* 2.32); and, second, as the site of Julius Caesar's assassination (the Senate met in the large curia space in the courtyard behind the theatre). Indeed, one account (Plutarch, *Caesar* 61) has Caesar falling at the feet of Pompey's statue. Keen to reinscribe recent history, the theatres of Balbus and Marcellus were inaugurated during the reign of Augustus, while, in 'his' theatre, Pompey's statue was moved away from its prominent position overlooking the street (Suetonius, *Augustus* 31.5) and the curia space was converted into public latrines (Dio, *History* 47.19). Public toilets were important civic amenities that were found across the empire (Figure 7.8). They improved the quality of everyday life and, despite their rather base role, were not overlooked by imperial benefactors.) To give some idea of scale, the smallest of these three theatres could seat 7500, while Pliny estimates that 40,000 could fit in the Theatre of Pompey (*Natural History* 36.115); today, the Royal Opera House in London seats 2200, and the Metropolitan Opera House in New York 3800. Meanwhile, the

FIGURE 7.8 Public latrines, such as this one in Ostia, had a social function: 'Vacerra haunts the public loos, where he sits all day – not shitting, just cadging a meal' (Martial, *Epigrams* 11.77). This practice extended to private houses: the villa at Settefinestre, near Cosa, built in 75 BC, boasts a communal lavatory that could have seated twenty people at a time. Photo © C.M. Dixon.

Colosseum had a capacity of 45,000, and an astonishing 265,000 spectators could watch the chariot races at the 635-metre-long Circus Maximus. Present-day comparisons might be the Rose Bowl Stadium, California (92,542), Melbourne Cricket Ground (100,000) and London's Wembley Stadium (the second-largest in Europe, with a capacity of 90,000). While ancient seating estimates should be treated with caution, recent studies at the Theatre of Pompey suggest that they may not be quite as far fetched as scholars once thought; and it is worth noting that, as there were no individual seats, these ancient buildings probably had quite flexible capacities.

Some Roman theatres, such as the one at Orange and the Composite one at Verulamium, took advantage of natural slopes, as their earlier Greek counterparts had done, while the theatre in Palmyra was built into the ground, possibly to keep it cool. Many others, however, were freestanding, and their stage buildings were elaborate affairs, often used to house imperial portrait statues. Provincial buildings were often built on a smaller scale out of local materials: for instance, the amphitheatre/theatre at Verulamium could seat only 2000 spectators and consisted of piled turf revetted with stone walls. Similarly, the theatre at Palmyra only had thirteen rows of seating *in total*; compare this with the fourteen rows that Augustus reserved for the equestrian class alone in Rome's theatres. Despite assertions that Greek audiences were never lured into the sinful temptations of the Roman games, archaeological evidence suggests that Greek theatres in Asia Minor, such as the one at Ephesus, were remodelled not only to increase seating capacity and create vaulted entrances but to provide a water source and the protective barriers commonly used in Roman hunts and *naumachia* (but seldom required for theatrical performances).

INFRASTRUCTURE

Despite its elaborate entertainment venues, Roman architecture was more than just a pretty façade. Practical elements such as roads, walls, bridges and aqueducts formed the vital framework that linked the aforementioned buildings both in Rome itself and throughout its vast empire. The extension and retention of an empire required the construction of walls to discourage attackers from attacking towns and, in the case of Hadrian's Wall in Britain, to demarcate the Romans' northernmost frontier. Roads and bridges were needed for speedy communications and the swift deployment of troops, while aqueducts were essential for the supply of water (see *Via Appia* and *Aqua Appia* in Chapter 2; Map 5, no. 4). Permanent defences were built to an elaborate standard pattern that involved digging ditches thirty Roman feet deep and a hundred feet wide (a Roman foot was 29.59 centimetres). The earth that had been excavated was built up into a mound behind the ditch and supported on either side by a retaining wall made of standard-sized blocks of tufa rock. The end result was about fifteen metres deep and fifteen metres high. Hadrian's Wall was built between AD 122 and 127 on the orders of the emperor Hadrian. Its purpose was to facilitate the control of the border and to keep in their native northern zones the tribes who had been defeated by Agricola at Mons Graupius, near Aberdeen, in AD 84.

The empire was held together by its network of roads, which branched out from all the main towns and linked with the quickest and safest sea routes. The building and upkeep of these roads were the responsibility of the state; military roads in the provinces were constructed by the army, usually with some additional forced labour from the local people. According to an 'itinerary' compiled in the reign of Antoninus Pius (AD 138–161), there were approximately 22,400 kilometres of metalled or paved roads in second-century AD Italy; in Gaul there were 14,000 kilometres; in Spain 11,200 kilometres; in Britain (parts of which were still unknown) 4500 kilometres; in Africa 14,000 kilometres; and in Asia 15,200 kilometres. All of these were provided with milestones – there were five Roman feet to a *passus* (pace) and 1000 paces to a Roman mile (*mille passus* or *mille passuum*), which was thus 1.48 kilometres. In AD 68 a special messenger reached Clunia (northern Spain) from Rome (a distance of 2000 kilometres) in six and a half days; the following year another messenger travelled from Mainz to Rome (2100 kilometres) in nine days. In addition to milestones, key junctures and points of entry were marked in cities from Gaul to Syria with triumphal arches, which could represent military conquest (the Arch of Titus in Rome and the Arch of Orange in France) or imperial munificence (Trajan's arch at Benevento). In the east these structures sometimes took the form of a *tetrapylon* (Greek) or *quadrifrons* (Latin for 'four gates') at a crossroads, such as Septimius Severus' arch at Lepcis Magna and the *tetrapylon* at Palmyra.

Early Roman bridges were made of wood, and this tradition continued until the end of the empire for military bridges. (If necessary, the army had to be able to destroy bridges easily, to stop the enemy using them.) However, the construction of more permanent river crossings began under Augustus; the ornate, five-arched bridge at Ariminum (Rimini), which dates from his reign, is still in use. At Alcantara in Spain, six arches of unmortared granite blocks, the two centre ones fifty-five metres above the water, carry the road across the river Tagus. This bridge was built in about AD 106, and an inscription in a nearby temple reads: 'The celebrated Lacer built this bridge with supreme skill to endure through the ages to eternity.' He did and it still does. Similarly, Trajan's architect, Apollodorus of Damascus, is famous not only for his monumental buildings in Rome but for his bridge-building exploits during the emperor's military campaigns.

While modern audiences marvel at large tiers of arches in the countryside, such as the famous Pont du Gard near Nîmes, which brought fresh water from the mountains in a covered channel down an imperceptible gradient (just 2.5 centimetres over the course of the bridge), the majority of Rome's water transport (and some of her most impressive engineering) was accomplished through underground siphons and pipes or tunnels bored through hills. The Romans knew the rule of dynamics: that water always rises to the level of its source. The Claudian aqueduct, begun by Caligula and finished by Claudius, had a seventy-kilometre-long channel and started its final overhead descent to Rome twelve kilometres from the city. This and ten similar structures brought water to the urban population and they all had to be continually maintained, as is evidenced on the inscription of the Porta Maggiore, where the Claudian aqueduct entered the city (Figure 7.9; Map 5, no. 8). The municipal water board, which maintained the system, consisted of 460 slaves whom Claudius had taken on to his personal staff, with a special commissioner, a freedman, in charge. In AD 97 Nerva appointed as inspector of aqueducts Sextus Julius Frontinus (*c.* AD 40–103), a former governor of Britain. In his exhaustive report on the system, Frontinus estimated that over 1000 million litres of water came into Rome every day through the eight aqueducts which were then operational.

FIGURE 7.9 Porta Maggiore. This double arch, made of travertine and located at the Porta Praenestina, was built by Claudius in AD 52. It carried channels from two aqueducts (the *Aqua Claudia* and the *Aqua Anio Novus*), which ran behind the inscription. The three levels of text record the original project under Claudius (which brought water from the 45th and 62nd milestones outside the city), as well as subsequent work carried out by Vespasian (AD 71) and Titus (AD 81), both of whom record the dilapidation of the aqueduct over a decade. The gate is well preserved because it was built into the later Aurelian Wall (AD 271). Photo © imageBROKER/Alamy.

The aqueduct represented a triumph on a number of levels. First, only a militarily secure place could ever contemplate leaving something as potentially vulnerable as its water supply out in the open countryside (it was probably for this reason that Etruscan and Greek cities preferred wells). Second, while it used natural phenomena such as gravity and pressure to carry water across vast distances, the aqueduct was also a triumph over nature, a means to support public baths, latrines and other amenities, as well as irrigate farmland. Despite having only rudimentary tools, the Romans were able to manipulate the laws of nature in unprecedented ways to create buildings that would be unparalleled in size and ingenuity for more than a millennium. While they borrowed from the styles and visual language of numerous cultures, it is their innovative use of science, technology and manpower that survives as the most impressive legacy of Roman architecture.

FURTHER READING

* indicates sourcebook

Adam, J.-P., *Roman Building: Materials and Techniques*, Routledge, 1999.

Barton, I. (ed.), *Roman Public Buildings*, Exeter University Press, 1995.

Barton, I. (ed.), *Roman Domestic Buildings*, Exeter University Press, 1996.

Beard, M. and Henderson, J., *Classical Art: From Greece to Rome*, Oxford University Press, 2001.

D'Ambra, E., *Roman Art*, Cambridge University Press, 1998.

Dunbabin, K., *Mosaics of the Greek and Roman World*, Cambridge University Press, 2001 (new edition).

Elsner, J., *Imperial Rome and Christian Triumph*, Oxford University Press, 1998.

*Humphrey, J.W., Oleson J.P. and Sherwood, A.N. (eds), *Greek and Roman Technology: A Sourcebook: Annotated Translations of Greek and Latin Texts and Documents*, Routledge, 1997.

Kleiner, D.E.E., *Roman Sculpture*, Yale University Press, 1994 (new edition).

Ling, R., *Roman Painting*, Cambridge University Press, 1991.

Ling, R., *Ancient Mosaics*, Princeton University Press, 1998.

Ramage, N.H. and Ramage, A., *Roman Art: Romulus to Constantine*, Prentice-Hall, 2004 (new edition).

Rodgers, N., *The Architecture of Ancient Rome*, Lorenz Books, 2013.

Sear, F., *Roman Architecture*, Routledge, 1998.

Stewart, P., *Roman Art*, Oxford University Press, 2004.

Ward-Perkins, J.B., *Roman Imperial Architecture*, Yale University Press/Pelican History of Art, 1992 (new edition).

Wilson Jones, M., *Principles of Roman Architecture*, Yale University Press, 2003 (new edition).

8 ROMAN LITERATURE

LANGUAGES AND SOURCES

Wandering immigrants to the Italian peninsula brought with them their own dialects of ancient speech. Three of these, Umbrian, Oscan and Latin, emerged as contenders for the ultimate language of the region. Latin, which was spoken from about 800 BC in the comparatively small area of Latium, became enriched by features of local Sabine and Etruscan speech, and much more significantly by Greek. Legend has it that Greek settlers came to Italy shortly after the Trojan War, which was fought around 1220 BC. Certainly, there was a Greek trading post in the Bay of Naples by 775 BC. The fifty years or so following the traditional date for the founding of Rome (753 BC) coincide with the composition of the Greek epic poems, the *Odyssey* and the *Iliad*, and the establishment and circulation throughout the Greek world of the Greek alphabet.

The domination of one dialect over another is usually due to external rather than linguistic features – the south-eastern dialect of English became the standard form because London, where it was spoken, was the centre of government, and where the English printing industry emerged. In the case of Latin, Roman military expansion caused it to become the common language of the whole Italian peninsula, the western Mediterranean and the Balkans, and the second language, if not the first, wherever else Rome's conquests lay.

From the Latin alphabet is derived the English alphabet; and, to all intents and purposes, they are the same. Without the benefit of a time machine, no one knows exactly how Latin was pronounced and few pronounce Latin the way we now believe it was actually spoken. Instead, there are various modern 'standards' which tend to follow national boundaries. It is worth trying to get to know the way the Romans pronounced it, however, since much of Latin literature was expressly written to be delivered out loud.

Not that the Romans were without books. The Latin word *liber*, originally the inner part of the bark of a tree which even more ancient Italians had used as a writing surface, to the Romans meant anything that was written. The equivalent of our 'book' was *volumen* (volume), meaning 'roll'. This literally was a roll of papyrus (see Figure 8.1) up to ten metres long and thirty centimetres wide, with a rod fixed at each end, on which the work was written in columns about ten centimetres wide. To read a book, rolling up the used portion with the left hand while unrolling the rest with the right, required both dexterity and strength, though libraries provided reading desks to help with this. (The word 'library' also comes from *liber*.) Julius Caesar had the idea of opening a public library, but the project lapsed on his death, so the credit for founding the first one in Rome goes instead to Asinius Pollio (76 BC–AD 4). Publishers employed teams of educated slaves to do the copying, and booksellers advertised and sold the results of their labours. Importunate acquaintances were an occupational hazard for authors, in precisely the same way as they can be today:

> Whenever we meet, Lupercus, you immediately say, 'May I send my boy to pick up a copy of your new book? I'll give it back as soon as I've read it.' Lupercus, don't bother the boy: it's a long way to my district, and I live up three flights of stairs, long ones, too. You'll find what you want much nearer. I guess you're often in the Argus shopping precinct. Opposite the forum of Caesar there's a bookshop whose front is covered with advertisements: you can see at a glance which poets are available. Ask for Atrectus – he's the owner – and he'll get down for you from the first or second shelf a Martial, smoothed with pumice-stone and bound in purple, for 5 denarii. 'You're not worth that,' I hear you say? You're a sensible chap, Lupercus!
>
> **(Martial, *Epigrams* 1.117)**

The most striking feature of Latin is its use of inflections – that is, changes in the form of a word to indicate, for example, gender, number, case, person, degree, voice, mood or tense. The order of words in a sentence was flexible and could be varied for the sake of emphasis, different minutiae of meaning, or simply rhythm. So *chiasmus* (a word order of ABBA) allows an author to place words in physical locations that befit those words' meanings: for example, in '*innumeris tumidum Pythona sagittis*' (Ovid, *Metamorphoses* 1.460), the words 'swollen Python' (*tumidum Pythona*) are literally surrounded by 'innumerable arrows' (*innumeris sagittis*). Similarly, interlocking word order (ABAB) can also allow for alliteration and *onomatopoeia* (creating a sound like the action implied): for example, '*eliso percussis aere pennis*' ('slicing through the air with beating wings'; Ovid *Metamorphoses* 1.466) captures both the sound and the rhythm of wings as they flap through the air. These nuances are not easily conveyed in English translations.

Alliteration was widely used in both verse and prose, but rhyme only rarely, and then usually internally, in prose. Poetry was written in prescribed metre patterns,

FIGURE 8.1   Oxyrhynchus Papyrus (P. Oxy 6.2331). This third-century AD papyrus, a Greek poem describing the labours of Hercules, was discovered by archaeologists in a collection of manuscripts dating from the first to the sixth century AD in a rubbish heap. Preserved by the dry heat, papyri are often destroyed in attempts to unroll them. Scholars at Oxford University are now using scanners to study and digitally 'unroll' their secrets, without compromising the source. Photo courtesy of the Egypt Exploration Society.

made up of short and long syllables, arranged in 'feet', a feature that defined Roman poetry as much as rhyme defined English poetry until the twentieth century.

As a result of these many linguistic differences and styles in composition, a translation can never recapture all aspects of the original, but a good one can reflect its spirit: the meaning, flavour and often even the flow. Translation is a craft of the creative imagination. Just as a translation should always be into the first language of the translator, so the translator must be a skilled exponent in that language of the medium into which the original is being translated, whether it is prose or verse. The flexibility as well as the precision of Latin were well suited to the verse forms which Roman poets employed. There have been numerous prose translations of Virgil, and many others in verse. John Dryden, who was Poet Laureate 350 years ago, was certainly not the most accurate translator, yet he managed to capture the stateliness and possibly the spirit of the original:

> Arms, and the man I sing, who, forc'd by fate,
> And haughty Juno's unrelenting hate,
> Expell'd and exil'd, left the Trojan shore.
> Long labours, both by sea and land, he bore,
> And in the doubtful war, before he won
> The Latian realm, and built the destin'd town;
> His banish'd gods restor'd to rites divine,

> And settled sure succession in his line
> From whence the race of Alban fathers come,
> And the long glories of majestic Rome.

(*Aeneid* 1.1–7; trans. John Dryden)

It is easy to identify a number of differences in style, language and readability when comparing Dryden's beautifully romantic, 'artistic', but far from literal version with a more recent (prose) translation of the same passage:

> This is a story of war – and the story of a warrior, the first of the fugitives from Troy to make his way to Italy. Constantly driven off course by fate, or by the power of the gods, and harassed by Juno's relentless anger, he came to shore at last in Latium – but even there a long and bitter conflict lay ahead of him before he could establish a city and a home for his ancestral gods.
>
> But his descendants would be the founding fathers of Alba Longa, and one day they would build the walls of everlasting Rome.

(Trans. G.B. Cobbold (2005), p. 3)

The readability of a translation can play a fundamental role in how an audience both understands and identifies with literature. Like Roman readers, we are all products of our own time and purveyors of our own language, and it is for this reason that ancient literature, like Shakespeare's plays, continues to be recast in new translations in successive eras.

Equally less rigid are the genres of Latin literature, many of which are modern constructs. The ancient literature was much more interdisciplinary in nature and the idea that ancient authors saw themselves purely as historians, novelists, comic playwrights, scientists, 'didactic', 'elegiac' or 'lyric' poets is misleading. It can also distort our understanding of the Roman literate audience, who, much like modern audiences, probably read works from ever one of these genres.

ENNIUS

Quintus Ennius (239–169 BC) is regarded as the father of Latin poetry. He has been referred to as the 'Chaucer of Roman literature', which is misleading in that Chaucer's birthplace was London and early on he had access to the royal court, whereas Ennius was born of Greek parentage in Rudiae, Calabria, the 'heel' of Italy. As well as Greek, however, he spoke Latin and the local Oscan dialect. As a subject of Rome, he served in Sardinia in the Second Punic War. He was still there, presumably as a member of a garrison, in 204 BC, for there he met Cato, then praetor, who took him back to Rome.

Ennius lived frugally, writing and earning a living by teaching the sons of the nobility, with whom he was on good terms. He was granted Roman citizenship in 184 BC.

Ennius wrote over twenty stage tragedies, mainly on Greek themes, as well as some comedies and occasional verses. His main work, on which he was engaged for the last twenty years of his life, was a massive verse history of Rome up to his own day (albeit omitting the First Punic War) in eighteen books. For this, he abandoned the rough and barely perceptible rhythms of earlier Latin poets for the musical measures of the hexameter, which he forged into the epic medium later used by Virgil. We have only fragments of Ennius' work, totalling some 600 lines, which may not be his best, but he was often quoted by later writers.

COMEDY: PLAUTUS AND TERENCE

The first comic dramas that the Romans saw were based on the Greek 'new comedies' of the kind staged in Athens between about 400 and 200 BC (Figure 8.2). Their hallmarks included stratagems and counter-stratagems, stock characters (young

FIGURE 8.2   The principal writer of Greek 'new comedy' was Menander (342–c. 292 BC), whose situation comedies influenced Plautus and Terence. This second-century or early first-century BC mosaic from Pompeii illustrates a scene from his *Ladies at Lunch*, of which only a few lines survive. Photo © C.M. Dixon. Courtesy of del Ministero dei Beni e delle Attività Culturali e del Turismo – Soprintendenza Speciale per i Beni Archeologici di Pompei, Ercolano e Stabia.

lovers, scheming slave, family hanger-on) and standard situations (obstacles to young love, mistaken identities, revelations of true identity), with some musical accompaniment.

Titus Maccus Plautus (254–184 BC) was not the first of these Roman dramatists, but twenty-one plays attributed to him by Terentius Varro have survived. This, in itself, is a measure of his popularity; but also, in spite of being based on earlier Greek models, his work retains a raw freshness of its own. He devised ways of adapting Greek verse metres to the Latin language, and introduced to audiences whose taste had tended towards farce and slapstick several varieties of literary comedy, such as burlesque and domestic and romantic pieces, in which verbal fireworks replaced crude banter. He also surmounted the problem of playing consecutive scenes, without any breaks between them, in front of a standard backdrop, usually a street with the entrances to two houses.

Plautus was born in Sarsina, a small village in Umbria, but left home early to go to Rome. He seems to have been stage-struck, for he first worked as a props man and then, with the money he had earned, set himself up in the same kind of business. When that failed, he took a job turning a baker's handmill, which he was able to give up after writing his first three plays. Shakespeare's *Comedy of Errors* is based on Plautus' *The Brothers Menaechmus*; and the protagonist of Plautus' *The Braggart Soldier* is the prototype of the Elizabethan stage boaster, whose appearance in *Ralph Roister Doister* by Nicolas Udall (1505–1556) marks the beginning of English comedy written for public performance.

Publius Terentius Afer (*c.* 185–159 BC) was brought to Rome as a slave, possibly from Africa. He took his name from that of his owner, Terentius Lucanus, who educated him and gave him his freedom. The story goes that he submitted his first play, *The Girl from Andros*, to the curule aediles (one of whose functions was to act as municipal entertainment officers); they referred him to Caecilius Statius (*c.* 219–*c.* 166 BC), the most popular playwright of the day. Caecilius was at dinner when Terence called, but immediately began to read the play aloud. He was so impressed that he invited Terence to join the dinner guests and share the couch of honour with him. The play was first performed in 166 BC, and Terence wrote five more before he died while on a trip to Greece to find further plots. He was only about twenty-six. His plays are better plotted than those of Plautus and indeed some of the originals he adapted.

The comedy of manners effectively began with Terence. He was adept at employing the double plot, especially to illustrate different characters' responses to a situation, and at developing the situation itself. There is more purity of language and characterization than in Plautus, which may account for Terence being nothing like as popular in his own day as he would become later. The French philosopher and writer Denis Diderot (1713–1784) said that of all writers of comedy only Terence and Molière (1622–1673) had the gift of individualizing their characters in a timeless way.

LYRIC POETRY: CATULLUS AND HORACE

Lyric poetry has come to mean that in which the writer claims to present their own thoughts and feelings. Originally, it simply meant poetry or a song accompanied by the lyre, for which the Greek poets used a variety of metres. The Romans adopted the metres, though not necessarily the accompaniment, and employed them in a rather more precise form to express themselves poetically.

Gaius Valerius Catullus (*c.* 84–54 BC) was born in Verona, in the north of Italy, probably of a moderately rich family. Certainly, when he arrived in Rome in about 62 BC, it was not to look for a job. He became one of the wave of 'new poets' who reacted against their elders while, from the evidence of his own poetry, boozing, whoring and generally living it up (if he is to be trusted). Catullus, at any rate, moved in high circles, especially if the woman he calls Lesbia in his poems, and with whom he had a blazing affair, was Clodia, the emancipated and profligate sister of Cicero's arch-enemy Publius Clodius and the wife of Metellus Celer, consul in 60 BC. In this case she would have been rather older than her ill-starred lover. In 57 BC, Catullus was the guest, or camp-follower, of Memmius, governor of Bithynia, to whom Lucretius dedicated *De Rerum Natura*. He died soon after returning to Italy.

Catullus was not a prolific writer. We have just 116 poems, varying in length from 2 to 408 lines, and a few brief fragments, which probably represent the whole of his published work. Many of them are bitingly observant cameos of friends and enemies (among the latter was Julius Caesar), chance meetings and alfresco sexual encounters, in which he is often coarse but always amusing. Others, including his longest (Poem 64), an account in hexameters of the wedding of Peleus and Thetis, have mythological themes, but still show a depth of poetic emotion. His shorter poems, mocking the 'cobwebs in his purse' by inviting friends to a party at his house, as long as they bring food, wine and women (Poem 13), or ridiculing pretentious young dandies adopting a Greek accent (Poem 84), are witty and entertaining.

However, it is the love/hate poems to Lesbia/Clodia – passionate, tender, often bitter – that are Catullus' most famous works, and they remain some of the most poignant, expressive and painfully accurate descriptions of love's tumultuous path. In the first of the two poems below, one can see the vivid and timeless emotions of love's discovery (it is a reworking of one of Sappho's poems – appropriate for a lover named 'Lesbia'). Meanwhile, love's abandonment is evoked in the second poem, which is perhaps Catullus' most commonly quoted work (probably on account of its brief yet brutal accuracy).

> He sits opposite and constantly watches you and hears you sweetly laughing. It takes all my senses away from me, makes me wretched: for as soon as I see you, Lesbia, there is no sound in my throat, my tongue is tied, a slender flame spreads

through my limbs, my ears ring with their own sound and my eyes are covered in double darkness.

(Catullus, Poem 51 ('When Love Strikes') 4–10)

I hate and love. Why do I do this? maybe you ask.
I don't know. But I can feel it happening and I'm in agony.

(Catullus, Poem 85 ('When Love Departs'); trans. Clive Letchford)

One cannot discount the parallels between Catullus' affair with Lesbia and Shakespeare's with his 'dark lady' of the sonnets, and especially between Catullus' denunciation of his mistress as a whore (Poems 37 and 58) and Shakespeare's of his as 'the bay where all men ride' (Sonnet 137). But of all English poets, Byron is probably nearest to Catullus in temperament, habits and poetic genius. Byron himself may have recognized this, for while still in his teens he translated two of the poems (3 and 51) into, unfortunately, some of his lesser verse.

Whereas Catullus often wrote in the passions of the moment, his successor, Quintus Horatius Flaccus (Horace; 65–8 BC), had the leisure and the time to marshal his thoughts into lines which display more grace and artifice than those of Catullus, but less emotion. Horace was born in Apulia, the son of a freedman who had acquired a small estate by collecting taxes on sales at agricultural auctions. Horace was taken by his father to Rome, where he was sent to the best educational establishments. At eighteen, Horace went to Athens to continue his education but was caught up in the civil war following the assassination of Julius Caesar. He fought on the wrong side at Philippi – as a legionary commander in the army of Brutus. He was pardoned for this lapse of loyalty, but when he returned to Rome he found that his father's estate had been confiscated. He became a civil service clerk and in his spare time wrote verses which caught the eye of Virgil, who introduced him to his own patron, Gaius Maecenas (c. 70–8 BC). A few years later Maecenas set Horace up in a farm near Tibur at the foot of the mountains to the east of Rome.

Horace's lyric poetry comprises his 17 epodes and 103 odes in 4 books. The former are on a variety of political and satirical themes, plus a few love poems. Most are written in an iambic metre – a longer line followed by a shorter one – which is known as the 'epode', or 'after song'. The first three books of odes were written between 33 and 23 BC and reflect the events of the time. The opening line of the fourth verse of the ode below is the celebrated saying '*dulce et decorum est pro patria mori*':

Let a tough young man be glad to learn to endure harsh conditions and shortages on demanding military training. Let him harry the fierce Parthians on horseback, bringing terror with his spear, and let him spend his life in danger under the stars. The mother of a warring tyrant will see him from the enemy walls, her full-grown daughter too, and sigh: alas, I hope the royal fiancé, inexperienced in battle, doesn't provoke this lion, fierce to touch. He is seized by a bloodthirsty anger as he goes through the middle of the slaughter. It is a welcome privilege to die for one's country.

(Horace, *Odes* 3.2.1–16; trans. Clive Letchford)

Horace's odes are regarded as his finest works. His others include *Carmen Saeculare*, a poem to various gods, commissioned by Augustus to celebrate the saecular games in 17 BC (a *saeculum* was an interval of 100 or 110 years); three books of epistles, of which the third is generally known as the literary essay *Ars Poetica*; and two books of satires. (The Latin root of 'satire' meant a medley of reflections on social conditions and events, rather than the pointed, witty criticism evoked by the word today.)

From remarks in his own poems and from a biography by Suetonius, Horace appears to have been short and rotund, with dark hair that turned grey early. He also seems to have been a bit of a hypochondriac, but this did not stop him enjoying to the full his life, his work and the position the latter gave him in society.

VIRGIL

The *Aeneid*, the epic of the empire of Rome and of Roman nationalism – for its poetry and poetic sensibility arguably the most influential poem in any language – is unfinished (see Chapter 1). And its author asked his friends, just before he died, to burn it. Literary executors, faced with just this problem throughout history, have usually responded with commendable common sense and regard to posterity, as they did in this case.

Publius Vergilius, or Virgilius, Maro (70–19 BC), was born in Cisalpine Gaul. He had a good education in Cremona and Milan before going on to study in Naples and Rome. He does not appear to have been very fit, which may explain why he wrote at the family farm (until it was confiscated in 41 BC after the Battle of Philippi). He appealed against the decision and was reinstated on the orders of Octavian. In 37 BC he published a series of bucolic episodes (*eclogues*) that were loosely based on a composition by the Hellenistic pastoral poet Theocritus (fl. *c.* 270 BC). He then wrote four books of didactic verse about farming known as the *Georgics*. Though these show Greek influences, the agricultural activities he describes (corn-growing, viticulture, cattle-breeding, bee-keeping) are Italian and the message is both topical and nationalistic, with its emphasis on traditional agricultural industries, a return to the old forms of worship, and cooperative working for a profitable future.

By this time, Octavian (still only thirty-three) was emperor in all but title and name, and he approached several writers about composing an epic poem to record his achievements. Virgil accepted the assignment, but on his own terms: he would write an epic of Rome's mythological antecedents. Augustus frequently asked after the poem's progress and, apparently, was not disappointed with either the pace or the product. In 19 BC, Virgil met the emperor in Athens; then, instead of touring Greece as he had intended, accompanied him back to Rome. He caught a fever and died a few days after landing at Brundisium. He was unmarried and, largely thanks to his patrons, a comparatively rich man.

Virgil had started the *Aeneid* eleven years earlier and had composed 10,000 lines in that time. But his epic must be viewed as unfinished as it awaited final revision and polishing at the time of his death. After outlining Rome's glorious destiny as a city (Book 8; see Chapter 1) and her legendary conflicts with Carthage and Egypt, exemplified in Aeneas' relationship with the foreign queen Dido (Figure 8.3), the story ends on a dramatic climax. Turnus, king of the Rutuli, stakes everything on single combat with Aeneas. They fight, Turnus is wounded, and he makes a heroic speech: 'Whatever happens to me, I have deserved it, I will not beg for my life – you must do what you must do. But if you have any feeling for a parent's loss, I implore you to take pity on my father Daunus' (*Aeneid* 12.931–934). Aeneas frowns, hesitates and is on the verge of forgiving Turnus when he spots on his opponent's shoulder the belt of his dead ally and friend Pallas, which Turnus has clearly stripped from Pallas' corpse in an utter breach of mythological chivalry:

> And just a glimpse was enough to remind Aeneas of how much he had grieved for Pallas, and his compassion was driven out by a burst of terrible rage.
>
> 'Did you hope to escape me, still dressed up in what you have stolen from my friend? But now it is Pallas – not I – who offers you up for sacrifice. It is Pallas who gives you this final wound, and Pallas who makes you pay your debt at last – with your own degenerate blood.'
>
> He drove his sword hot and deep into Turnus' heart. And Turnus' limbs became chilled and slack, and his protesting spirit fluttered away into the shadows.
>
> **(Aeneid, 12.945–952; trans. G.B. Cobbold (2005), pp. 336–337)**

The *Aeneid* is a continuation of Homer's *Iliad*, to stress the connection between Rome and the heroes of Troy, with strong echoes of the wanderings of Odysseus in the *Odyssey*. The gods' continuous intervention and their bickering as to which of their favourite mortals shall triumph are in tune with the traditional notions of 'divine intervention' that Augustus would advocate. To modern readers, Aeneas may seem a character lacking in personality: in 1914 the American poet and critic Ezra Pound described him as a 'stick'. To Virgil and his contemporaries, however, Aeneas

FIGURE 8.3 Though Virgil referred to the Britons as 'totally cut off from the whole world' (*Eclogues* 1.66), Britain in Roman times was not entirely a cultural backwater. This fine fourth-century AD mosaic pavement, found at Low Ham in Somerset, illustrates incidents from the first and fourth books of the *Aeneid*. On the right, Aeneas' ships arrive at the African coast. At the top, a naked Venus, goddess of love, presides over a meeting between Dido, queen of Carthage, and Aeneas, with Cupid, in the guise of Aeneas' son Ascanius, between them. On the left, Aeneas and the queen go hunting; and at the bottom, sheltering together from the storm engineered by Juno, they embrace. In the central panel Venus stands between cupids with raised and lowered torches, signifying that Aeneas will live and Dido die. Photo © Somerset County Museums.

embodied the Stoic ideal, accepting what fate threw at him and impassively pressing on towards his personal destiny.

Literary debts to Virgil are legion. This pagan poet even became a prophet of Christianity in Dante's (1265–1321) *Divine Comedy*. Virgil, in the personification of Human Reason, is the poet's guide to the Gates of Paradise. Among the British poets who have implicitly or openly acknowledged his influence are Chaucer, Gavin Douglas, Marlowe, Shakespeare, Milton, Dryden (of course), Pope, Keats and Tennyson. The American-born T.S. Eliot (1888–1965) wrote in his essay 'What is a Classic?' (1944):

> [Aeneas] is the symbol of Rome; and, as Aeneas is to Rome, so is ancient Rome to Europe. Thus Virgil acquires the centrality of the unique classic; he is at the centre of European civilization, in a position which no other poet can share or usurp.

ELEGIAC POETRY: PROPERTIUS AND OVID

Sextus Propertius (*c.* 50–*c.* 15 BC) was born near Assisi in Umbria, but his family, like Virgil's, was dispossessed in the proscriptions of 41 BC. His father died when he was a child, and his mother sent him to Rome to be educated for a career in the law. Instead, he turned to literature and published his first book of elegies in about 26 BC. Through this he acquired fame and an introduction to Maecenas, and though he resisted persuasion to compose patriotic verses, he was encouraged to write three more books before his early death from an unknown cause. Many of his poems describe his love for 'Cynthia' (called Hostia in real life), who appears to have been a freedwoman and a courtesan, providing another example of 'Augustan morality' as an ideal, rather than a common practice (see Chapter 6) .

> Just as Ariadne lay exhausted on the deserted shores while Theseus' boat was sailing away; just as Cepheius' daughter, Andromeda, lay down for her first sleep after being freed from the hard rock; just as a Thracian Bacchant collapses onto the grassy bank of the river Apidanus, tired from her continuous dancing; just so did Cynthia seem to be resting, breathing gently, her head supported on her outstretched arms. Meanwhile, I was dragging my drunken footsteps back home and the slaves were keeping the torches alight well into the night.
>
> **(Propertius, 1.3.1–10; trans Clive Letchford)**

Propertius' poems, like the walls of a middle-class home (see Chapter 7), are peppered with allusions to Greek myths, which he uses as models for his ideal love and lover. This ideal, however, is often contrasted with a more melancholy and self-effacing reality and wonderfully flawed human characters.

We have enough background for Publius Ovidius Naso (Ovid; 43 BC–AD 18), chiefly from evidence in his own poems, to form a picture of a literary philanderer. However, we do not know for what crime, at the height of his powers and popularity, he was banished by Augustus, for life, to the Roman equivalent of Siberia – a small, bleak place called Tomi (modern Constanta) on the west coast of the Black Sea.

Ovid was born into an ancient equestrian family at Sulmo in the mountains east of Rome. Destined for a political career, he studied rhetoric and law. He married at sixteen but divorced shortly after (the first of many transgressions against Augustus' campaign for family values). After doing a grand tour of Greece, Asia Minor and Sicily, accompanied by a companion/tutor, he held minor legal and administrative posts in the civil service, but abandoned politics for poetry in about 16 BC, when he married again (although his wife died just two years later). He combined his pursuits of poetry and pleasure in *Amores* (*Love Poems*) and *Ars Amatoria* (*The Art of Love*). These were not so much erotic as irresponsible in that they appeared to condone adultery. Augustan law had made this a public offence, and Augustus, who banished his own daughter Julia because of it in 2 BC, clearly took the issue very seriously (see Chapter 6). The *Ars Amatoria*, which was published the very next year and provided helpful advice on how to cruise for women in public venues, clearly ran afoul of Augustus' ideology. The passage below, a tutorial on how to pick up ladies at sporting events, beautifully illustrates how little has changed in the courtship ritual over the past 2000 years:

> Don't let thoroughbred horse-racing escape your attention either. The spacious Circus has many convenient opportunities. You don't need fingers to trace out your secret messages, nor do you have to find out things through a series of nods. You can sit right next to your woman – no one will stop you – and push your side against hers as much as you can. It is good that the seat markings force you together, even if you do not want it. The rule of the place is – you've got to touch the girl. Next, you should look for a good opening line and say some words suitable for public consumption. Make sure that you ask enthusiastically whose horse it is. Whichever horse she supports, support it as well – straight away. Whenever the crowded procession passes with its ivory statues of the gods, greet the goddess Venus with enthusiastic applause. If any dirt happens to fall into the lap of your girl, then you should flick it off with your finger. Even if there isn't any, flick some imaginary dirt off. Any excuse you like is suitable for your duty towards her. If her cloak slips down too far and touches the floor, gather it up and carefully lift it up from the dirty ground. Straight away, as a reward for your duty, and with her permission, her legs will present themselves to your eyes.

> **(Ovid *Ars Amatoria* 1.135–158; trans. Clive Letchford)**

Nine years later, Ovid was exiled. He continued to compose poems, but his carefree days were over: the collection was titled *Tristia* (*Sadness*). He reveals (*Tristia* 2.207) that the reasons for his exile were 'a poem' (presumably from *Ars Amatoria*) and 'an error'. Whatever these were, Ovid had to go, and *Ars Amatoria* was banned from Rome's three public libraries. He was never recalled to the city, even after the death of Augustus. Even in his despair, however, Ovid retained his sense of humour: he composed one story about the anthropomorphic travels of his own book in Rome, which ends when it finds a library where his works have been banned.

It is difficult to capture the genius of Ovid in translation, particularly when he employs verbal effects and ingenious and delicate deployment of verse forms in his

FIGURE 8.4 Part of a wall painting from Pompeii of the legend of Europa and the bull, one of many stories of transformation woven into Ovid's *Metamorphoses* (2.837–875). Europa, daughter of the king of Phoenicia, was attracted by a fine white bull while she played with her companions. It was Zeus in disguise, and he acted so tame that she was tempted to climb on to his back. He carried her away over the sea to Crete, where he revealed himself to her. They had three sons, who were adopted by the king of Crete, to whom Zeus married off Europa. Photo © C.M. Dixon. Courtesy of del Ministero dei Beni e delle Attività Culturali e del Turismo – Soprintendenza Speciale per i Beni Archeologici di Pompei, Ercolano e Stabia.

couplets to amuse his readers (see above). Perhaps partly because of this translation problem, the fifteen books of *Metamorphoses* (*Transformations*), written entirely in hexameter, have become his most enduring and influential work (Figure 8.4). This vast collection of linked myths and legends was widely drawn upon by later Roman and European writers, including Chaucer, and parts of it were translated into English by William Caxton (1480), Dryden (1699) and more recently by the Poet Laureate Ted Hughes.

EPIGRAM AND SATIRE: MARTIAL AND JUVENAL

Epigram is a Greek term meaning 'inscription', often in verse, on a tombstone or accompanying an offering. Subsequently, it came to stand for almost any occasional short poem. The form was widely used in Rome until, in the hands of Martial, it became the medium for short, pointed, witty sayings about people and the hazards of daily and social life, usually in elegiacs, but in other metres too. Marcus Valerius Martialis (*c.* AD 40–104) was a Spaniard from Bilbilis who arrived in Rome in AD 64 and was taken up by his literary fellow countrymen Seneca and his nephew Lucan until, in the following year, they were purged by Nero. Thereafter, Martial lived in a third-floor flat on the slope of the Quirinal hill, scraping a living by writing verses for anybody and any occasion. He even claimed to write them on labels for gifts which guests were given at a party. The verses ultimately did well, for he published several books of them, and ended up owning a farm in the country as well as a house in Rome. He was a hack, a parasite and, when it suited his interests, as it did when writing about Domitian, an unctuous flatterer. However, he was also witty, coarse and frequently poetic, and he pioneered a form of literature which has had, and still has, many exponents.

Perhaps mocking the moralizing tendencies of more conventional literature, Martial targeted a very different (non-elite) audience. For example, he addresses Lesbia, a street walker with a penchant for including a wider audience in her 'show':

> You always do your dirty little deeds in unguarded, open doorways – you don't hide them away. You are more pleased by a voyeur than a participant; you don't like your pleasures hidden away. Prostitutes drive away any witnesses with curtains and bolts; a gaping hole in a brothel wall is unusual. At any rate, learn discretion from Chio and Ias; whores find cover even in graveyards for their filthiest acts. My analysis doesn't seem too harsh, does it?
>
> I'm not telling you not to get fucked.
>
> I'm just telling you not to get caught.
>
> **(Martial, 1.34; trans. Clive Letchford)**

One of Martial's friends – if a man of his nature and bent could be said to have had any – was Decimus Junius Juvenalis (c. AD 55–c. AD 140), the most graphic of the Roman satirists and the last of the classical poets of Rome. As far as we can tell, he was born in Aquinum, the son of a well-to-do Spanish freedman. He may have served as commander of an auxiliary cohort in Britain and possibly held civic offices in his home town before venturing to Rome. During the reign of Domitian, he seems to have been exiled to Egypt, undoubtedly for saying or writing something offensive to the emperor, but not sufficiently offensive to suffer execution.

We have sixteen of his satires, published between about AD 110 and 130, in the reigns of Trajan and Hadrian. They attack various social targets, including homosexuals, living conditions in Rome, women, extravagance, human parasites and vanity, while moralizing on such subjects as learning, guilty consciences (see Chapter 6) and the army's treatment of civilians. They boast sarcasm, invective and broad humour, though of a kind that today would probably be penned by a crusading journalist, rather than a satirical poet.

THE NOVEL: PETRONIUS AND APULEIUS

The romance in prose was a literary form used by the Greeks in the third century BC. In the hands of two Roman writers in particular, the novel took on a very different aspect. Hovering between prose fiction and satire in its senses of both 'medley' and 'ridicule' is the *Satyricon* of Gaius Petronius (d. AD 66), known also as Petronius Arbiter from his rather inappropriate job title of *elegantiae arbiter* (style guru), in which capacity he organized Nero's personal revels. *Satyricon* is also the original picaresque novel, a kind of bisexual odyssey of two men and their boy around the towns of southern Italy. We have only fragments, the best known of which is the account of the wealthy freedman Trimalchio's dinner party (see Chapter 6 for more extracts). Although deliberately overdrawn, this splendidly illustrates the manners and mores of the Roman nouveaux riches:

> We all join in the applause which the servants have started and attack this amazing dish with a smile on our faces. Trimalchio is no less pleased by his trick and says, 'Carver, carve 'er!' A waiter with a long knife immediately steps forward and, making extravagant gestures in time to the music, hacks away at the arrangement. You would think he is a gladiator fighting from a chariot while the water-organ is playing. Even so Trimalchio keeps saying in a persistent way, 'Carver, Carve 'er.' Suspecting that the frequent repetition of this word is a part of his joke, I'm not embarassed to ask the person reclining next to me about this. He has seen this sort of thing rather a lot and says, 'Do you see the man who is carving the food?

He's called Carver. Every time Trimalchio says "Carver" he is both addressing him and giving him his order.'

(Petronius, *Saytricon* 36; trans. Clive Letchford)

It is not clear whether Petronius' account of this ridiculous dinner party was designed to mock only aspiring freedmen like Trimalchio, or also the aristocratic behaviour at court which such men tried so desperately to mimic.

A victim of one of Nero's periodic purges, Petronius died with considerable style and urbanity. According to Tacitus, he slowly bled himself to death, while conversing, eating and even sleeping, having committed to paper a 'list of Nero's most perverted acts, classified according to the novelty of the performance, with male as well as female partners, and their names, which he dispatched to the emperor under seal' (*Annals* 16.19).

Lucius Apuleius was born in about AD 125 at Madaura (see Map 4), North Africa. According to his own account, he married a rich widow much older than himself, and was then accused by her family of sorcery (he was certainly much interested in magic and its effects). He conducted his own defence and was acquitted. His novel *Metamorphoses*, better known as *The Golden Ass*, is a rollicking tale of the supernatural, told in the first person. It describes how Lucius dabbles in magic, is given the wrong ointment by the maid who is also his bed-mate, and is turned into an ass. Several good stories are spliced into the action, including an excellent version of the legend of Cupid and Psyche. The conversion of Lucius to the cult of Isis after he is turned back into human form gives the ending a religious significance as well as a narrative twist. Apuleius himself became a priest of Osiris and Isis, and was also a devotee of Aesculapius, god of medicine. He seems to have had no problem squaring his religious convictions with organizing gladiatorial shows for the province of Africa.

HISTORIANS: CAESAR, LIVY, TACITUS, SUETONIUS AND PLUTARCH

History was not necessarily a separate genre in ancient Rome. Indeed, Rome's first history was composed by the poet Ennius (although it survives only in quotations in later sources; see above). Many of Rome's historians have already been discussed in this book (Chapters 1–4), as an understanding of their accounts and approaches is directly related to the events they recorded. This section, therefore, will provide a more general treatment of them.

The original Roman records, with the names of the principal officials for each year, were inscribed on white tablets called *fasti* (in the keeping of the *pontifex maximus*) and displayed to public view. We know that the first historian to write in Latin was Cato the Elder (see Chapter 2), but his history of Rome has been lost.

Hence, the earliest surviving account of contemporary events is Julius Caesar's seven-book record of his campaigns in Gaul, *De Bello Gallico* (*Gallic War*, see Chapter 3). Objective only in that he mentions – but does not dwell on – his failures (responsibility for which he tends to attribute to either the weather or his subordinates), this account was written in the third person with a clear, no-nonsense style. It was probably a serial publication (more like modern journalism), written to supplement his dispatches to the Senate, and was likely used by his PR team to promote his image in Italy. His *De Bello Civili* (*Civil War*) is a more impressive oratorical and political document, employing carefully selected facts and linguistic legerdemain to assign blame for Rome's internal strife almost entirely to his opponents.

Titus Livius (Livy; 59 BC–AD 17; see Chapters 1 and 2) lived most of his life in Rome, had two children, and was a close acquaintance of Augustus and Claudius. It was the latter who first encouraged Livy to write history. His full history of Rome – from Aeneas to 9 BC – comprised 142 books, of which we have 35, plus synopses of the others. His style can be both moralizing and romantic in recreating dramatic characters from Roman history with eloquent speeches. A strong proponent of the Augustan regime, Livy expresses pride in Rome's humble origins while constantly contrasting the city's past with the grandeur of the present. He often uses the past for didactic purpose: to illustrate how Augustus' 'traditional' Roman values had played a fundamental role throughout Rome's history. While the episodes he describes may not always be historically accurate (see Chapter 2) , they are faithful accounts of human nature and, therefore, presumably seemed credible to his Roman audience.

Cornelius Tacitus (*c.* AD 55–*c.* AD 117; see Chapter 3) was a senator, consul in AD 97, and governor of the province of Asia in AD 112. An excellent public speaker, he published a book on oratory in his twenties, followed by two series of histories, covering the emperors Tiberius to Domitian, known respectively as the *Histories* and the *Annals*. Just over four books of the *Histories* survive, describing the years AD 69–70: the reigns of Galba, Otho and Vitellius, and the beginning of that of Vespasian. The surviving *Annals* books cover parts of the reigns of Tiberius, Claudius and Nero. Tacitus also wrote a short and flattering biography of Agricola, as well as *Germania*, a graphic report on the land and people of Germany. He was a witty writer as well as a shrewd, if partisan, observer and commentator, and an upholder of the ancient virtues. His writings were lost until the fifteenth century, but thereafter they soon influenced the political thinking of the Italian statesman Niccolò Machiavelli (1469–1527). Tacitus' philosophic attitude to history is also reflected in the monumental *History of the Decline and Fall of the Roman Empire* by Edward Gibbon (1737–1794).

Gaius Suetonius Tranquillus (*c.* AD 70–*c.* AD 140) held a succession of posts in the imperial court, becoming director of the imperial libraries and then chief of

Hadrian's personal secretariat, which gave him access to archive material on earlier reigns. His series of biographies of the Caesars (see Chapter 3) is one of many biographical and antiquarian works by Suetonius to have survived intact. He was, with Plutarch (AD 46–120), who wrote in Greek, the originator of the modern biography.

Plutarch's *Parallel Lives*, which provides biographies of famous Greeks and Romans in pairs, provides some juicy comparisons, but also tends to moralize events and people at the expense of critical analysis. Regardless, his works are the basis for some of the most colourful characters in subsequent works, including Cleopatra in Shakespeare's *Antony and Cleopatra* and his Coriolanus.

As we move forward into the 'Golden Age' of Rome under Trajan, our sources on the emperors become more sparse. Though some of Rome's greatest historians lived at this time, few chose to document the grandeur that preceded the fall. As a result, we have been left with the few accounts, each limited in its own way, that were discussed in Chapter 4.

PHILOSOPHY AND SCIENCE: LUCRETIUS, SENECA AND PLINY THE ELDER

In the dark, confused days presaging the end of the republic, voices were abroad which questioned prevailing views about the natural and spiritual worlds. Some of these belonged to the Epicureans (followers of the Greek philosopher Epicurus from the fourth century BC), whose tenets included both a fascination with the physical senses and a rudimentary theory of atomic matter. In a modern context, Epicureanism is often associated with a love of food and drink, if not hedonism, and this can be somewhat misleading. Ancient Epicureans sought to understand (and enjoy) the human experience through a harmony of body and mind, and a study of natural causes. These values are documented in *De Rerum Natura* (*On the Nature of Things*) a work of great learning and poetry by Titus Lucretius Carus (*c.* 99–*c.* 55 BC), whose rejection of spiritual gods and images in favour of science anticipates the modern dilemma between biological theories (e.g. evolution) and religion. Lucretius invests Venus, whom he invokes at the beginning of the poem, with an overall creative power in nature, before exploring the composition of matter and space in atomic terms, followed by discussions of the mind, feelings, sex, cosmology, anthropology and meteorology. It is a mark of his skill that he succeeded in presenting all of this in the language and metre of poetry.

This philosophical poem – of which we have the first six books, some 7500 hexameters – is unique in Latin. True to the interdisciplinary spirit of the Roman world, it reads like a cross between a science treatise by Richard Dawkins and a psychological self-help book. While the language is often unwieldy (even in translation), the aim of Lucretius' arguments is conveyed beautifully in a summary composed by J.D. Duff, the editor of the fourth edition of H.A.J. Munro's translation:

> sweet though it is to see from a place of safety, the storm tossed sailor or the battling soldier, far sweeter it is from the heights of Philosophy to look down on men lost in error and struggling for power and wealth; what blindness not to see how little is needed to rid us of pain and bring us innocent pleasure; often merely fresh air and fine weather, not palaces nor banquets . . . It is not wealth or birth or power, nor armies and navies that can free us from fear of religion and death and all the cares of life: reason alone can deliver us from all such empty terrors
>
> **(Lucretius, _De Rerum Natura_ 2.1–61 (1920 edition), pp. xiii–xiv)**

Apart from his writings, we know almost nothing about Lucretius, save for a story recorded hundreds of years later by St Jerome (fourth century AD), who tells us that he was poisoned by an aphrodisiac, went mad, wrote poetry in his lucid spells, and committed suicide at the age of forty-four. This account is unlikely to be true (Jerome was probably motivated more by Christian prejudice than by any desire to record the historical truth). However, there is a chance that Lucretius took his own life after his great project proved too much for him.

His work was an inspiration to a number of late republican authors, including Virgil, who refers to it in the _Georgics_ – 'Lucky are those who have been able to find out the reasons for things and who have crushed under foot their fears, their unavoidable fate and the clamour of the avaricious underworld' (2.490; trans. Clive Letchford) – as well as a number of scholars during the Enlightenment. In a time of political and social insecurity, Lucretius preached not 'hedonism' but rational thought; while he acknowledged the human fascination with suffering (such as watching a battle from the comfort of the stands), he advocated a higher fulfilment of the mind and body in simple pleasures, not elaborate feasts, luxurious homes or military triumph.

Freedom from the fetters of human ambition and the fear of death were echoed in another form of philosophical belief in the late republic: Stoicism. The term comes from the Greek _stoa_, referring to the colonnaded portico in Athens where the philosopher Zeno (335–262 BC) held discussions with his disciples. Its teachings were brought to Rome in 156–155 BC by his successor, Diogenes of Babylon. They reflected some of the traditional characteristics which Romans aimed to emulate, and which were to be enshrined in Virgil's _Aeneid_ (see Chapter 1) and endorsed by Cicero (see Chapter 2) in his philosophical work _Tusculanae Disputationes_ (_Discussions at Tusculum_). Seneca and Marcus Aurelius (AD 121–180), the 'philosopher emperor' (see Chapter 5), were both devotees. In English to be stoical means 'keep calm and carry on' in a state of resignation to fate, as does Virgil's hero, Aeneas. This is a simplification of a basic Stoic credo – that a single divine will (or God) controls everything in the universe. All activity is incorporated in the *logos*, the 'rational order' or 'meaning' of the universe. Everything is part of a wider 'reason' or good, a concept which Christianity would adopt and promote.

The fundamental difference between Epicureanism and Stoicism was that in the latter 'virtue' or 'duty' (rather than pleasure) was the key to attaining spiritual enlightenment. The Romans valued *virtus*, which comes from the word *vir* (man) and means something akin to manliness or mental as well as physical strength. With the help of *virtus*, one can more readily accept the circumstances of life and one's station in it. Stoics also declared that there was no difference between people of one station and those of another: whether male or female, Greek or barbarian, enslaved or free.

Stoicism in practice, however, did not always live up to the values it projected in theory, as one can see in Lucius Annaeus Seneca the Younger (4 BC–AD 65), the tutor and then victim of the emperor Nero, and the first patron of Martial (see Chapter 3). The second son of Seneca the Elder, he was born in Córdoba, Spain, arrived in Rome as a youth, and was soon influenced by the Stoics. In his philosophical writings (12 dialogues and 124 epistles to his friend Eucilius survive), he comes across as a moral philosopher whose aim was to live correctly through the exercise of reason. His *Naturales Questiones* (*Scientific Investigations*) is an examination of natural phenomena from the point of view of a Stoic philosopher. The moral pretensions he advocated were less clear in his actions, however: he condoned various dynastic murders, was banished for eight years under suspicion of having an affair with one of Caligula's sisters, and on his return, although he curbed the worst excesses of his pupil Nero, he grew very rich in the process. His *Apocolocyntosis* (*Pumpkinification*; a pun on *apotheosis* – 'the act of becoming a god') is a wicked skit on the deified Claudius which lampoons the emperor's employment of freedmen (something Seneca, with his supposed Stoic values, should have applauded).

We also have ten of Seneca's verse tragedies. These are solid, lyrical and bleak in their tragic vision, allowing no escape from evil or defence against the brutality of fate. It is perhaps not surprising that this message eventually came to irritate the teenage Nero. From Seneca's example, Elizabethan and Jacobean dramatists took the five-act structure and the cast of secondary characters, who serve to report on events off stage and elicit private thoughts (especially those of the heroine through a female confidante). The violent and gruesome *Thyestes* is the archetypal revenge tragedy, such as Kyd, Tourneur and to a certain extent Shakespeare (in *Hamlet*) exploited.

Gaius Plinius Secundus (AD 23–79), better known as Pliny the Elder, was concerned with natural phenomena throughout his life and at the time of his death, while attempting to record the eruption of Vesuvius in AD 79. He was born at Como of a wealthy family, practised law in Rome, and saw military service. He probably went to ground during the reign of Nero, returning to public life only in AD 70, after the accession of Vespasian. He held several senior government posts, including that of deputy governor of northern Spain, and wrote thirty books of Roman history as well as thirty-seven books of his *Natural History*. The latter, his only surviving work, covers many subjects, ranging from physics, geography and ethnology to zoology, botany, medicine and metallurgy, with digressions into anything else that interested him. He drew his material from many written sources. For example, in Book 20, on 'medicines derived from garden plants', he lists 1606 drugs and cites the works of 52 writers. It is thanks to his work that we have an understanding of Rome's buildings and art collections, as well as the perils of the stingray and the Roman solution for dandruff (see Chapter 7).

LETTER-WRITERS: CICERO AND PLINY THE YOUNGER

Much has already been said of Cicero the man, the political and forensic orator, and the statesman (see Chapters 2 and 3), and a number of his speeches and philosophical works, in which field he established a tradition of Roman writing, survive from the hand of this master of style and rhetoric. To the student of Roman life, however, the four collections of his letters, edited shortly after his death in 43 BC, are of even greater and more immediate interest: 'To his Brother Quintus', a soldier and provincial governor who also died in the proscriptions; 'To his Friends'; 'To Brutus', the conspirator; and 'To Atticus', who was Cicero's closest friend and confidant. Some of these letters were undoubtedly intended for ultimate publication – what public and literary figure does not have this eventuality in mind? – but, taken as a whole, they are refreshingly revealing about Cicero himself. From his catastrophic misjudgements of character (see Chapter 2) to the bitchy nicknames he gave to public figures – both his allies, such as Pompey, whom he called 'Pasha', and his enemies, such as Clodius Pulcher, 'Pretty Boy' – Cicero's letters paint a vivid picture of a wonderfully flawed individual and his day-to-day existence at the end of the Roman republic.

Gaius Plinius Caecilius Secundus (*c.* AD 61–*c.* AD 112), known as Pliny the Younger to distinguish him from his even more eminent and industrious uncle and adoptive father, clearly assumed his correspondence would be published within his lifetime, too. He showed early literary promise – writing a tragedy in Greek verse when he was just thirteen – and became a distinguished orator, public servant and philanthropist (aspects of his character that are constantly reinforced in his letters). He married three times and though he had no children he was awarded, as Martial and Suetonius had been, honorary status as a 'three-child parent', which bestowed certain privileges, including exemption from taxes. Not that Pliny lacked funds: he endowed a library at Como, a school for children of free-born parents, and a public baths, while the interest on an even larger sum was left in his will to provide for his 100 freedmen and fund an annual public banquet.

His letters range over private and public topics, including his first-hand account of the eruption of Vesuvius; his detailed description of his villa (2.17; see Chapter 7); news of a haunted house in Athens (7.27) and of a tame dolphin (9.33); and his official report to Trajan on the Christians (10.97), in his capacity as governor of Bithynia in Asia Minor, and his request for a policy decision on how to deal with them (see Chapter 4).

FURTHER READING

Readable translations of the works of all the major authors referred to in this book are available in Penguin paperback editions. Good modern versions in English of Apuleius, Caesar, Catullus, Cicero, Horace, Juvenal, Livy, Lucan, Lucretius, Ovid, Petronius, Plautus, Propertius and Suetonius are also published in paperback by Oxford University Press. The translations in the Loeb Classical Library (Harvard University Press) series tend to be more old fashioned, but the editions include the Latin texts as well.

Braund, S. Morton, *Latin Literature*, Routledge, 2001.

Cobbold, G.B. (trans.), *Vergil's Aenied: Hero, War, Humanity*, Bolchazy-Carducci, 2005.

Harrison, S. (ed.), *A Companion to Latin Literature*, Blackwell, 2004.

Howatson, Margaret (ed.), *The Oxford Companion to Classical Literature*, Oxford University Press, 1997 (new edition).

Janson, T., *A Natural History of Latin*, trans. N. Vincent and M. Damsgaard Sørensen, Oxford University Press, 2004.

Kenney, E.J. and Clausen, W.V. (eds), *The Cambridge History of Classical Literature II: Latin Literature*, Cambridge University Press, 1982.

Kraus, C.S. and Woodman, A.J., *Latin Historians*, Oxford University Press, 1997.

Lucretius, *On the Nature of Things*, trans. H.A.J. Munro, ed. J.D. Duff, Routledge, 1920 (4th edition).

McLeish, K., *Roman Comedy*, Bristol Classical Press, 1991.

Mellor, R., *Tacitus*, Routledge, 1994.

Poole, A. and Maule, J., *The Oxford Book of Classical Verse in Translation*, Oxford University Press, 1995.

Rutherford, R., *Classical Literature: A Concise History*, Blackwell, 2004.

Sharrock, A. and Ash, R., *Fifty Key Classical Authors*, Routledge, 2002.

Oxrhynchus Papyri website: http://www.papyrology.ox.ac.uk.

9 THE ROMAN ARMY

The growth and consolidation of the Roman empire is beautifully illustrated in the development of her army. Beginning with an army of citizen farmers who campaigned in the summers under temporary generals and yearly consuls in the regal period and the early republic (seventh to fourth centuries BC), Rome's army changed as her territories expanded in the third to first centuries BC from a temporary conglomeration of Italian farmers to a more formalized, permanent and professionalized force, which employed men from all over the Mediterranean as well as international tactics (e.g. at the Battle of Zama; see Chapter 2). Like Rome's political sphere in the late republic, the army was increasingly controlled by individuals (generals), many of whom came from Rome's most prestigious families. These generals not only recruited armies (starting with P. Scipio Africanus during the Punic Wars) but took a greater role in organizing (see discussion on 'Marian mules', Chapter 2), paying and gaining land settlements for their soldiers. The role of the army also changed from one based solely upon protection to one of financial and political support:

> the soldiers did not serve the interests of the state, but only of those who had recruited them and they gave their support to these people not because of the compulsion of the law, but because of personal inducements; they fought not against enemies of Rome but against private adversaries.
>
> **(Appian, *Civil Wars* 5.17)**

The situation deteriorated at the end of the republic into a series of bloody civil wars that set Romans against Romans. In the aftermath, the emperor Augustus responded by creating the first centralized system of organization for the Roman army, which addressed the social, political, administrative and economic roles that the Roman army had come to play.

THE NEW MODEL ARMY

Formerly, legions had been raised as needed, and disbanded when no longer required. But maintaining peace throughout the empire and with those outside its boundaries called for permanent forces stationed a long way from Italy. After the Battle of Actium, Augustus had under his notional command several armies comprising what remained of some sixty legions, many of which had fought against each other under rival commanders. He retired 100,000 veterans, many of whom he settled in colonies. He removed, insofar as he could, potentially subversive elements, and discharged men who were surplus to his requirements. He retained twenty-eight legions as a standing army, at which strength, give or take the odd legion, it remained for the next 200 years. These he disposed about the provinces of the empire, with concentrations at potential trouble-spots such as Syria and along the Rhine and the Danube. To maintain the loyalty of the legions to himself, provinces in which there were military units were under his control (imperial provinces), and he appointed the governors; governors of other provinces were appointed by the Senate (senatorial provinces). In this arrangement, many of the most fruitful provinces remained under imperial control.

Augustus nominated sixteen years as the term of service in the legions, followed by a further period of four years in reserve – to be in reserve meant staying with the legion but being excused normal duties. At the end of a man's service, he would received a set gratuity. In AD 5, the term of full-time service was raised to twenty years plus an unspecified period as a reservist, and the gratuity was fixed at 12,000 sesterces, equivalent to about fourteen years' pay for a legionary (Julius Caesar, at the beginning of the civil wars, had doubled his soldiers' pay to 225 denarii a year). The following year, Augustus established, with an initial gift from himself, the *aerarium militare*, a national fund for the payment of the gratuities, financed by levying taxes on inheritances and sales at auction. A soldier's pay, however, would continue to be paid out of the imperial revenues. To avoid encumbrances on the march (and to stop provincial women from inheriting large sums of Roman money), soldiers were forbidden to marry while on active service, though this did not prevent those on garrison duty setting up house and raising families with local women or camp-followers (called *contubernalis*).

A legion was commanded by a legate, in republican times a senior politician assigned to the post for a limited period, after which he might proceed to a provincial governorship. Caesar used a flexible system whereby a legate might, if circum-stances warranted it, command two or three legions. Augustus promoted men of ability, promise and proven loyalty to himself, who had served in some capacity as state officials, to military appointments as legates commanding individual legions.

THE LEGION

Under the republic, new **legions** were assigned serial numbers, with numbers I to IV reserved for those raised by consuls; those levied elsewhere were allocated higher numbers. Whatever the system, and it is still not fully understood, at any one time several legions might have the same number. To avoid confusion, each also came to assume a title or nickname, reflecting the circumstances of its formation, the name of its founder, the place where it was raised, or the front where it had served with distinction. So there was a First German as well as a First Italian legion, and a Second Parthian as well as a Second Trajan's Brave. A legion's own standard, often referred to as its 'eagle', was carried wherever it went. The eagle was the rallying point for troops in battle and a signal as to where the main action was; to lose it to the enemy was both a disaster and a disgrace. The *aquilifer*, who carried the legion's standard, ranked in seniority only just below a centurion and was also responsible for the safe-keeping of the legion's pay-chest. The *imaginifer* bore a second standard, with an image or the emblem of the emperor and, later, portraits of the imperial family too. Both wore animal skins over their uniforms, with the heads drawn up over their helmets.

A legion was a self-contained unit which even on the march could rely on its own resources for weeks on end. The legionaries themselves did all the manual work of digging, construction and engineering. Every man carried trenching tools and a pair of stakes which at each stop became part of the camp palisade. He also had to shoulder, or carry attached to his person, clothes, a cooking-pot, rations and any personal possessions, as well as his weapons and armour. Each legion also had a complement of specialists and craftsmen, known collectively as *immunes* ('exempt from normal duties'): surveyors, medical and veterinary orderlies, armourers, carpenters, hunters, even soothsayers. The surveyors went ahead of the column of march to select and lay out the site of the night's camp; it was always constructed to the same pattern and surrounded by a ditch, a rampart and a palisade, all of which had to be built afresh each time. Leather tents, each of which slept eight men, were carried separately by mules. At legionary headquarters or in the forts that defended the empire there was a wider range of non-combatant staff, including clerks to look after and process the paperwork, paymasters and military police (Figure 9.1).

In the field, a legion consisted of ten cohorts, each divided into six centuries of eighty men, each under the command of a centurion. The legionary legate was assisted by six younger officers – the military tribunes. These were short-term political appointees; the next step up for the senior tribune (*tribunus laticlavius*) was a seat in the Senate. The senior professional soldier in the legion was likely to be the camp prefect (*praefectus castrorum*). He was usually a man of some thirty years' service, and was responsible for organization, training and equipment. Day-to-day responsibility

FIGURE 9.1 Scene from Trajan's column. In the band below, legionaries are building a fortification. In the foreground (left), a medical orderly in a field dressing station patches up a leg wound, and (centre) a Dacian prisoner is brought before the emperor. Behind (left to right) standards are borne into battle; two musicians carry their *cornua* (circular trumpets used in battle to transmit orders); and carts, driven by mules, transport supplies on the march. Photo © Deutsches Archäologisches Institut, Rome: Anger, Neg. D-DAI-Rom 1989.0762.

was therefore in the hands of the centurions, the most senior of whom (*centurio primi pili*) commanded the first century of the first cohort, which consisted of five double centuries. Centurions did not march; they rode on horseback. They could also inflict corporal punishment – the twisted vine-staff each carried was not just an emblem of rank.

Augustus' system was a positive encouragement to social mobility. What you did, and how you did it, mattered more than who you were. A permanent army offered equestrians career structures as officers at the same time as the expansion of empire opened up for them military and civil posts in the provinces. Centurions could achieve equestrian rank, with the opportunities of status and wealth that it afforded.

OTHER UNITS

The legions were supported by auxiliary forces, composed of inhabitants of the empire who were not citizens of Rome, and who often brought their own military skills to add bite to time-honoured Roman infantry tactics. All squadrons of cavalry were auxiliaries, each one divided into troops of thirty men. While some auxiliaries fought as infantry and were equipped like legionaries, others retained their native dress and weapons, and served as archers, slingers, spearmen or broadswordsmen. Originally auxiliaries were led by their own chiefs, but in imperial times they were brought within an overall chain of command under Roman officers. From the reign of Claudius onwards, an auxiliary and his immediate family qualified for Roman citizenship after twenty-five years' service (a further extension of social mobility).

Under the empire, the only armed forces in Italy were the *cohors praetoria* (imperial guard) and the *cohortes urbanae* (city cohorts), who garrisoned Rome itself and whose presence was to prevent unrest rather than ward off possible attack from outside (which was unthinkable) and act as a police force. The imperial guard was a crack unit whose members wore a special uniform and received double pay, in addition to the bribes which they were routinely offered in the guise of bonuses for their allegiance. When the emperor went on campaign, the imperial guard went with him. In AD 6, Augustus recruited a further force, mainly from freedmen, the *vigiles*, 7000 strong, which patrolled the streets of Rome and served as its fire brigade. Continued imperial support of the *vigiles* is evident in Ostia, where a house of the fire brigade has been discovered, containing a shrine and numerous imperial statue bases.

Up to the time of Augustus, mastery of the seas had been achieved by ad hoc measures and largely foreign naval skills and crews. Augustus established a standing fleet of ships which were his own property and which he manned with free-born provincials and his own freedmen. His successors saw the wisdom of this initiative, and under the emperor's overall command there were established a number of regional flotillas: two for Italy (based at Misenum and Ravenna), and the rest to help control the provinces, centred on Mauretania, Egypt, Syria, the Black Sea, the Danube (which had two: upper and lower), the Rhine and Boulogne. The last of these, the British flotilla, was used by Agricola in AD 84 to soften up the opposition in Scotland with lightning raids along the east coast; it also discovered the Orkneys and established that Britain was an island.

WEAPONS AND TACTICS

The deployment of the Roman infantry in battle depended on its mobility. Apart from his hobnailed heavy sandals (the emperor Caligula, whose name means 'Little Boots', was born on campaign and named after these sandals), a legionary's legs were bare except in the colder climates, where tight-fitting knee-breeches were the order of the day. The most usual form of helmet was bronze, with a skull-cap inside and projections to protect the back of the neck and the ears and cheeks. A legionary carried on his left arm a cylindrical leather shield which was shaped to fit his body and was about 1.2 metres long. It was also useful as a siege weapon: a body of men crouched underneath their locked-together shields could approach a wall undeterred by missiles fired from above. Not unnaturally, this formation was known as the **'tortoise'** (*testudo*; Figure 9.2). On the march a man carried two javelins of different weights, each two metres long and with a metal head. One of these went into battle with him; he would hurl it at the enemy when in range, before getting down to the serious business of fighting hand to hand with his short, double-edged, thrusting and stabbing sword.

Battles were largely fought with 'conventional' weapons. The artillery of the time, of which the largest and most effective weapon was known as the *onager* (wild ass) because of its kick, was used as siege batteries. Each century, however, was allocated a mechanical arrow-shooter which was deployed in battle. A Roman general's

FIGURE 9.2 Image of *testudo* formation on Trajan's column (photo of a cast in the National Museum of Romanian History). This scene depicts use of the *testudo* formation during the siege of a Dacian city. Despite the odds against them (a fortified area and a clear bottleneck situation at the gates), the order and discipline of the Roman soldiers allow them to outstrip their less organized enemies, who are depicted sprawling in death at the bottom of the relief. Photo © CristianChirita/Wikimedia Commons.

objective was to break up and, if possible, break through the enemy lines by sheer force of concerted numbers and by manipulating his infantry. Horsemen were mainly employed to head off attacks by the opposition's cavalry and to pursue stragglers.

One example of typical Roman tactics and the *testudo* formation is the **Battle of Caer Caradoc**, which secured southern Britain for Rome in AD 51 (Figure 9.3). The battle was fought between the Briton chieftain Caratacus and the Roman general Publius Ostorius Scapula, founder of Rome's first colony of veterans in Calmulodunum (Colchester) and a *municipa* in Verulamium (St Albans). Our knowledge of this battle comes from Tacitus, whose histories are uniquely objective (without imperial propaganda). However, as in all our accounts of Roman Britain, Tacitus recorded only one side of the story. Caratacus positioned his troops on a hill flanked by two rivers of variable depths (the Severn and the Teme). This base was fortified with stone ramparts, making it difficult to approach and even harder to overpower. The Roman army crossed the Teme, and, under heavy missile attack, assumed the *testudo* formation while they approached and dismantled the crudely made stone ramparts (Tacitus, *Annals* 12.35).

The Romans pursued the Britons as they fled further up the hill and broke their lines so they were caught between fighting heavily armed legionaries and lightly armed auxilaries. Caratacus' wife, children and brothers were captured, but the chief himself managed to escape, only to be turned over to the Romans by Briton queen

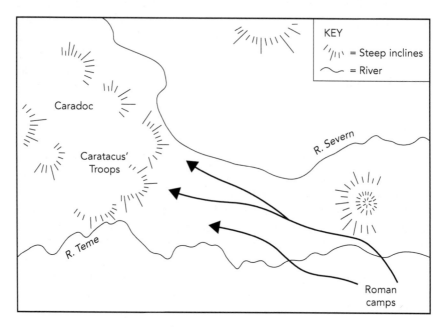

FIGURE 9.3 A reconstruction of the Battle of Caer Caradoc.

Cartismandua, who had signed a treaty with the invaders (Tacitus, *Annals* 12.36). The whole family was then taken to Rome for a triumphal procession, and Caratacus spoke so nobly that he was pardoned by the Senate, which compared the battle with some of Rome's greatest victories (Tacitus, *Annals* 38).

The Battle of Caer Caradoc illustrates the skill of the Roman army in a number of areas: technology (crossing the river and dismantling the fort), organization (the *testudo* formation) and strategy (catching the enemy between two lines of soldiers with different skills and weapons).

CONSOLIDATING AND PATROLLING THE EMPIRE

In republican times, the empire had been allowed to expand as opportunity and circumstances allowed, and as the Senate decreed. Augustus recognized the need for a specific foreign policy and saw that to undertake random wars of aggression, which were often attritional, in pursuit of new conquests was an uneconomic and unsatisfactory method of exercising it. Military success was a Roman way of life, but Augustus would ensure that it was gained by consolidating provinces and their defences, without enabling any commander to aspire to an overwhelming personal following among his troops. However, this policy, which also required the recruitment and training of local soldiers in order to sustain manpower on the frontiers, had dangerous and unforeseen consequences. In AD 9, during the Battle of the Teutoburg Forest, Publius Quintilius Varus lost three complete legions, three cavalry regiments and six auxiliary cohorts, after being enticed into unfamiliar territory between the rivers Weser and Ems by Arminius (*c.* 18 BC–AD 19), a German chieftain of the Cherusci but also a Roman citizen, who fomented a rebellion against Rome. Varus committed suicide, the Romans retired permanently to the west bank of the Rhine, and new Germanic tribes moved into the region which the Romans had vacated.

Augustus advised Tiberius not to try to extend the boundaries of the empire. His immediate successors were either too suspicious or too frightened of the army to do much else, with one notable exception – Claudius' invasion of Britain in AD 43. Three years earlier, Claudius had altered the status of Mauretania from client kingdom to two provinces. Thrace, too, had been a client kingdom in the time of Augustus, and in AD 46 Claudius defused an ugly situation by making it a province. That was that, as far as the extent of the empire was concerned, for more than fifty years. Then, in AD 101, Trajan crossed the river Danube and entered Dacia, without waiting to give a chance to the treaty agreed between his predecessor Domitian and Decebalus, king of Dacia. This campaign resulted in a great victory but dubious long-term advantage (though modern Romanian is derived from Latin), and Roman troops finally evacuated from Dacia in AD 275.

In AD 106 Trajan assumed into Roman 'protection' the area which became the province of Arabia and controlled the main caravan route to the coast of Judaea. In AD 114 and 115 he also annexed Armenia as far as the Persian Gulf, and overran Mesopotamia, but these were tactical acts of immediate military expediency which were promptly reversed by his successor, Hadrian, in AD 117.

LIFE IN THE ROMAN ARMY

Some legions remained on the same station for many years; others were deployed as the situation demanded. The Second Augusta, raised by Augustus himself, and the Twentieth *Valeria Victrix* ('Strong and Victorious') spearheaded the invasion of Britain in AD 43; they were also among the last to be evacuated in AD 400, though a detachment from the Twentieth was sent to Mainz on the Rhine in AD 270 to help deal with an uprising there. The Twentieth was also Agricola's strike-force in northern Britain, and it was probably his successor who constructed the fortress at Inchtuthil in Perthshire as its headquarters. This, the most northern of all Roman permanent fortifications, occupied an area 457 metres square and was to have been a purpose-built city in miniature, with streets and full administrative, residential and leisure amenities, including separate houses for each of the officers and a hospital containing sixty five-bedded wards opening off each side of a wide corridor of the rectangular building. However, it was abandoned while still under construction and then systematically destroyed to prevent it falling into the hands of the enemy.

Clearly there was significant social as well as geographical mobility in the Roman empire and its army. The British Museum houses the tombstone of one G. Saufieus, a Macedonian soldier of the Ninth Legion Hispania who was quartered at Lincoln. (His legion lost 2000 soldiers during Boudicca's rebellion in 60–61 AD.) Born in Heraclea, he was a member of the Fabian voting tribe (with a citizen's rights) who died after twenty-five years' service in Britain. Another soldier's tombstone, found in Cirencester, records the life of Sextus Valerius Genialis, from Holland, who joined a Thracian (modern Bulgaria) cavalry regiment, served for twenty years, and died in Colchester before Boudicca's rebellion (Figure 9.4). While one may assume, on the basis of their names, that army regiments were formed on a regional basis, it is clear from such tombstones that this was not always the case. Both G. Saufieus and Sextus Valerius Genialis joined army regiments named after regions far from their home provinces and ended up in yet another distant area of the empire. Their epic journeys were recorded on their memorials, as was the fundamental role that the army played in their lives: the age of each man appeared on his tombstone, but so did the length of time he served as a soldier.

FIGURE 9.4 Tombstone of Sextus Valerius Genialis from Cirencester, now in the Corinium Museum, Gloucester. Genialis – a Frisian tribesman (from modern-day Holland) but a member of the Thracian first cavalry regiment (from modern-day Bulgaria), which was based in Colchester before Boudicca's rebellion, c. AD 43–61 – illustrates the truly cosmopolitan nature of the Roman army. He died at forty, after twenty years' service, and the distinctly military image of an armoured man on horseback, spearing a defeated and disarmed opponent, reflects both the occupation of the deceased and the Roman army's superior fighting skills. © Cotswold District Council, courtesy of the Corinium Museum.

Letters on wooden tablets discovered at Vindolanda (near Hadrian's Wall) reveal aspects of daily life and administration among the soldiers – from accounts of men who held various positions in Britain and requests for supplies to an invitation to a child's birthday party. These tablets create an image of the Roman army as a community that incorporated women, slaves and soldiers from across a vast empire. The evidence of the **Vindolanda tablets**, and *ostraca* (small shards of pottery inscribed with similar information) in the eastern empire, also attests to high levels of literacy among the soldiers, many of whom had to be able to read and write to carry out their administrative tasks. In addition to learning battle tactics, Roman soldiers received an education in writing, medical, construction and/or engineering skills that could be used long after their military careers were over.

The Roman army was responsible for the production of the walls, roads and milestones which defined the empire, even it its furthest frontiers. The extent of the occupation of a region was bounded by a *limes* (plural: *limites*), which simply meant a 'path' or 'track'. Then it came to refer to the military road which linked the permanent forts housing the units of a legion, whose task it was to discourage hostile military gatherings beyond the 'line', keep the peace and allow free movement of trade across it. Thus *limes* came to mean 'boundary' or 'frontier' and the English word derived from it to signify something which 'may not be passed'. Sometimes, as in the case of Hadrian's Wall and the Antonine Wall in Britain, the *limes* was an actual wall. Hadrian's bold decision to review (rather than extend) the physical boundaries of the empire resulted in a different kind of action throughout the empire. In addition to his wall in Britain, he strengthened (with a wooden palisade) the defences of the Rhine, which, together with those on the upper Danube, consisted of 170 forts and fortresses. In Africa, where problems could be expected from cavalry, he devised a combination of a deep, wide ditch and a low stone wall.

The army's role not only as soldiers but as administrators, builders and engineers is depicted on Trajan's column. A young Roman seeing such images may well have been seduced by the opportunities for social mobility, travel and education that joining the army seemed to offer. However, for those who dreamed of travel, adventure, glory and a decade of commitment-free sexual escapades, the reality (e.g. laying roads and building walls in damp and cold Britian, or standing watch all day in the scorching heat of the Syrian desert) may have been somewhat less rosy. Most military service was tedious, but it could also be very risky, even before the fighting began: sea travel was dangerous (and many Romans could not swim); wounds (even something as minor as a splinter) could prove fatal; and dying far from home was commonplace.

FURTHER READING

* indicates sourcebook

Bowman, A.K., *Life and Letters on the Roman Frontier: Vindolanda and its People*, British Museum, 1994.

*Campbell, B., *The Roman Army, 31 BC–AD 337: A Sourcebook*, Routledge, 1994.

Erdcamp, P. (ed.), *A Companion to the Roman Army*, Blackwell, 2007.

Goldsworthy, A., *The Complete Roman Army*, Thames & Hudson, 2011 (reissue).

James, S., *Rome and the Sword: How Roman Warriors and Weapons Shaped Roman History*, Thames & Hudson, 2011.

Keppie, L., *The Making of the Roman Army: From Republic to Empire*, Routledge, 1998 (new edition).

Pollard, N. and Berry, J., *The Complete Roman Legion*, Thames & Hudson, 2012.

Sidebottom, H., *Ancient Warfare: A Very Short Introduction*, Oxford University Press, 2004.

Webster, G., *The Roman Imperial Army of the First and Second Centuries AD*, Constable & Robinson, 1996 (new edition).

Vindolanda website: http://vindolanda.csad.ox.ac.uk/.

10 CHRISTIAN ROME: THE FALL OF THE ROMAN EMPIRE AND ITS LEGACY (AD 330–PRESENT)

> The decline of Rome was the natural and inevitable effect of immoderate great-ness. Prosperity ripened to the principle of decay; the causes of destruction multiplied with the extent of conquest; and as soon as time or accident had removed artificial supports, the stupendous fabric yielded to the pressure of its own weight.
>
> **(Edward Gibbon, *The History of the Decline and Fall of the Roman Empire* 4.173–174)**

The traditional ideologies and historical framework which Rome's early emperors had sought to institutionalize in her monumental buildings became a liability in a new Christian world, where pagan traditions were not immediately reconciled with Christian values. That Rome retained her pagan values is attested not only in the number of Christian churches which remained outside the city walls until the fifth century AD but also in the continuation of pagan games and festivals throughout that century (the last Lupercalia festival, for example, was recorded around AD 494, when Pope Gelasisus criticized a Roman senator for 'streaking about' in the buff). The historian Ammianus Marcellinus, who lived in Rome in the fourth century and fought as a soldier, captures this fluctuating world, which struggled at times to reconcile the prejudices of Christians and pagans alike. Although his manuscript survives only as a fragmented codex from between AD 353 and 378, it reveals a flame of traditional Roman culture as it flickers into oblivion; or, as Gibbon would suggest, collapses upon itself.

THE FALL OF ROME (AD 330–476)

Constantine had intended that, upon his death, the rule of the empire should devolve to a team of four: his three sons – Constantine II (*c.* AD 316–340), Constantius II (AD

317–361) and Constans (*c.* AD 322–350) – and his nephew Dalmatius. To form a tetrarchy on a dynastic principle was, however, more than the system could stand. Dalmatius was murdered, the brothers bickered, their armies fought, and the empire was in splinters once again. The failure of dynasty was a lesson even Rome's leaders would never learn, to her great peril.

Valentinian (AD 321–375) was nominated as emperor by the troops at Nicaea, on condition that he appoint a joint ruler. What happened next is described by Ammianus Marcellinus, writing some twenty-five years after the event, in his continuation of the histories of Tacitus:

> Now, after Valentinian had been acclaimed emperor in Bithynia, he gave orders that the army should march in two days' time, and called a meeting of his senior officers, as though he intended to seek sound advice rather than follow his own inclinations. When he enquired who would be the best person to be his partner in running the empire, everyone was silent, except Dagalaifus, the master of the cavalry, who answered confidently: 'If you love your family, great emperor, you have a brother; if you love the state, choose someone else to invest with this office.' Valentinian was not pleased, but made no comment, hiding his thoughts. By a forced march, the army reached Nicomedia on 1 March [AD 364], where he appointed his brother Valens as chief of his personal staff, with the rank of tribune . . . Having concluded that he was already overwhelmed by the amount of urgent business and that there should be no further delay, on 28 March he presented Valens on the outskirts of the city and proclaimed him Augustus. There was universal acceptance of the appointment – no one dared oppose it.
>
> **(History 26.4)**

Valentinian and Valens (*c.* AD 328–378) made an amicable east–west division. However, the citizens of the empire, particularly the Christians, continued to struggle with dogmatic debates about Jesus' divinity and his relationship with his father, which had been discussed as early as AD 325 at the first council at Nicaea, where a number Christian leaders had met to try to establish an ecumenical, or 'universal', doctrine from the church. The results of their deliberations survive today in the Nicene Creed and the celebration of Easter as a keystone in the Christian calendar. However, from the very beginning Christians had a variety of practices and interpretations of doctrine that were not easily reconciled. The more lengthy version of the Nicene Creed which is used was instituted sixty years later in the first council of Constantinople (AD 381) and it differs in several respects from the original.

The empire was briefly united again in AD 394 under Theodosius I (*c.* AD 346–395), the 'Great'. He was a Christian who had been baptized in AD 380, and it was he who effectively made Christianity the official religion of the empire by sanctioning the destruction of the great cult Temple of Serapis in Alexandria, and by passing measures prohibiting pagan practices. Ammianus describes the Temple of Serapis, including a branch of the famous library at Alexandria, as the glory of the empire (*History* 22.16). His account predates the destruction of the temple (and library) in AD 391, when Theodosius passed an act of intolerance on pagan worship. Theodosius also revenged the lynching of one of his army commanders by inviting the citizens of Thessalonica to a show at the circus and then massacring them in their seats, a lapse for which the archbishop of Milan persuaded him to do public penance. Ammianus notes that there was not only acrimony between pagans and Christians, but increasing divisions within Christianity itself, observing at one point that not even the savage beast is as deadly to mankind as Christians are to each other. Just as Christian accounts of pagan practice are dismissed as biased, Ammianus, a pagan, may have had a similar bias; however, he is one of the last pagan voices in Roman history and he does endeavour to be objective. A century after Christianity was accepted by Constantine, the circle of persecution was complete: in AD 415, the first Christian witch hunt resulted in the murder of Hypatia, a neo-Platonic philosophy teacher and mathematician in Alexandria, who was dragged to a church and stripped before she was killed.

At some point in the fourth century AD a fierce nomadic people known as the Huns set out inexorably westwards from their homelands on the plains of central Asia, triggering equally destructive movements among the tribes in their path. They displaced the Alani, who then displaced the Vandals from their territories between the Vistula and the Rhine, who in turn swept through Gaul, Spain and into North Africa. Also displaced in this orgy of migration were the Ostrogoths (Bright Goths) and Visigoths (Wise Goths), who bordered on the Roman empire immediately on the other side of the lower Danube, and had in various guises fought implacably with Rome before. Britain was now abandoned to the determined waves of Picts, Scots and Saxons who had threatened to overwhelm the land, and the former outpost's legions were rushed to the final defence, no longer of the empire, but of Rome itself.

Under Theodosius' sons Arcadius (*c.* AD 378–408) and Honorius (AD 384–423), the eastern and western parts of the Roman empire finally divided, despite attempts to represent solidarity with monuments in the Roman Forum honouring a successful campaign in Libya (Figure 10.1). Their decision to kill Flavius Stilicho – a half-Vandal, half-provincial general whom Gibbon describes as 'Rome's last great general' after describing the peace he brokered (thought bribery) with Alaric the Visigoth (d. 411) – was shortsighted. His murder sparked others and created dissent among many, who began to look elsewhere for leadership. Without a strong general or the solidarity Honorius and Arcadius sought to proclaim, the city of Rome was captured and sacked by Alaric in AD 410.

Pope Leo I (r. AD 440–461) negotiated terms with Attila the Hun (*c.* AD 406–453) to leave Italy after he had ravaged it (AD 452), but in AD 455 the Vandals sacked Rome

FIGURE 10.1 Dedication to the three emperors – Honorius, Arcadius and Theodoisius – in the Roman Forum, c. AD 402–406. This dedication, in front of the Arch of Septimius Severus, was erected by the Senate to honour the *fides* and *virtus* of the emperors after one of the Gothic Wars. The marble block had previously formed part of an equestrian statue (a hoof print is still visible on one side, as are Greek letters on the bottom right corner), illustrating that late antique Rome was the 'city that ate itself'. This monument, along with an Arch of Honorius (much smaller than Severus' arch), was meant to show solidarity, but the erasure of Flavius Stilicho's name illustrates the increasingly volatile political environment in Rome. Photo by Gregor Kalas, Professor of Architecture at the University of Tennessee, who has recently reconstructed the late antique Roman Forum as part of the 'Visualizing Statues' project (http://inscriptions.etc.ucla.edu).

from the sea. The final act of this drama was played out in AD 475–476. The Roman empire in the west was now, to all intents and purposes, merely Italy, and its proud armies had been reduced to a mixed bag of Germanic mercenaries. Orestes, formerly secretary to Attila, was appointed military commander-in-chief by Julius Nepos, whom Leo I (emperor of the east, AD 457–474) had sent to Italy to take up the vacant position of emperor of the west. Orestes responded by marching his troops on Ravenna, to which Honorius had transferred the imperial court in AD 404. Nepos fled, and Orestes, having waited in vain for some official authorization from the east, nominated his fourteen-year-old son Romulus emperor of the west, with himself as head of internal and external affairs. However, when he refused to honour requests for land grants from the mercenaries, which had been granted to their predecessors in the service of the empire, they turned to their commander, Odoacer (d. AD 493), who agreed to meet their demands if they would recognize him as their king.

Rome, the city that had once gorged itself on grain from Egypt, Libyan figs, Spanish olive oil and peppercorns from India, was now struggling for survival. Imports were declining as the empire collapsed, and the large latifundia farms of the late republic were long gone, as were the farmers who could have been recruited to serve in a local army. Rome's great buildings were falling into ruin or being cannibalized for other constructions, including a number of churches, many of which were created in the shadow of former temples and law courts (often called 'basilicas'). Indeed, the form of the modern Christian church, with a long central aisle ending in an apse, has its origins in the Greek 'king's court'.

Nearly 1000 years after Rome had expelled her kings, the empire reverted to a kingship. In AD 476, Odoacer, feeling that an emperor was now unnecessary, killed Orestes and deposed Romulus Augustulus. He then informed Zeno (emperor in the east, AD 474–491) that he would be happy to rule as king of Italy under Zeno's jurisdiction. The Roman empire in the west was at an end. The Roman Catholic Church now assumed the role of unifying the lands and peoples which had formerly been Roman, organizing its sphere of influence along Roman lines.

There is rarely a single cause for truly catastrophic disasters. Civilizations less stable and less well organized than Rome have survived inert autocracy, economic failure, political and administrative incompetence, chronic internal disunity, plague, class barriers, corruption in high places, decline of moral standards, and the necessity of radically changing the structure and status of the workforce. Ultimately, what hastened the end of the Roman empire was the failure of the very instrument by which it had been founded – the Roman army. The policy of dividing it into frontier forces and mobile field forces which could be dispatched to trouble spots had its disadvantages. However effective communications might be, the infantry always had to march to its destination – in training, recruits were required to march twenty miles in five hours, but that would be about the most an army could travel on foot in a day.

The creation of more mobile armies simply meant that each one was weaker, at a time when heavy losses had been incurred in the civil wars in which prospective emperors engaged and in fighting off the invasions of Italy and of Gaul.

The eastern Roman empire, largely by reason of its geographical situation, was bypassed by the hordes of invaders. It was, in any case, less vulnerable to outside attack than the west, and its internal political stability was greater. Between AD 364 and 476, there were sixteen emperors in the west but only eight in the east (and those figures do not take into account usurpers who did not make it to the top, of which there were only two in the east in those 112 years).

THE EASTERN EMPIRE

Byzantium, capital of the eastern empire, had first been reconstructed in the time of Septimius Severus not just as a Roman city, but modelled on Rome itself, on and around seven hills. The building of a racecourse on the lines of the Circus Maximus where there was insufficient space for it was not beyond the skill and ingenuity of the architects. It was constructed on the flattened summit of a hill, with one end of the stadium suspended over the edge on massive vaulted supports. Eastern influence led to the development of a distinctive style of Byzantine architecture, with the dome the predominant feature and interiors richly decorated, all of which are exemplified in the surviving church of Hagia Sophia (Figure 10.2). The history of this building is a testament to the troubled times: a church was built on the site by Constantine, restored by Constantius II in AD 360, but burned down in AD 404 in a series of riots following the exile of the emperor Arcadius' wife. A second church (some of which survives, mostly underground) was commissioned by Theodosius and finished in AD 415, but this burned down in AD 532, during the rule of Justinian, when much of the city was destroyed in the Nika rebellion. This rebellion began as a riot between two sets of fans (the Blues and the Greens) in the stadium before developing into a full-scale revolt. The widespread destruction gave Justinian an unanticipated opportunity to indulge his passion for building and led to the golden age of Byzantine architecture. Hagia Sophia, designed by Anthemius to be much larger than any of its predecessors, was just one of four major new churches. It boasted a main dome which, unusually, was built on a square base; this was replaced in AD 555 by one with forty arched windows around its circumference. Hagia Sophia became a mosque in 1453, but since 1935 it has been a museum. Churches based on its design have been built across the world, including St Sophia in Galston, Scotland (1885–1886).

Justinian ruled from AD 527 to 565, and was said to have been eighty-three when he died. He was born in Illyricum, the son of a Slavonic peasant, and was appointed joint emperor in AD 527 by his uncle Justin, who died a few months later. Justin had

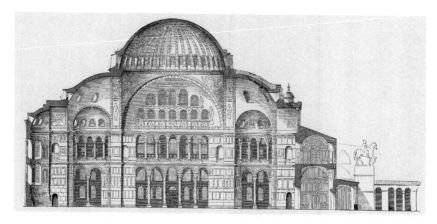

FIGURE 10.2 Architectural reconstruction of Hagia Sophia. This building, possibly the greatest surviving example of Byzantine architecture, featured golden niches and ceilings that would inspire the basilica of San Marco (Venice), which includes spoils, including a bronze *quadriga* statue, 'rescued' by the Venetians during the Ottomans' sack of Constantinople. The lower levels are filled with rich polychrome marbles from across the empire – green (from Laconia), yellow (from Numidia), red and white (from Caria) – grey granite and purple porphyry (Egypt). After seeing the finished Hagia Sophia, Justinian famously boasted, 'Solomon, I have outdone thee.' Wikicommons Wilhelm Lübke/Max Semrau.

risen through the ranks of the army to be emperor, allegedly without ever learning to read or write. He had not, however, spared the education of his nephew, whose ambitious aims included stamping out corruption in government, refining and upholding the law, uniting the churches in the east, and taking Christianity forcibly to the barbarians in the west, thus recovering for the empire territories that it had lost. In pursuit of this last aim, his skilled generals Narses, formerly employed as an imperial eunuch, and Belisarius tore into the barbarian kingdoms and restored to the empire, albeit only temporarily, its former African provinces and northern Italy, including the city of Rome itself. At the same time Justinian himself recaptured southern Spain while that region was in the throes of a civil war.

Before becoming emperor, Justinian had committed the solecism of marrying an actress called Theodora. Until her death in AD 548, however, she proved an admirable foil and a supportive wife, on the one hand standing up for persecuted members of the heretical Monophysite sect (whose views she supported), and on the other comforting and encouraging her husband at times of stress, notably during the Nika rebellion. While the eastern empire was largely Greek in its mores, it still upheld Roman law. The Justinian Code (AD 528–529) brought together all valid imperial laws. In addition Justinian issued a revised and up-to-date 'Digest' (AD 530–533) of the works of the classical jurists, and a textbook on Roman law (AD 533). He is also credited with introducing into Europe the culture of the silkworm.

After Justinian, the eastern empire was Roman in name only. In AD 1053 the church of the east split with the church of Rome and in due course begat the church of Russia. On 29 May 1453, Constantinople and its emperor Constantine XI fell to the Turks and the forces of Islam, who had already overrun what remained of the empire's narrow footholds along the coast of the Sea of Marmara.

THE LEGACY OF ROME

The remarkable thing about the civilization of Rome is not that it ultimately collapsed, but that from such minute beginnings it survived for so long under so many external and internal pressures. It lasted long enough and the pressures were resisted firmly enough for many Roman practices and traditions, even before the Christian era, to become entrenched in modern life.

While it was not in the Romans' nature, or necessarily in their interest, to invent startling labour-saving devices, their systematic attitude to measurement enabled them to establish the basis of a calendar, and to devise methods to assess distances with great accuracy. They turned building into a science and gave a new impetus to hydraulics. The contribution of Roman law to European law is incalculable, and from the Romans come the traditions of impartial justice and trial by jury. Banking, insurance, public hospitals, the postal system, the daily newspaper, the fire service, motorways (and motorway hotels), public libraries, central heating, glass windows, apartment blocks, sanitation, drainage and sewers, social benefits and public education are all Roman institutions. So is that universal common bond and basis of social life throughout the modern world which they called *familia* and we recognize as the family, the extended family, or the family unit.

Except for the addition of three letters, the alphabet used today for the English language, as well as for the Romance languages (French, Italian, Spanish, Portuguese and Romanian), German, Scandinavian and other European languages, is that which the Romans developed and refined for their own use. Further, the Romance languages themselves are firmly based on Latin, as is one-third of the English language. The success of Latin as the foundation of so much of modern language is not just due to the fact that it was possible to use it eloquently for the expression of literary forms – and without a close acquaintance with Latin literature on the part of writers in other languages, there would be virtually no English or European literature before about 1800 – but also because it could be employed so precisely to express points of law, science, theology, philosophy, architecture, agriculture and medicine.

Latin remained the language of scholarship and prose in western Europe during the Middle Ages and the Renaissance; it is the language of the Roman Catholic Church; and it survives within the English language in the form of many tags, phrases and abbreviations. Latin was also the language for education, uniting scholars, lawyers, philosophers and theologians for centuries across Europe with a common grounding in Latin literature. Even as different languages emerged, such as early Italian in Dante's *Divine Comedy* (*c.* 1308–1321), Virgil remained an iconic guiding figure in both the language and the text.

There are many correlations between pagan and Christian holidays. For example, the party spirit and generosity that defined the Roman Saturnalia (around the winter solstice) survive in the Christian holiday of Christmas, while aspects of the sexually charged Lupercalia (13–14 February) persist on St Valentine's Day. Similarly, Roman art and architecture provided models for many European artists in the late antique, medieval and Renaissance periods, as well as for architects working in more recent times, such as those who designed the Capitol Building in Washington, DC, St Paul's Cathedral in London and the palace square in St Petersburg.

Rome's imperial system, both its titles and its imagery, survive in many modern terms that are synonymous with power: emperor (*imperator*), prince (*princeps*), tzar (Caesar), duke (*dux*). Charlemagne (AD 742–814) adopted the title 'Imperator Romanorum', brought about a Carolingian renaissance of art and minted coins, in addition to redefining the western empire. Pope Sixtus IV (r. 1471–1484), who retained the title *pontifex maximius*, restored the *Aqua Vergina* (to provide an alternative water source to the Tiber), restored churches, repaved and rebuilt roads, cleared out the Campus Martius, built the Ponte Sisto, and began the Capitoline collection of Roman artefacts (such as the Capitoline wolf; see Figure 1.2). Napoleon (1769–1821) used the Justinian Code as a model for his new system of law, and invoked the Roman ideology and iconography of empire (Figure 10.3) during his campaigns in Europe and Africa, calling himself 'emperor of the French', erecting triumphal arches in Paris with the symbol of the eagle, and bringing back historical spoils for what was then renamed the Musée Napoléon.

More recently, Benito Mussolini (1883–1945), 'il Duce', manipulated Rome's historical past, bringing back the image of *fasces* in his Fascist reforms, rebuilding a new centre, the Piazzale del Imperatore, between the site of Augustus' *Ara Pacis* and his mausoleum and commissioning a new version of Augustus' *Res Gestae* (Figure 10.4). Mussolini also has the distinction of being the last world leader to import an obelisk, found by Italian soldiers in Axum, Ethiopia, and transported to Italy as a spoil of war and a symbol of empire in 1937. Originally Egyptian monuments to the sun god Ra, obelisks are now more commonly associated with the Roman assertion of imperial power. Examples were moved to Rome by Augustus after his victory over Egypt and by Constantine to Constantinople, and others were later erected in the

FIGURE 10.3 François Rude, *Napoleon Awakening to Immortality* (1845). This image of Napoleon, sitting up as he awakens to everlasting life, represents a combination of Roman funerary imagery in his reclining posture (like the Sarcophagus of the Spouses; Figure 1.3) and the ideal classical style of Augustus' public portraits – looking ahead, with a serene and ageless expression (like the Prima Porta statue; Figure 3.4). Dressed in military regalia, with the *corona civica* ('civic crown') and *capite velato* ('covered head'), while a dead eagle lies at his feet, the portrait evokes the consolidation of military, political and religious power in one man. Musée D'Orsay, Paris. Photo © Musée d'Orsay, Dist. RMN-Grand Palais/Patrice Schmidt.

Place de la Concord in Paris (1833), on London's Embankment (1878) and in Central Park in New York City (1881). Mussolini's obelisk has the further distinction of being the only one ever to be repatriated: it was carefully dismantled and flown back to Ethiopia in 2005. These monuments, which climb desperately towards the sun, have

FIGURE 10.4 Dedication of Augustus' *Res Gestae* by Mussolini. This modern copy of Augustus' *Res Gestae* (restored in 2005 and incorporated into the Ara Pacis Museum) survives on the *Via Ripetta*, across the street from Augustus' mausoleum (where the original version was erected). This wall is all that remains of a pavilion erected by Mussolini in 1938. Hitler was fascinated by this monument during his visit to Rome in that year and described Mussolini as 'the founder of a new imperium'. Photo by author.

come to represent both the ambition and the transience of imperial power: past, present and future.

Studying the Romans is, in many respects, like holding a mirror up to the modern world. It is a rare opportunity to observe both what has changed over the course of 2000 years and what remains fixed in the human experience. Despite all our advances in technology, science and medicine, are we any more successful at overcoming human nature? Gibbon's reasons for the decline of Rome (outlined at the start of this chapter) could just as easily be attributed to civilization in his time or in the present. Ultimately, it is both their humanity and their ambition to surpass those who had come before them – in control, in exploration and in enjoying life – which make the Romans such an inspiring and illuminating subject. In examining their character, we gain a better understanding of our own.

FURTHER READING

Bowersock, G.W. and P. Brown (eds), *Late Antiquity: A Guide to the Post-Classical World*, Cambridge University Press, 1999.

Elsner, J., *Art and Culture in Ancient Rome*, Cambridge University Press, 1996.

Gibbon, E., *The History of the Decline and Fall of the Roman Empire*, ed. J.B. Bury, Methuen, 1909 (2nd edition).

Jenkyns, R. (ed.), *The Legacy of Rome*, Oxford University Press, 1992.

Jensen, R.M., *Understanding Early Christian Art*, Routledge, 2000.

Lenski, N., *The Cambridge Companion to the Age of Constantine*, Cambridge, 2005.

Mitchell, S., *A History of the Later Roman Empire AD 284–641*, Oxford University Press, 2006.

Rousseau, P. (ed.), *A Companion to Late Antiquity*, Blackwell, 2008.

Ward-Perkins, B., *The Fall of Rome: And the End of Civilization*, Oxford University Press, 2005.

For a brilliant reconstructions of the buildings, monuments and statues in the late antique Roman Forum, see 'Visualizing Statues', a collaborative project between Diane Favro, Christopher Johanson and Gregor Kalas undertaken at the Experiential Technologies Center at the University of California, Los Angeles, with funding from the National Endowment for the Humanities: http://inscriptions.etc.ucla.edu/.

Appendix 1

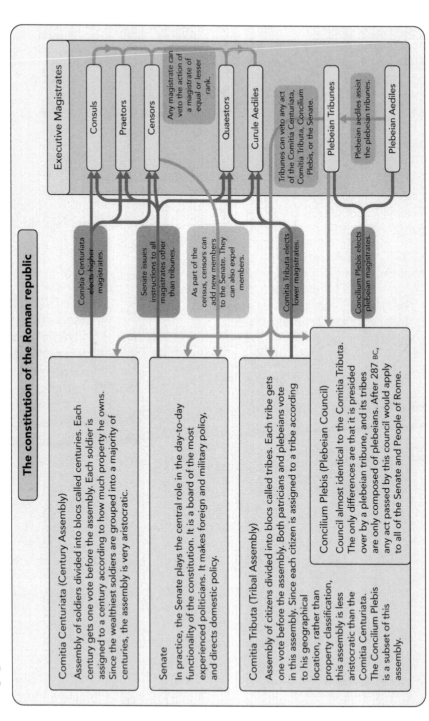

The constitution of the Roman republic

Comitia Centuriata (Century Assembly)

Assembly of soldiers divided into blocs called centuries. Each century gets one vote before the assembly. Each soldier is assigned to a century according to how much property he owns. Since the wealthiest soldiers are grouped into a majority of centuries, the assembly is very aristocratic.

Senate

In practice, the Senate plays the central role in the day-to-day functionality of the constitution. It is a board of the most experienced politicians. It makes foreign and military policy, and directs domestic policy.

Comitia Tributa (Tribal Assembly)

Assembly of citizens divided into blocs called tribes. Each tribe gets one vote before the assembly. Both patricians and plebeians vote in this assembly. Since each citizen is assigned to a tribe according to his geographical location, rather than property classification, this assembly is less aristocratic than the Comitia Centuriata. The Concilium Plebis is a subset of this assembly.

Concilium Plebis (Plebeian Council)

Council almost identical to the Comitia Tributa. The only differences are that it is presided over by a plebeian tribune, and its tribes are only composed of plebeians. After 287 BC, any act passed by this council would apply to all of the Senate and People of Rome.

Executive Magistrates

- Consuls
- Praetors
- Censors

Any magistrate can veto the action of a magistrate of equal or lesser rank.

- Quaestors
- Curule Aediles

Tribunes can veto any act of the Comitia Centuriata, Comitia Tributa, Concilium Plebis, or the Senate.

- Plebeian Tribunes

Plebeian aediles assist the plebeian tribunes.

- Plebeian Aediles

Comitia Centuriata elects higher magistrates.

Senate issues instructions to all magistrates other than tribunes.

As part of the census, censors can add new members to the Senate. They can also expel members.

Comitia Tributa elects lower magistrates.

Concilium Plebis elects plebeian magistrates.

Appendix 2

ROMAN NAMES AND NOMENCLATURE: A BRIEF INTRODUCTION

A year of reading Virgil can offer little help when trying to decipher a Roman building inscription or reading a simple funerary epitaph. Public language, written in block capitals, contains abbreviations of names and common words that can be confounding for the uninitiated. However, a basic understanding of these names and the formulae is easily learned. This appendix offers an introduction to Roman names, both how they are recorded and what they reveal about an individual. A further discussion and slideshow on the companion website titled 'How to read a Roman inscription' offers a tutorial on reading Roman monuments and provides a list of common abbreviations.

Roman nomenclature was originally a simple process by which family names were passed down, originally to the firstborn son and later to all members of the family, including manumitted slaves. In the early republic, a man named Marcus would pass his *nomen* (name) only on to his firstborn son, a tradition that remains in some societies today. Eventually, all sons took the name Marcus, which became a *praenomen* (pre-name), and were also given a second name, such as Tullius, as their *nomen* (e.g. Marcus Tullius). As noble families propagated, the combination of two family names was no longer sufficient (or, perhaps, was simply confusing). A third name, called a *cognomen* (literally a 'known name'/'nickname') became popular as early as the fourth century BC with figures such as Appius Claudius Caecus ('the Blind') or Appius Claudius Caudex ('Blockhead') (see Chapter 2). *Cognomen*, not unlike slave names such as Felix ('Lucky'), were often taken in jest or refer to a family's agrarian roots: for example, Lentulus ('Lentil') and Cicero ('Chickpea'). Roman citizens who were successful in battle in the republic (and members of the imperial family during the empire) could be given the honour of an *agnomen* (e.g. P. Cornelius Scipio Africanus, which referred to his victory in the Battle at Zama in North Africa; see Chapter 2).

By the late republic, the *praenomen* was often abbreviated (see chart below): for example, M. Tullius Cicero. With imperial titles, such as Tiberius Claudius Nero, the first two names were sometimes abbreviated (e.g. 'Ti. Cl.') on monuments. Imperial names, often popular during the lifetime of an emperor (and given to all manumitted slaves of the imperial household), are often used for dating purposes, as they can indicate a time after which (*terminus post quem*) a person was likely to be born.

Family names were also passed on to daughters and household staff. Cornelia (mother of the Gracchi, daughter of P. Cornelius Scipio Africanus), Tullia (daughter of Cicero) and members of the imperial family (e.g. Julia, the daughter of G. Julius Octavius, and Agrippina, the daughter of M. Agrippa and Julia) record this practice. Slaves, who were often given 'pet' names or names relating to their origins (e.g. Philematio had a Greek name; see Chapter 6), took one or two of their patron's names upon manumission (e.g. Philematio became Aurelia Philematio, attesting to her connection with that family).

ROMAN CITIZEN

M(arcus) Statius M(arci) f(ilius)
Gal(eria tribu) Maximus

'Marcus Statius Maximus,
son of Marcus, of the Galeria voting tribe'

SLAVE

Felix M(arci) s(ervus)

'Felix, slave of Marcus'

FREEDMAN

M(arcus) Statius M(arci) l(ibertus) Felix   'Marcus Statius Felix, freedman of Marcus'

DAUGHTER

M(arcia) Statia M(arcus) f(ilia)

Marcia Statia, daughter of Marcus

MOST COMMON LATIN *PRAENOMINA*

APP	Appius
A/AV/AVL	Aulus
C/G	Caius/Gaius
CN/GN	Cnaeus/Gnaeus
D	Decimus
L	Lucius
M/ (= five-stroke M)	Manius
M	Marcus
N	Numerius
P	Publius
Q	Quintus
SER	Servius
SEX	Sextus
S	Spurius
TI	Tiberius
T	Titus
V	Vibius

COMMON ABBREVIATIONS

AN/ANN	*ann(is)/ann(orum)*	years
AVG	*Augustus; augustalis*	Augustus; augustalis
BM	*b(ene) m(erenti)*	well-deserving
COH	*coh(ors)*	cohort
COS	*co(n)s(ul)*	consul
C R	*c(ives) R(omani)*	Roman citizens
D D	*d(ecreto) d(ecurionum)*	by decree of the council
D M	*D(is) M(anibus)*	to the spirits of the departed
EX TEST	*ex test(amento)*	according to his/her will
F	*f(ilius/a)*	son/daughter
F/FEC	*f(ecit)*	he/she made it (i.e. set it up)
F C	*f(aciendum) c(uravit)*	he/she saw to its setting up
H F	*h(eres) f(ecit)*	the heirs made it
H S E	*h(ic) s(itus/a) e(st)*	here he/she lies
L	*l(ibertus/a)*	freedman/freedwoman
LEG	*leg(io)*	legion
	leg(atus)	governor

MIL	*mil(es)*	soldier
P	*p(osuit)*	he/she placed (it)
P M	*p(ontifex) m(aximus)*	high priest
P P	*p(ater) p(atriae)*	father of his country
	p(ro) p(raetore)	with the powers of a praetor
PRAEF	*praef(ectus)*	prefect
PRAET	*praet(or)*	praetor
S P Q R	*S(enatus) P(opulusque) R(omani)*	the Senate and People of Rome
S T T L	*s(it) t(ibi) t(erra) l(evis)*	may the earth lie lightly upon you
TRIB POT	*trib(unicia) pot(estate)*	with tribunician power
V C	*v(ir) c(larissimus)*	most distinguished gentleman
VIX	*vix(it)*	he/she lived
V S L M	*v(otum) s(olvit) l(ibens) m(erito)*	willingly and deservedly fulfilled a vow

Appendix 3

HISTORICAL TIMELINE

The origins of Rome

(Most of these dates are approximate)

1220	Destruction of Troy.
1152	Traditional date of founding of Alba Longa.
1000–750	Phoenician expansion overseas.
1000	Latins settle in Latium.
814	Traditional date of founding of Carthage.
775	Euboean Greeks establish trading post in Bay of Naples.
753	Traditional date of founding of Rome.
753–510	Period of the kings in Rome.
650	Etruscans occupy Latium.
616–578	Tarquinius Priscus.
578–534	Servius Tullius.
534–510	Tarquinius Superbus.
510	Ejection of kings.
505	Final defeat of Etruscans.

The republic

509	Establishment of the republic. First consuls.
496	Romans defeat Latins at Lake Regillus.
451/450	The Twelve Tables.
390	Gauls sack Rome, but withdraw in return for ransom.

338	Latin league of states dissolved.
327–290	Samnite Wars.
321	Disaster at Caudine Forks.
283	Final capitulation of Etruscans.
280–275	Pyrrhus leads Greek cities in south of Italy against Rome.
265	Rome now holds all Italy south of river Arno.
264–241	First Punic War.
241	Western Sicily becomes first Roman province.
239–237	Rome annexes Corsica and Sardinia.
227	All Sicily and Sardinia with Corsica become provinces.
218–202	Second Punic War.
218	Hannibal invades Italy.
216	Hannibal defeats Romans at Cannae.
202	Battle of Zama.
197	Spain annexed and divided into two provinces.
191	Rome completes conquest of Cisalpine Gaul.
184	Cato elected censor, having been consul in 195.
167	End of third war against Macedonia, which is divided into four self-governing regions.
167–160	Maccabaean revolt in Judaea.
153	Roman year begins on 1 January.
149–146	Third Punic War.
146	Destruction of Carthage and Corinth. Province of Africa established.
144	Dedication of temples to Hercules Victor by Lucius Mummius Achaicus.
133	Tiberius Gracchus is tribune of the people. Pergamum bequeathed to Rome and in 129 becomes the province of Asia.
123–122	Gaius Gracchus is tribune of the people.
121	Transalpine Gaul becomes a province.
107	First consulship of Marius.
102–101	Marius defeats Teutones and Cimbri.
100	Sixth consulship of Marius.
91–88	Social War between Rome and Italian allies.
88	First consulship of Sulla. Having marched on Rome, he departs for the east, where Mithridates has massacred Roman citizens.
87	Marius and Cinna capture Rome.
86	Seventh consulship of Marius, who dies on 13 January.
83	Sulla lands in Italy, and is joined by Crassus and Pompey.
82–80	Sulla is dictator. Proscriptions and constitutional reforms.
78	Death of Sulla. The beginning of the end of the republic.

Transition

74	Bithynia and Cyrenaica become provinces.
73–71	Slave revolt of Spartacus.
70	First consulships of Pompey and Crassus.
67	Pompey crushes the pirates.
66–63	Pompey defeats Mithridates and reorganizes the region.
63	Consulship of Cicero. Conspiracy of Catiline. Caesar is elected *pontifex maximus*.
60	'First triumvirate' of Caesar, Crassus and Pompey.
59	First consulship of Caesar.
58–50	Caesar's Gallic Wars. The whole of Gaul becomes part of the empire.
55–54	Caesar's invasions of Britain.
52	Pompey appointed sole consul.
49	Pompey authorized to deal with Caesar, who crosses the Rubicon, signifying that he comes as an invader. Pompey leaves for Greece. Caesar is dictator for eleven days.
48	Caesar defeats Pompey at Pharsalus.
48–47	Caesar in Egypt.
47	Caesar defeats Pharnaces at Zela.
46	Caesar is appointed dictator for ten years.
45	Final defeat of Pompeians in Spain. Caesar returns to Rome.
44	Assassination of Caesar.
43	First consulship of Octavian. Formation of second triumvirate: Octavian, Antony and Lepidus. Proscriptions, in which Cicero dies.
42	Caesar is officially deified. Brutus and Cassius are defeated at Philippi. Cisalpine Gaul is incorporated into Italy.
31–23	Successive consulships of Octavian/Augustus.
31	Battle of Actium.
30	Antony and Cleopatra commit suicide. Egypt is annexed.
28	Octavian is awarded the title of *princeps*.
27	Octavian renounces his special powers; he accepts the provinces of Spain, Gaul and Syria for ten years, and assumes the name of Augustus. Agrippa builds the original Pantheon.

The empire: Julio-Claudians and Flavians

23	Augustus is awarded full tribunician powers for life, with extended *imperium*.
9	Dedication of *Ara Pacis*.

AD

4	Augustus adopts Tiberius, who is granted tribunician powers for ten years.
9	Varian disaster.
13	Augustus' control of his provinces is renewed for a further ten years.
14	Census enumerates five million Roman citizens. Death and deification of Augustus.
18	Death, in banishment, of the poet Ovid.
31	From Capri, Tiberius denounces Sejanus, on whom the Senate pronounces the death sentence.
33	Probable date of the crucifixion of Jesus of Nazareth under Roman law.
41	Assassination of Caligula. Claudius becomes emperor.
43	Invasion of Britain, part of which becomes a province.
44	Achaea and Macedonia become subject to the Senate. Judaea reverts to being a province.
46	Achaea is annexed.
48	Claudius registers about seven million citizens of Rome, and opens the way for more provincials to be senators.
61	Revolt in Britain of Boudicca.
64	Great fire of Rome.
66–74	First Jewish War.
69	Year of the four emperors.
74	Vespasian confers Latin rights on all parts of Spain.
78–84	Agricola is governor of Britain.
79	Eruption of Vesuvius.
80	Fire in Rome. Opening of Colosseum.
96	Assassination of Domitian. Senate elects Nerva to succeed him.

The 'five good emperors'

97	Nerva adopts Trajan as co-ruler and successor.
101	Trajan invades Dacia, which is finally annexed in 106.
104	Death of the poet Martial.
113	Dedication of Trajan's column.
114–116	Trajan conquers Mesopotamia.
c. 117	Death of the historian Tacitus.
117	Accession of Hadrian. Roman empire is at its greatest extent.
122	Hadrian in Britain.

c. 126	Rebuilding of the Pantheon in its present form.
132–135	Second Jewish War.
139	Accession of Antoninus.
c. 140	Death of the poet Juvenal.
142–143	Building of Antonine Wall in northern Britain.
161	Accession of Marcus Aurelius.
161–166	Parthian Wars, followed by plague.
167	Barbarian invasions across the Danube.
178	Further risings of Marcomanni and other tribes.
180	Accession of Commodus.

The Severan and disintegration of dynastic rule

192	Murder of Commodus brings the Antonine dynasty to an end.
193	Septimius Severus proclaimed emperor and marches on Rome.
194	Severus defeats Pescennius Niger and campaigns in Mesopotamia.
195	Severus defeats Clodius Albinus and departs for a second Parthian war.
203	Erection of arch of Severus in the Forum.
208	The imperial family leaves for Britain.
211	Severus dies at York.
212	Caracalla has his brother Geta murdered. All free inhabitants of the empire are now entitled to Roman citizenship.
226	The *Aqua Alexandrina*, the last of Rome's eleven significant aqueducts, is operative.
235	Assassination of Alexander Severus and his mother.

Third-century crisis?

238	Year of six emperors.
242–3	Roman victories over Goths and Persians.
250	Widespread persecution of Christians by Decius.
251	Gothic invasions of the empire.
257	Edict of Valerian against the Christians.
259–274	Imperium Galliarum, breakaway state of Gaul.
260	First edict of toleration for Christians.
270	Aurelian proclaimed emperor while campaigning against the Goths.
270–273	Revolt of Zenobia.
271	Aurelian defeats Vandals and Alamanni, and begins fortifications: Aurelian Wall in Rome and defences of other cities.

275   Assassination of Aurelian while on his way to fight the Persians.

283   Carus subdues the Quadi and Sarmatians but dies en route to fight the Persians.

Recovery: Diocletian and Constantine

284   On the death of Carus' son, Diocles (later Diocletian), cavalry commander of the imperial guard and suffect consul in 283, is proclaimed emperor.

286   Maximian is promoted to Augustus, with responsibility for the west. Carausius declares himself ruler of Britain and part of northern Gaul.

287–290   Diocletian campaigns on the Danube and in the east.

293   Galerius and Constantius appointed Caesars. Murder of Carausius by Allectus.

c. 297   Diocletian begins dividing the provinces into smaller units.

303   Edict against the Christians. Diocletian visits Rome for the only time.

305   Abdication of Diocletian and Maximian. Galerius and Constantius are Augusti.

306   Death of Constantius at York.

308   Galerius appoints Licinius as Augustus.

309/310   Constantine and Maximinus, who is Galerius' nephew and adopted son, are recognized by Galerius as Augusti.

312   Vision of Constantine. He becomes sole ruler of the western empire.

313   Death of Diocletian. Edict of Milan, ending persecution of Christians.

315   Erection of arch of Constantine.

322–323   Victories of Constantine over Sarmatians and Goths.

324   Licinius is defeated and killed, making Constantine sole ruler of the empire.

325   Council of Nicaea; formation of Nicene Creed.

330   Dedication of new capital city, Constantinople.

332–334   Great victories over Goths and Sarmatians.

337   Baptism and death of Constantine. Constantine II, Constantius II and Constans are recognized as Augusti.

Christian Empire and the fall of Rome

340   Constans defeats and kills Constantine II.

350   Constans is replaced in a coup by Magnentius, and then murdered.

353   Magnentius' suicide results in official reprisals against his supporters in Britain.

361	Constantius dies in Cilicia while marching to oppose Julian, who has been declared Augustus by his troops. Julian enters Constantinople as emperor, having publicly declared his paganism.
363	Julian dies of wounds. Jovian is declared emperor.
364	Jovian dies. Valentinian is elected emperor. He chooses his brother Valens to rule the east.
368–374	German wars.
375	Death of Valentinian.
378	Death of Valens.
379	Theodosius I, supreme commander against the Goths, succeeds Valens.
388	Maximus, who has had to be recognized by Theodosius as Augustus over Britain, Gaul, Spain and Africa, is defeated and executed. The ruler of the western empire is once again Valentinian II (d. 392), son of Valentinian.
391	Theodosius passes measures banning paganism.
395	Death of Theodosius. His elder son Arcadius is emperor in the east, and his younger son Honorius emperor in the west. The division of the empire is now permanent.
401	Alaric the Visigoth invades Italy.
404	Honorius transfers his court to Ravenna.
408	Death of Arcadius, who is succeeded by his son Theodosius II.
410	Alaric sacks Rome. Rescript of Honorius, allegedly informing the inhabitants of Britain that they must organize their own defence against the Saxons.
418	Honorius grants Visigoths federate status in Gaul.
423	Death of Honorius.
429–438	Publication of Theodosian Code of laws.
439	Vandals occupy most of North Africa, north-west Spain, and Visigoths, Burgundians, Alans and Franks almost all of Gaul.
440–461	Leo I is pope.
450	Death of Theodosius II.
451	Attila the Hun invades Gaul, but is defeated for the only time.
452	Attila invades Italy, but withdraws under persuasion from Pope Leo.
455	Vandals sack Rome from the sea.
476	Romulus Augustulus (aged fourteen) is deposed by Odoacer, a Germanic mercenary commander, who informs Zeno, emperor in the east, that he will rule under his sovereignty. Establishment of a Gothic kingdom in Italy, and the end of the Roman empire in the west.

The eastern empire

527	Justinian succeeds his uncle as emperor in the east.
528–529	Code of Justinian.
530–3	Digest of Justinian.
532	Nika revolt in Constantinople.
532–537	Building of Hagia Sophia.
559	Justinian's retired general Belisarius delivers Constantinople from the Huns.
565	Death of Justinian.
622	Traditional date for the founding of Islam.
760	Foundation of Turkish empire.
1053	Split between church of Rome and the church in the east.
1453	Fall of Constantinople to Mehmed II and the Turks. End of the eastern Roman empire.

Appendix 4

LITERATURE TIMELINE

BC

753	Traditional date of founding of Rome.
c. 750–c. 725	*Iliad* and *Odyssey* of Homer, Greek epic poet.
c. 630	Birth of Greek lyric poet Sappho.
c. 620	Birth of Greek lyric poet Alcaeus.
c. 496/5–406	Sophocles, Greek writer of tragedies.
c. 480–c. 425	Herodotus, Greek historian.
469–399	Socrates, Greek philosopher.
c. 465–c. 386	Aristophanes, Greek writer of comedies.
c. 460–c. 400	Thucydides, Greek historian.
c. 429–347	Plato, Greek philosopher.
c. 342–c. 292	Menander, Greek writer of comedies.
341–270	Epicurus, Greek philosopher.
254–184	Plautus, writer of comedies.
240–207	Livius Andronicus writing plays and verse in Latin.
239–169	Ennius, writer of tragedies in verse.
234–149	Cato 'the Censor', historian and general writer.
c. 215	Fabius Pictor, first Roman historian, writing in Greek.
c. 200–c. 118	Polybius, Roman historian who wrote in Greek.
c. 185–159	Terence, writer of comedies.
116–27	Varro, scholar and critic.
106–43	Cicero, orator and letter-writer.
100–44	Julius Caesar, military historian.
c. 99–c. 55	Lucretius, poet and philosopher.
86–35	Sallust, historian.

c. 84–54	Catullus, lyric poet.
c. 70–8	Maecenas, patron of literature.
70–19	Virgil, epic and pastoral poet.
65–8	Horace, lyric poet.
59–AD 17	Livy, historian.
c. 50–*c.* 15	Propertius, elegiac poet.
43–AD 18	Ovid, elegiac and narrative poet.
c. 40	Vitruvius writing treatise on architecture.
4– AD 65	Seneca the Younger, philosopher and scientist.

AD

23–79	Pliny the Elder, historian and scientist.
37–*c.* 100	Josephus, Jewish historian who wrote in Aramaic and Greek.
39–65	Lucan, epic poet.
c. 40–*c.* 104	Martial, writer of verse epigrams and satire.
c. 46–*c.* 120	Plutarch, Roman historian and biographer who wrote in Greek.
c. 55–*c.* 140	Juvenal, writer of verse satire.
c. 56–after 117	Tacitus, historian and biographer.
c. 61– *c.* 112	Pliny the Younger, letter-writer.
66	Death of Petronius, author of *Satyricon*.
c. 70–*c.* 140	Suetonius, biographer.
c. 125	Birth of Apuleius, novelist.
c. 160	Appian, Roman historian, writing in Greek.
c. 165–*c.* 235	Cassius Dio, Roman historian who wrote in Greek.
c. 330–*c.* 395	Ammianus Marcellinus, Roman historian.

Appendix 5

GLOSSARY OF LATIN TERMS IN THE TEXT

aerarium militare: military fund.

ager publicus: (literally public lands) owned/acquired by the state but often leased to private individuals.

amicus (plural: *amici*): friend.

aquilifer: (literally eagle-bearer) bearer of the chief standard of a legion.

atrium: hall.

candidatus (plural: *candidati*): (literally clothed in glittering white) one standing for election to office.

cena: dinner.

centurio primi pili: commander of the first century of the first cohort.

cliens (plural: *clientes*): (literally listener) client, follower.

coemptio: form of marriage by pretended purchase.

cohors praetoria: praetorian guard, imperial guard.

cohors urbana: city cohort, city guard.

comitia centuriata: assembly by centuries.

comitia curiata: assembly by wards.

comitia tributa: assembly by tribes.

concilium plebis: meeting of the people.

confarreatio: form of marriage incorporating an offering of bread.

consul suffectus: deputy (or 'substitute') consul.

curia (plural: *curiae*): senate house; a tenth part of one of the three original tribes of Rome.

cursus honorum: (literally course (race) of honours) the steps by which a politician moved upwards in seniority from post to post.

damnatio memoriae: the condemnation of an individual (often an emperor) in the form of desecration of that person's name on public monuments.

decemvir (plural: *decemviri*):   one of a committee of ten.

devotio: act of self-sacrifice.

dextrarun iunctio: the linking of hands; common in a marriage ceremony.

dignitas: often translated as self-respect.

dilectus: (literally choosing) an army recruitment operation.

diocesis: division.

divi filius: son of a god.

domus: house, home.

eques (plural: *equites*):   horseman, knight.

familia: family, household.

fasces: bundle (of rods and an axe), carried before officers of state; it was also the badge of Mussolini's party in Italy, hence the name Fascists.

flamen (plural *flamines*):   priest of a particular god.

flamen dialis: priest of Jupiter.

frumentum: grain, military rations.

genius: birth-giving spirit.

gens: tribe, clan.

gravitas: dignity, integrity.

honestiores: citizens of honourable circumstances.

humiliores: citizens of humble circumstances.

imaginifer.   image-bearer.

immunis (plural: *immunes*):   exempt (from normal duties).

imperator.   commander (the title conferred by his troops on a victorious general); emperor.

imperium: command, power.

impluvium: basin for collecting rain.

indigitamenta: spirits attendant on a deity.

in flagrante delicto or *flagrante delicto*:   (literally with the crime blazing) redhanded.

intercessio: the right of a magistrate to veto the actions of any inferior magistrates and a special privilege of the tribune of the plebs which applied to all offices save that of a dictator or interrex.

instinctu divinitatis: literally by divine inspiration.

jentaculum: breakfast.

lar (plural: *lares*):   spirit of the household.

lar familiaris: special household spirit.

larvae: see *lemures*.

latus clavus: broad stripe (on a toga, indicating senatorial rank).

lemures: mischievous spirits of the dead.

levitas: lightness, inconstancy.

liber: written work or division of a work.

libra: Roman pound weight (= 327 grams).

limes (plural: *limites*):   path, line, frontier.

ludi circenses: events in the arena.

ludi scaenici: theatrical events (at the games).

magister (plural: *magistri*):   magistrate, officer of state.

maiestas: treason.

manes: spirits of the dead.

manus: (literally hand) husband's legal power over his wife.

mille passus or *mille passuum*:   1000 paces (= one Roman mile).

mos maiorum: custom of our ancestors.

municipium (plural: *municipia*):   town possessing the right of Roman citizenship.

naumachia: sea-fight.

nemus: grove.

nobilitas: nobility, fame, recognition.

novus homo: (literally 'new man') first of his family to achieve high office; upstart.

numen (plural: *numina*):   divine will, divine power.

omen (plural: *omina*):   sign, omen.

optimates: (literally the best) members of society (many of whom were senators) in the mid–late Republic with traditionalist politics.

ostraca: broken fragments of pottery (plural) reused for writing purposes.

palla: robe of a woman.

passus: pace (= five Roman feet); see also *mille passus*.

pater (plural: *patres*):   father, senator.

paterfamilias: head of the household (male).

patria potestas: authority of the head of the household, authority of the father.

pecunia: money.

pecus: head of cattle (the original Roman monetary unit).

penates: spirits of the larder.

peristylum: colonnade.

pietas: duty, devotion, loyalty.

pilum: a heavy Roman javelin used in battle.

plebiscita: decree of the people.

plebs urbana: city plebs.

pontifex (plural: *pontifices*):   priest.

pontifex maximus: chief priest.

populares: the people's men, who sought populist reforms in the mid–late republic.

praefectus castrorum: camp prefect, camp commander.

praeses: chairman.

prandium: lunch.

primus inter pares: first among equals, a term applied to Augustus.

princeps: first, chief.

proconsul: proconsul; provincial governor after his term of office as consul.

pro praetore: propraetor; provincial governor after his term of office as praetor.

prorogatio: prorogation, extension of a period of office.

provocatio: challenge, appeal.

quindecimvir: member of a committee of fifteen.

rector: supervisor.

respublica: state, commonwealth.

retiarius: gladiator armed with a trident and net.

rex sacrorum: king of religious rites.

salutatio: greeting of clients in the house of the patron.

senatus consultum: decree of the Senate.

senatus consultum ultimum: extreme decree of the Senate.

socius (plural: *socii*):   ally.

spina: (literally spine) wall dividing the race-track.

tablinum: multi-purpose room.

terminus: boundary stone.

toga praetexta: robe of a child.

toga virilis: robe of a man; see also *latus clavus*.

tribunus laticlavius: senior military tribune, entitled to wear a broad purple stripe
  on his tunic; see *latus clavus*.

tribunus plebis: tribune of the people.

triumviri: (literally the three men) attributed to the informal first triumvirate
  (Caesar, Pompey and Crassus) and then the more formal second triumvirate
  (Octavian, Antony and Lepidus). It derives from minor magistrate boards in the
  Republic such as the *tresviri monetales* (three magistrates in charge of the mints).

usus: (literally use) practice, custom.

vestibulum: entrance-hall.

vicarius: deputy (to an emperor).

victimarius: attendant at a sacrifice, slaughterer.

vigiles: watchmen, night-guards.

villa: country house.

virtus: manliness, strength, worth.

volumen: roll, volume.

INDEX